CHRISTIAN FAITH & PUBLIC POLICY

THINKING AND ACTING IN THE COURAGE OF UNCERTAINTY

Richard John Neuhaus

AUGSBURG PUBLISHING HOUSE
Minneapolis, Minnesota

CHRISTIAN FAITH AND PUBLIC POLICY

Copyright © 1977 Augsburg Publishing House

Library of Congress Catalog Card No. 76-27086

International Standard Book No. 0-8066-1554-0

Scripture quotations unless otherwise noted are from the Revised Standard Version of the Bible, copyright 1946, 1952, and 1971 by the Division of Christian Education of the National Council of Churches.

MANUFACTURED IN THE UNITED STATES OF AMERICA

Contents

HN31
N48
1977
CETS

Part I: FOUNDATIONS

What We Believe and Why It Makes a Difference—The Presence of God in the World—The Politics of God—The Many Worlds of "the world"—Liberation and Modesty—Justice and Power—Themes and Metaphors That Can Help—Changed Understandings of God's World—The Political Order—State and Church

Prayer and Proclamation—Cultivated Civic Virtue and Piety —The Internal Politics of Christian Community—Individual Christian Vocation—Research and Education—Advocacy by Groups and Individuals—Corporate Statements—Official Leadership—Political Implementation

The Political Task—The Church and the Political Task—Values in Public Policy (Social Order, Justice, Liberty, Equality)— Calculating Costs and Benefits

Part II: DIRECTIONS FOR PUBLIC POLICY

The Nation-State—International Law and Organizations—The United Nations—Ideological Conflict—Multinational Corporations—War, Arms and Disarmament—America's Peace-keeping Responsibilities

We stand on a mountain pass in the midst of whirling snow and blinding mist, through which we get glimpses now and then of paths which may be deceptive. If we stand still, we shall be frozen to death. If we take the wrong road, we shall be dashed to pieces. We do not certainly know whether there is any right one. What must we do? "Be strong and of a good courage."

James Fitzjames Stephen,
Liberty, Equality, Fraternity
1873

Moreover it is required of stewards that they be found trustworthy. But with me it is a very small thing that I should be judged by you or by any human court. I do not even judge myself. . . . It is the Lord who judges. Therefore do not pronounce judgment before the time, before the Lord comes, who will bring to light the things now hidden in darkness and will disclose the purposes of the heart.

—St. Paul
1 Corinthians 4

Foreword

Christian Faith and Public Policy is intended to help Christians reflect on the meaning and direction of their public responsibility.

In this work Richard John Neuhaus examines the role of the church in the formulation of public policy, articulates a theological-social ethical conceptual framework for dealing with public policy, and suggests policy goals in several areas of concern today. The author's insightful comments, his prophetic observations, and his pastoral concern for the Christian community make this book a distinctive contribution to thought and action. It is a sensitive commentary on our nation's agenda as the United States begins its third century.

In preparing this book the author met with more than a dozen consultants to explore selected themes. His first draft was studied and discussed by forty persons representing a wide cross section of church and community interests.

Though this book has arisen out of processes developed by the Lutheran Council in the U.S.A., it does not reflect an official position either of the Council or its participating church bodies. It is the contribution of Richard John Neuhaus in conversation with various consultants. As such, it is offered as an aid to continuing discussion, study, and action in and by the Christian community.

Bryon L. Schmid, Director
Social Study and Planning
Lutheran Council in the U.S.A.

A Word to the Reader

It is not new for Christians to address themselves to issues of public policy. Church bodies and their agencies have, over the years, developed numerous studies and position papers and have frequently issued formal statements on a wide range of public policy questions. This study should be seen as part of that history of concern for public policy. It is undertaken in the hope of providing a coherent attempt to relate Christian faith and public policy.

In addition, I hope the study will help advance Christian thought and action in the political arena. As a statement of posture or perspective, the emphasis is on the context within which Christians exercise public responsibility. But context means little unless it is filled with particular content. Therefore the larger part of this study is given to discussing specific policy issues facing us now and, we expect, in the future. I hope that the connection between theory and practice, between theology and policy, will be evident to the reader throughout.

The study is titled "Christian Faith and Public Policy." Faith must be active in love that is in pursuit of justice. Illuminating what that sentence may mean in our society and world is the purpose of this study. Admittedly, it is an ambitious project. I hope it will be judged as much by the seriousness of its intent as by the success of its achievement, or lack thereof.

What is meant by public policy? "Public policy" does not encompass the whole of life but those matters which deal with the ordering of public life together in communities, nations, and in the world. More specifically, public policy treats of those issues which are subject to the political process. As the reader will see, in a democratic society such as that of the United States, the "political process" must be de-

7

fined very broadly indeed. It involves not only electoral politics but also the courts, voluntary associations, the media, and a host of other participants. Public policy has to do with the laws, the institutional arrangements, and the formal and informal controls by which we attempt to order our common life in response to an ever elusive vision of the Commonwealth.

The study is offered in two main parts. Part I is a theological statement of the theory behind any effort to relate Christian faith to public policy and identifies the means and ways by which Christians exercise their responsibility for public policy. The first part also includes some guidelines ("testings for decision") which emerge from and interact with our theological perspective. These "testings" suggest the directions pursued in Part II where we take up specific public policy issues. The study is supplemented by a bibliography "for further reading." The books and articles noted there will also give the reader further insight into the larger conversation which informs the author's approach to specific questions.

Obviously, the study has had to be selective in deciding which policy questions to treat. I tried to choose those which seem of greatest moment to the church, the nation, and the world. I have also attempted to anticipate some issues and directions which are not (yet?) receiving much consideration in American public discourse.

Of course this study does not represent the official position of any church body or Christian agency. Nor need there be an official position on all these issues. The study is the contribution of an author in conversation with several consultants and a number of reviewers and commentators. Its chief aim is to advance continuing discussion, study, and action throughout the church. I hope it will also offer guidance to Christians in the individual and corporate exercise of their citizenship, assist those who are called to speak to public policy on behalf of the churches, and be a helpful point of reference to church bodies and agencies as they participate in the ongoing debate about the kind of society and world in which God intends his children to live together.

I am very grateful to the consultants and many others who were involved in the project that produced this book, especially the following: Dr. Duane L. Addison, Dr. Robert Benne, Dr. Peter Berger, Dr. George W. Forell, Dr. Loren E. Halvorson, Dr. Harold Haas, Dr. Eleanor H. Haney, Dr. Karl H. Hertz, Dr. Victor Hoffmann, Sen. Ernest Hollings,

Dr. Paul Jersild, Dr. Dale G. Lasky, Dr. Eugene W. Linse, Jr., Dr. Merle Longwood, Dr. Ralph L. Moellering, Dr. Larry Rasmussen, Congressman Paul Simon and Ms. Susan Thompson. We have agreed on the formulation that the book "represents the views of the author in conversation with consultants." Especially in Part 2, where I deal with specific policies, an effort is made to accommodate the sometimes conflicting views of the several consultants. While I am finally responsible for the presentation of issues, particular nuances are the valuable contribution of others who sometimes had a different angle on both the "what" and the "why" of positions taken. In all this I am especially indebted to Byron Schmid of the Lutheran Council in the USA for his insights and unflagging patience.

Finally, the reader should not overlook the two quotations on the flyleaf of this book. In working on this project, I was newly impressed by the elements of risk, fallibility, contingency, and awareness of ignorance that must mark thoughtful engagement in public affairs. Certitude is a great comfort and places limited demands on courage; courage is tested by uncertainty. Readers looking for ringing manifestos will sometimes be disappointed to discover only tentative suggestions; those looking for final answers might be frustrated in finding only a statement of alternative possibilities. There is a place for ringing manifestos, final answers, and the definitive "thus saith the Lord." Too often, however, what passes for prophetic pronouncement is merely the posturing of unwarranted certitude.

The greater and more common sin of Christians, however, is to be paralyzed by uncertainty. It is a failure of courage and, finally, a failure of faith; it is the refusal to live and act, also in the political realm, in radical dependence upon God's forgiving and correcting love. It is the hope of all of us involved in producing this study that it will embolden many to embrace more fully both the ambiguities and the obligations of Christian citizenship.

RJN
Brooklyn, NY

1

A Theology of
Christian Faith and Public Policy

What We Believe and Why It Makes a Difference

Many Christians believe that a study such as this is illegitimate and doomed from the start. They believe there can be no valid meeting point between church and public policy; the church lives exclusively in the sphere of the sacred, in the realm of eternal verities. Not only *need* it not concern itself about the secular world; it *must* not. The church is seen as the divinely instituted alternative to, and refuge from, the secular world. This viewpoint is antithetical to the biblical and classical Christian understanding of the church in the world.

Nonetheless, this viewpoint has made significant inroads among the churches. The reasons for this are no doubt complex. Some of them have to do with denominational histories, others are related to inadequate or misunderstood theological concepts. And some reasons simply reflect the sinful indifference that is common to all humanity and has plagued also the church from its very beginnings. Whatever the reasons, there are those who believe that any engagement in public policy blurs the line between the "children of light" and the "children of darkness." Others view such engagement as, at best, an optional task that may be embraced by some Christians. Yet others are fearful—not without reason—that the resources and authority of the church might be captured or used by political movements that are alien or even hostile to authentic Christian faith. The idea that the church should be isolated from public policy or that political concern is optional for the Christian community must be repudiated theologically. The fear that the church might be used in an illegitimate manner requires a sensitive response and great strategic care in relating Christian witness to public affairs.

Christians should be scrupulously honest in their analysis of social problems, even when—indeed, especially when—such honesty gets in the way of the short-range advancement of a favored policy. They should readily acknowledge areas of moral ambiguity, carefully distinguishing between positions that are religiously imperative and those that are formed by prudential judgment about which Christians may validly disagree. As will become evident throughout this study, that distinction is both problematic in theory and difficult in practice. Christians must be cautioned against thinking a position is religiously imperative simply because they feel very strongly about it. In sober fact most decisions, although informed by theological insight, are exercises in prudential judgment through the use of God's gift of reason.

The churches should nurture the expression of diverse viewpoints among their members, while at the same time clearly and publicly articulating the consensus that may be shaped around specific issues. (We will return to the ways in which these goals may be achieved.) Above all, the effort to relate Christian faith to public policy must be firmly grounded theologically. Protest or advocacy that is offered *in the name of the church or of the Christian faith* must be clearly related to the Word of God, both law and gospel, by which the community of faith lives and offers itself in service to the world. All of this is done in full awareness of our fallible understanding of that Word and in unremitting reliance on God's correcting and forgiving love.

The Presence of God in the World

The nexus, or the point of linkage and tension, between faith and public policy is discovered at the very heart of Christian theology, namely in our knowledge of the Triune God. In the world of God the Creator we proclaim and act out the gospel of God the Redeemer, empowered by the community-building and sustaining life of God the Sanctifier. All the work of God is directed toward the fulfillment of his world. "God so loved"—not the church, not the born-again, not the righteous—but "God so loved the world that he gave. . . ." The church is for the world. In all dimensions of its life—*kerygma* (proclamation), *koinonia* (human solidarity) and *diakonia* (service)—the church is for the world.

Christian faith is not merely subjective religious experience, nor is it based on private illumination. The gospel is a *public* statement, based upon *public* evidence, subject to *public* debate, and asserting a *public* reality—namely, the future of the whole world of God's creating, redeeming and sanctifying activity. When Christians attempt to set faith against community, or Christian community against the world, they are setting God against himself. The church proclaims a Word *for* the world and *about* the world in obedience to the faithful God who has irretrievably pledged himself *to* the world. It is a Word of salvation *for* the world, not salvation *from* the world.

Not all the world knows what the world is about. In the end time, when the kingdom of God is finally consummated, all human beings will acknowledge, to their eternal joy or regret, the rule of God. Christians understand themselves as people ahead of time. They are those who in the world have, by the grace of God, anticipated the rule of God and now call the world to respond in saving obedience to the Word of anticipation. That obedience will be vindicated in the end time. It is now obedience in hope, contingent upon the promise of what is yet to be and supported by the presence of that future now in Jesus Christ. That is, in Jesus the end time has appeared in our time.

When we say Christians are people ahead of time, we do not mean that they are in advance of the rest of the world in their ethical behavior. While this ought perhaps to be the case, we know that all too often it is not. The church is simply that community of people who accept, confess and celebrate Jesus the Christ as their Lord and Savior. It is solely by virtue of their relationship to the Christ that we speak of the church as people ahead of time. The natural or civil righteousness possessed by people outside the church frequently results in ethical behavior superior to that demonstrated by Christians. But Christians are called to set an example for the world also in their exercise of civil righteousness in obedience to Christ as Lord.

The Politics of God

What is yet to be is already happening. God, who is the Absolute Future, is himself now engaged in our present. In welcoming his rule in our lives, both public and private, we participate in the promised future. Christians are a pilgrim people, painfully aware that we are in exile from the kingdom for which we were made, but sustained by the knowledge that the exile is not permanent. Death, which appears as the final negation of all meaning, is not the last word. In the celebration of the presence of the Risen Christ we have a sure foretaste, even here in the wilderness, of the Promised Land. Our hope-filled focus on the future in no way detracts from the urgency of the here and now. Indeed, in our faithful welcoming of the future in our present, we become instrumental to God's promise-keeping power to complete our present in the glory of his fullness.

This lively interaction between the present and the oncoming rule of God is nowhere more mightily symbolized and effected than in the church's celebration of the holy Eucharist. This eschatological moment, experienced by those who have through baptism already entered the new age, is the sign of the cosmic future, the future of the whole creation. Thus the Eucharist is also a signal to the world, revealing the one, universal hope for all of history. That is, even when, as in worship, the church distinguishes itself from the world, it does so for the world. The church's distinction from the world, a distinction which must never be comprised, is for the sake of altering the world to its own future—and, therefore, to the meaning of its own present.

The church's sacramental life is an effective symbolization of what might be called "the politics of God." In baptism, all that is deadly dies and a new creation is proclaimed. Baptism gives new life not only to the person baptized but is also a promise in solidarity with all life that emerges from the primordial deeps represented by the water of creation and rebirth. The Eucharist signals the communal solidarity, now in the bond of need and grace, that will one day be realized in the *polis* of the New Jerusalem. Absolution signals a liberation by which all other liberation movements pale in comparison, for forgiveness is the final breakthrough from sin and death to the perfect liberty of the children of God. The means of grace then are exercises in the politics of the ultimate to which all other politics are penultimate. It is important to say, however, that the secular ordering of human relations now is indeed pen*ultimate*. That is, the present political task participates, by the grace and power of God, in the ultimate re-ordering of reality that is his work in history and that will be consummated in the kingdom of God.

The church then is very much in the world. It is not in the world by unfortunate and temporary accident; it has no meaning apart from its mission in the world—to remind the world that the kingdom of God has not yet come in its fullness, to illuminate the incompleteness and rebellion that is a sinful world's resistance to the oncoming rule of God, to provoke and participate in the creation's yearning for what is yet to be, that is, for our promised fulfillment in God's being all in all.

The church shares fully in the world's history. That universal history is the striving of God toward the creation's culmination in the fullness of his being. He calls us to join him in that striving. That striving may involve great sorrow and sacrifice, for we know that the cross is the form of history on its way to the promised kingdom. Christians are those who have responded to God's call in the revelation of Jesus the Christ. This does not mean that Christians or the community of Christians that is the church are the only means God uses in his working in the world. To the contrary, in ways that transcend and sometimes confound our understanding, God uses all the forces of history toward his promised ends. He may even use those forces that are in professed hostility to the coming of his kingdom. The singularity of the church is to signal, interpret and anticipate what the whole of the enterprise of history is about.

The Many Worlds of "the world"

In all this we are engaged in a life-and-death struggle. In accord with the Scriptures, "the world" is to be understood in its several aspects. "The world" is God's creation and the object and arena of his redemptive love. This world is inseparable from—has no being apart from—God himself. In loving the world with relentless devotion, Christians participate in God's love for his own creation—a creation which includes our selves, our loves, our fears and hopes. At the same time, the Scriptures emphasize that "the world" is at enmity with God. That is, God's loving creation is in a "fallen" state, marked by rebellion, fragmentation, and the rule of death. This condition pervades every dimension of the world and of our existence in it.

The "fallenness" of the world is not merely a negative factor, a lack of perfection, an absence of desired good. It is a positive, active hostility to God and his saving purposes. This hostility is underscored in Christian faith's understanding of the demonic. In describing the powers of evil at work in the world Christians should not cringe from speaking of Satan and his minions. No lesser concept can do justice to the horror by which history has been and continues to be marked. Politics is by no means exempt from the rule of evil. Indeed it is an arena in which "the principalities and powers" of the present time persistently challenge the rule of God.

Also in the political realm, Satan would again and again seduce Christians and others into surrendering themselves to false signs of the kingdom's coming. He would obscure the distinction between the "now" and the "not yet," urging us to "come to terms" with the present as though it were permanent and not subject to God's judgment and change. He would have us confuse things as they are, or things as we would make them, with absolute and eternal truth. Thus he sometimes induces despair, persuading us that there is no promising future and all our striving is in vain. At other times he induces fanaticism, persuading us to identify our ideas or programs with the kingdom of God itself. Despair and fanaticism are closely linked in the strategy of the demonic. Both are painfully evident in the political realm. One leads to political withdrawal and indifference, the other to passionate engagement and aggressiveness, but both are premised upon mistaking some lesser and provisional truth—whether the present order or the order we project for the future—for the absolute and eternal truth revealed in the promise of God's coming kingdom. This mistake is in fact the lie by which "the father of lies" would seduce us. It is the lie by which "the world" is so largely and so tragically possessed.

When we speak, therefore, of the church being for the world and of our hope for the world we do not think of the world as merely neutral stuff to be molded according to some better design. No, the world is the battleground on which, in ways that surpass our understanding, a cosmic struggle is being waged between the forces of death and the forces of life. As Christians we believe the victory of life—that is, of God—has already been secured and signalled in the resurrection of Jesus from the dead. But that victory has not yet been consummated in historical reality; not yet does the lion lie down with the lamb; not yet are swords beaten into plowshares and spears into pruning hooks; not yet are all tears wiped away, or the poor exalted, or the haughty cast down from their thrones; not yet does every knee bow at the name of Jesus or every tongue confess that Jesus Christ is Lord. The world persists in resistance and rebellion against the resurrection fact and the kingdom that is its promise.

Thus "the world" may be used in different ways. Sometimes it is used in a purely descriptive way, meaning all of reality or creation, or Planet Earth, with its human history. Sometimes—as in "the church and the world"—it means all those who are not part of the community that celebrates Jesus Christ as Lord. At other times, "the world" refers to all the forces and forms of demonic hostility to the rule of God, as described above, forces and forms from which the church in the world is by no means exempt.

But, above all, the world is the object of God's creative love and the arena of his redemptive work. It is the creation within which the church would signal and proclaim the new creation. Its evil is not of its essence but of its tragic rebellion; its captivity is not forever. The liberation which believers now know in Jesus Christ is a sign of the world's future, for, if the world would but realize it, he is the world's Lord. What we now affirm by faith will one day be confirmed by sight. This is our Christian assertion against the false powers and fake promises of the present time. This is the truth that, in the political realm, makes possible sober realism without despair and passionate engagement without fanaticism.

Liberation and Modesty

In the end time the meaning of our time and all times will be revealed. The meaning of our time and of all times before the end time is the drama of the world's resisting or welcoming the rule of God. Until that time, it is the church's task to proclaim and to live in cooperative obedience with that rule. We are the saddest of people, for we see the foolishness of the world—and of ourselves in the world—resisting its promised future; we are the most joyful of people, for we live already now by the sure hope of God's final triumph. We are caught in between the "now" and the "not yet." That very captivity is our liberation; we are liberated from the illusion that what we yearn for can be satisfied short of the kingdom of God; we are liberated from the despair that is the death-like absence of transcendent hope.

Christians are liberated for the liberation of the whole world. Human beings are freed to act in the hope, not of immediate success, but of final vindication. They are freed to act in the knowledge that there is a forgiveness greater than our error. They are freed to believe that policy has a purpose that is not contingent upon the establishment of illusory utopias but that can participate, although always in a preliminary way, in God's purpose through history. The very modesty with which we are enabled to view our efforts and designs is not reason for discouragement but is a liberation from the pretension of believing that our efforts must be definitive if they are to have any meaning at all. The knowledge of provisionality is the antidote to the pretension that has, especially in the political realm, plagued humanity with "definitive" programs that have been as horrible in their triumph as they have been frustrating in their failure. It is enough that we can in the "now" participate in the "not yet." What is preliminary is grace, and grace is prelude to the glory yet to be revealed.

Provisionality and the liberating modesty it induces are crucial to the Christian understanding of the political enterprise. We seek a more just society; we expect absolute justice only in the kingdom come. God has not provided us with a plan for policy-making in search of a more just society. Yet there is no plan of our own devising that can be just if it is not kept subject to the judgment of God.

Love, which is the presence of God in our midst, is in search of justice. Finally it is love for God that compels us to seek moral excellence, and it is love that compels us to be fair to our sisters and brothers. A concept of justice that is based upon calculated self-interest, no matter how enlightened, is fragile indeed. A concept of justice that is calculated upon the assumption of a rational, harmonious, and completed creation is a dangerous illusion. Our search for justice is love's response to the presence of God in us and in all his children.

Justice and Power

What we call justice short of the kingdom of God is always a provisional arrangement subject to change and in fact always changing. Human law is, at its best, a provisional definition of justice. It is an accommodation "for the time being" of different and frequently conflicting senses of fairness. Because many, for reasons perverse or otherwise, would not abide by the accommodation, it is necessary to check their ability to violate it. In a healthy society, that check is mutually accepted within a political process which allows for further change. It is understood that the definition of justice, on any given issue at any given time, will seldom, if ever, be acceptable to all. The political process is the continuing pursuit of intimations of justice. Even in a healthy society, however, it is necessary to employ coercion against those who refuse to accept the self-limiting character of that continuing political process. The use of coercion is not only necessary because of human sinfulness. It is also necessary because we are so far from the final revelation of justice and therefore righteous people can disagree on its definition. The health of a society may be measured in part by the degree and frequency to which it must resort to coercion in order to enforce its definition of justice. A social order that is not kept open to the correcting and changing power of the future is a social order increasingly dependent upon the use of coercion in one form or another.

Coercion means more than legally prescribed rewards and punishments in order to encourage socially desired behavior. Coercion may be relatively "hidden," as in social, political or economic structures that compel certain choices and preclude others. Whether coercion is open and explicit—as in legally prescribed penalties—or concealed and implicit—as in structures that perpetuate powerlessness and poverty—it is usually used in the negative sense of limiting human freedom. While such limitations of freedom are necessary to the freedom of others and to the survival of the social order that is essential to the freedom of all, coercion is to be counted as a cost to be paid rather than as a value in itself.

Many efforts—none of them entirely satisfactory—have been made to define the difference between coercion (or force) and power. Enough to say that power—whether used by an individual, a group, or by the state—is often viewed more positively as an exercise of human freedom and fulfillment. It is not necessarily the case that power is always exercised *against* the power of someone else. Power, which is the ability to change or control things in society, may be exercised for others, in harmony with others, or with their free consent. Yet politics is an interaction of powers and is typically conflictual in character. While Christians are rightly disposed to favor cooperation over competition and harmony over conflict, not every conflict should be viewed as an evil.

Power itself is not evil. Indeed Christians affirm the power of God and hope for its final realization in his kingdom, which is the ultimate exercise of power. In our provisional moment, however, there is a multiplicity of powers contending for power. In such a situation, conflict is inevitable. Christians should resist the false notion of reconciliation that seeks to avoid or end all conflicts between powers, frequently to the further weakening of the less powerful. The reconciliation which we seek as Christians is based upon the triumph of right, of justice—in short, the triumph of the will of God. Conflict is frequently instrumental to a resolution that is more proximately just.

To be sure, conflict can also increase injustice. Therefore Christians have a discriminating and somewhat ambivalent view of conflicts of power. At least in our provisional moment, conflicts are inevitable. Often they are necessary to the realization of greater justice. No conflict other than the conflict between God and the demonic (which seldom, if ever, finds unambiguous form in the political realm) is absolute, however. While affirming the exercise of power, therefore, Christians should seek to relativize power conflicts, especially when violence is involved.

First, the claims of the several parties to a power conflict are relative to the power and will of God. In some instances Christians will try not to end conflict but to advance the cause of the party that they perceive, always fallibly, to be more in accord with the will of God. Then too, Christians should remind all parties to the conflict of their common humanity and their common accountability to God. Christians should courageously resist the temptation to let conflicts assume an absolutized nature that depersonalizes or dehumanizes opponents. Finally, and emerging directly from the two prior considerations, Christians will insist upon limits within which the conflict is acted out. (We will return to this question of limits in our discussion of "civility" as a public virtue and, later, in our approach to problems of war and peace.) These, then, are some of the factors which condition the Christian affirmation of the inevitability and necessity of conflicts of power. The aim is to keep conflicts open to the future, to resist the temptation of false "final solutions."

The openness of the social order is ultimately dependent on its being kept subject to God who is the Power of the Future. To say then, as we Americans do, that ours is a society "under God" is not to confirm things as they are but to assure the continuation of the search for the justice that is yet to be. Thus is the Christian's participation in the political process firmly grounded in the revelation of God's work in the world. Our God is the God of the whole creation. He shares fully in its suffering and ecstasy and manifests himself in both judgment and promise; he is Lord of both the extraordinary and the mundane, of the religious and civil orders, of the "now" and the "not yet." Were this not so, he would be something less than the one whom Christians mean by "God," the source and end of all that has been, is and will be. All this we assert both for the glory of God and for the sake of the world, for the future of the world is in his glory.

Themes and Metaphors That Can Help

There are a number of theological themes that can help us understand the connection between Christian existence and the political task. For example, we affirm a "theology of the cross" and thus underscore the limited and even tragic character of life in the world. The cross, however, is far from being an invitation to passivity or resignation in the face of suffering. Inseparably connected, as it now is, with the resurrection of Jesus, the cross is a call to commitment without counting the cost, and it is a promise that such commitment, made in communion with and in obedience to Christ, will be vindicated.

Because Christians affirm that "the finite is capable of comprehending the infinite," we do not delude ourselves about the final or definitive nature of the political tasks in which we engage. We do not need to be politically fanatic in order to be urgent about politics. We are able to give ourselves to the tasks of the partial, the unsatisfactory and the incomplete, confident in the knowledge that in Jesus Christ, God has designed to engage his perfect being in this far from perfect world.

Because Christians believe the church, the redeemed and redemptive community, is established and sustained by the public acts of preaching the gospel and administering the sacraments, we are not tempted to remove ourselves from the world as a community of moral perfection; nor can we think of the church as some kind of "invisible" or "spiritual" fellowship neither affected by nor affecting the real world of social and political change. We should oppose those who would remove the necessary tension between the church and the world, either by merging the two so that they become indistinguishable or by so separating them that they become irrelevant to one another.

Because we believe that we are "justified by grace through faith," the political arena does not for us smell of the anxious sweat of the search for salvation. The gift of grace is the salvation of being free. We are free, and therefore the slaves of no person or institution. We are free, and therefore free to be the loving servants of all. We are not paralyzed by the knowledge of our own sinfulness. Because we are "at the same time sinner and justified," we are free to act boldly, also in the political realm, trusting only and always the grace of God.

These, then, are some of the chief themes that shape our understanding of the connection between faith and the political task. To these themes we must add that of the "two kingdoms of God," or, as some would prefer, "the twofold kingdom of God." Some thoughtful Christians tend to believe that the two kingdoms concept has been so abused and misunderstood that it is past time to discard it entirely. Rightly understood, however, it can be helpful in relating Christian faith to the political task. The *intention* of the two kingdoms concept is essential; if we did not have such a concept we would have to invent something like it. There is an inescapable "twofoldness" in our understanding of church and society, of Christian faith and politics. In the different traditions of Christian history that twofoldness has been variously conceptualized. Some concept is necessary to avoid absolutizing the present political task, on the one hand, and denying to that task any redemptive significance whatsoever, on the other. Against the one error we must insist that the political task is *pen*-ultimate, against the other that the political task is pen*ultimate*. The two kingdoms concept is one way of keeping the political task in proper perspective.

Christians of all times have wrestled in formulating their experience of the "nowness" and "not yetness" of history. This has been expressed both in terms of the part of the world that has accepted the gospel, and in terms of that part of the world that has not accepted it. In that case the second part has sometimes been called, quite simply, "the world" as distinct from the believing community. Thus Christians are "in but not of the world." At other times other formulas have been employed. But always the dialectic must be kept alive; the tension must not be relieved by a premature synthesis between what is and what, by God's grace, is to be. Neither must the tension be relieved by a static formula of coexistence between life in the redeemed community and life in the rest of the world. That is the false relief which, it is often charged, the two kingdoms doctrine has been guilty of offering.

The two kingdoms concept reflects two basic ways in which God's rule is manifested and exercised. The two kingdoms of God's rule are sometimes described in terms of the right hand and left hand of God, or of the distinctions between redemption and creation, gospel and law, grace and power. But always and in all ways we intend to affirm the rule of the One God over all things.

To speak of the left-hand kingdom of God is not to suggest that the world outside the church is of secondary or incidental importance to God. It is to suggest that God's saving promise is revealed to the believing community, but it is revealed for the sake of the whole world. To speak of the realm of redemption is not to deny that there is redemptive activity in the realm of creation. The believing community now experiences and proclaims the redemption that is within and for the whole creation. Similarly, law and gospel, power and grace, evidence God's disposition toward the whole world, but the whole world does not acknowledge God's rule. The world is radically marred by the rebellion, incompleteness and fragmentation that we call sin. The church is the community ahead of time that now celebrates the rule of God that will be manifest to all in the end time.

The two kingdoms concept is, then, a restatement of the Pauline concept of the "two ages" represented by Adam and by Christ. By two kingdoms Luther also underscored God's two-fold rule of the whole world by both law and gospel. The purpose was not to divide the world into two hermetically sealed realms or to suggest that there was one kind of God for believers and another for nonbelievers. Two kingdoms does not imply a division between sacred and secular but is a *metaphor* that highlights the tension between the "now" and the "not yet" of Christian existence. Because the Christian lives in both the "now" and the "not yet," under both gospel and law, he distinguishes the two kingdoms in principle even though they interpenetrate in his Christian practice. It is important to emphasize that the Christian and the Christian community live and serve in both the right- and left-hand kingdoms, in both the "now" and the "not yet." Some may complain that this is confusing, but that cannot be helped. The "now" and the "not yet" interact in ways that violate neat categorization. So also with creation and redemption, gospel and law. The one certainty and object of our confidence is God himself who works in all these ways to fulfill the promise he has made to his church and his world.

These distinctions in principle may strike some as a sterile exercise in theological speculation. We know from history, however, that the failure to understand this twofold distinction (however it may be phrased) can lead to enormous religious and social consequences. Because of the failure to acknowledge the realm of the gospel, millions of Christians have been robbed of the freedom to which they are called in Christ. Because of the failure to acknowledge the realm of the law, millions of others, including Christians, have been subjected to social confusion and the tyranny which such confusion invites. If we neglect the kingdom of the gospel, we are deprived of hope for the world and of hope for ourselves within the world. If we neglect the kingdom of the law or try to replace it with the rule of the gospel, we confuse the "not yet" with the "now" and end up mistaking the present order for the new creation to which we are called. Either confusion is very bad theology and leads to disastrous social policy.

Changed Understandings of God's World

Of course it is not adequate merely to repeat the formulations of the 16th century. The last four hundred years have witnessed significant changes in both the theory and fact of the civil order and of the church's relation to that order. Luther and the other confessional writers lived in a time in which, under the Holy Roman Empire, it was assumed that the whole of society was in some sense Christian. Even those who were not "true Christians" knew what the faith was about and accepted its general picture of reality. God was in his heaven, ruling, and the church was his chief interpreter among men. Society stood under two great powers—the church and the state. The church was responsible for redemption and the state responsible for protecting and governing the society in an orderly manner. This was, in brief, the worldview of *corpus christianum.* Within that worldview,

Reformation theology placed a new stress on the relative independence of the civil realm from the church and underscored the possibility of God-pleasing Christian vocation in that realm of the "left-hand kingdom."

Later generations sometimes confused the two kingdoms concept, identifying the church with the right-hand kingdom and the state with the left-hand kingdom. Since the hands were not supposed to know what each order was doing (in practice that usually meant the church was not to mix in the business of the state), the consequences were disastrous for both church and state.

While the biblical and confessional doctrine of the church has not changed, the church's relationship to the society, and therefore to public policy, is now significantly different because of vast changes in what we have called the civil realm. One such change is the apparent end of *corpus christianum.* Secularization means not only that there are many more non-Christians in the society but also that the biblical picture of reality (regarding, for example, human nature, the purposefulness of history, notions of virtue and justice) cannot be taken for granted in personal and institutional behavior. Many welcome this process of secularization and insist that public policy must be formed in deliberate indifference to the truth claims and values of any religion, including the Judaeo-Christian tradition. Also many Christians celebrate at least a modified form of secularization as a force that liberates people from religious tyranny and underscores the significance of what God is doing in the world outside the church. A distinction is sometimes made between secularization and secular-*ism,* the latter being almost universally condemned by Christians as a quasi-religion that would exclude any idea of a transcendent God from personal and public life.

Because we insist on God's rule over the whole of life, we are in basic agreement with the public acknowledgement that ours is a nation "under God." In accord with Pauline teaching, we believe the state receives its authority from God and is accountable to God. Nor is it tolerable that the phrase "under God" be simply a symbol of "empty transcendence," devoid of any specific content. The God this nation is under is the God of Abraham, Isaac, Jacob and Jesus. Christians should not hesitate, indeed they have the responsibility, to name God in the public realm. Until relatively recently in American history, the state did not hesitate to name the God to whom it is accountable. Today some determined secularists would eliminate in word and practice the public acknowledgment that we are a nation "under God." Others insist that it must remain, at the very most, a reference to empty and unnamed transcendance. Yet others would replace the God of biblical religion with a vague deity presiding over some form of "civil religion." The church must, in faithfulness to its own message and in accord with the burden of the history of the American people, resist all these trends. The inevitable nature of secularization is not self-evident. The inevitability of secularization may be a self-fulfilling dogma propounded by secularists and accepted by too many Christians.

Today the issues of religious liberty and securalization are, in many minds, tied together in a false and confusing manner. As we shall note in our treatment of human rights and public policy, religious liberty is best grounded not in secularization but in the very truth claims of biblical religion. Today public discourse and public policy—especially as the latter is determined by court decisions—are dangerously muddled about the complex issues surrounding the notion of "separation of church and state." Many of these problems may not be resolved soon, as some may prove insoluble. But the principle should be clear: in the words of one theologian, "As Luther had to put the Church back under God's gospel, we have to put the state back under God's law." (This does not of course imply a theocratic form of government. Neither church nor state, nor a church-state, can legitimately equate its decisions with the will of God. The statement does mean that all human government must acknowledge a law above its own laws. Although the will and purpose of God may often be "hidden" from us, that acknowledgment is not made empty or less important because of that. Indeed it is precisely the hiddenness of God's will— Luther spoke of *Deus absconditus*—that makes that acknowledgment and the modesty it induces so imperative.)

We oppose the notion that the state should proclaim the gospel. Whether it be the Christian gospel or some new gospel, states that presume to proclaim the way to salvation lead to totalitarianism. We do insist, however, that the state acknowledge the law of the Creator God under whose judgment it exercises legitimate authority.

Secularization and the difficult issues it raises represents one major change from the 16th century understanding of the "civil realm." There are at least two other changes which demand more thorough theological attention than we are able to give them here. The first has to do with the changing definition of the state, and the second with the development of democratic political theory. As we shall see, the two are very closely connected.

In *corpus christianum* the whole of society was divided, although never very neatly for very long, between the church and the state. Sometimes a third order, the family, (which then included most of what we call the economic order) was given equal eminence. For most practical purposes "the state" meant everything outside the acknowledged purview of the church. In some totalitarian societies today, "the state" is synonymous with society itself. In a constitutional democracy such as the United States, however, we witness a pluralism of "authorities" in the civil realm. The rise of capitalism, for example, has created an economic order that is, while increasingly entangled with the state, still largely independent of the authority of what we call the state. Similarly, the emergence of voluntary associations has created an order that is frequently insistent upon its independence from the state. The same might be said of labor unions, the communications media, and certain sectors of education. While these are all in certain respects subject to the state, they are not, in our contemporary understanding, part of the state. And, of course, they are not part of the church. They are part of the larger social order.

To simplify, what we call the social order or simply "society" Christians of the 16th century often called the state. (It should be noted that for Luther and the 16th century confessors the left-hand kingdom of the civil realm was both more various and inclusive, often coming close to what we mean by the social order. The equation of the social order with the state was a later 19th century development that did much to bring the two kingdoms concept into disrepute.) By "state" today we usually mean "the government," which is but one participant, although a crucial participant, in the social order. Government today continues to possess some of the singular characteristics claimed for government in past times. For example, with exceptions such as defense of self and property, the government has a monopoly on the legitimate use of violence; it alone can declare war and claim to make decisions on behalf of all the members of a society. Other institutions, such as business corporations, can make rules for their members but only the government can make law for society. The government is also singular among social institutions in that it alone can make legitimate claim upon the loyalty of all the members of the society. That loyalty, and the obedience it entails, is, however, sharply qualified. It is qualified first by the "higher obedience" Christians owe to God in instances of conflict between the law of the state and the law of God. It is qualified second—and this is significantly changed from earlier times—by the modern understanding of democratic theory and its accompanying notions of governmental "legitimacy."

Just as St. Paul's understanding of the state in the first century, when he exhorted Christians to be "subject to the governing authorities," was not identical with Luther's understanding of the state when he similarly exhorted the Christians of the 16th century, so Luther's understanding is not identical with ours. We cannot, for example, simply reiterate the severe warnings of earlier times against disobedience to the state. Since by "the state" they frequently meant the social order itself, their warnings were rightly directed against the dangers of anarchy and social chaos. They had to oppose, as we must oppose, the illusion that human beings are inherently righteous and capable of living together independently of the law and of institutional orders. In short, they had to underscore, as we must underscore, the "not yetness" of the present age that must be ordered by the law rather than by the gospel.

If, however, we today use the term "state" in a way that equates the government with social order itself, we encourage a kind of docility to government that is incompatible with both the process and the rationale of democratic government. Democratic theory posits that governmental authority is derived from "the consent of the governed." The notion of the sovereignty of "the people" is not incompatible with our understanding, as long as that sovereignty is qualified by the meaningful affirmation of society "under God." (Technically, the term sovereignty cannot be qualified since it means supremacy over and independence from any source of authority. It is used here, however, in the widely accepted sense that the sovereignty of the people is subject to God or, in non-theistic language, to the Commonweal.)

The Political Order

Democratic theory, with its notion of legitimacy derived from the consent of the governed, is not incompatible with our understanding of civil authority. Since the ultimate source of authority is God himself, the consent of the governed can be an agency of that authority as much as "the divine right of kings" or some other concept was viewed as a legitimating agency in other times and places. One must ask, however, whether a more positive posture toward democratic government is not possible. Lutheranism, both in Europe and in the United States, has been criticized for failing to provide theological support for democratic society. That criticism must be taken seriously. At the same time we must insist that there is no one form of government or one political theory that is uniquely compatible with the life and mission of the church of Jesus Christ. Certainly the "two kingdoms" concept, no matter how imaginatively interpreted, precludes our calling any form of government or social order "Christian" in the theological sense of that term. (Sociologically, by virtue of its operative values, and statistically, by virtue of its membership, some societies may be said to be Christian. But theologically, by virtue of the functions appropriate to the civil realm and inappropriate to the community of the redeemed, no society can be equated with the church or can be ruled by the gospel.)

Because the church is catholic, both in space and time, it must not tie itself to any one notion of governmental legitimacy. We well know, for example, how culturally conditioned are our modern notions of democratic government. The United States in particular has had to learn most painfully the dangers inherent in thinking that our idea of democracy can be readily universalized in practice. These are among the strictures that should be placed on any effort to take a more positive theological stance toward democratic ideas of government. One would not, however, leave the impression that Christians are indifferent to alternative forms of government and the ideologies on which they are based.

Christians have traditionally placed the emphasis on the functional aspects of governmental authority. That is, legitimacy is determined not by some political theory about the "source" of authority but by whether or not a government does what governments are supposed to do. Usually with reference to Romans 13, the duties of government have been described in terms of restraining evil, rewarding good, securing civil peace and advancing the general well-being of the people. Since all governmental authority is "from God," it is sometimes suggested, we do not need to concern ourselves with questions about the "source" of governmental legitimacy. The problem with this apparently simple functional approach is that the definition of function makes substantive assumptions. For example, the idea of what it means to advance the general well-being of the people is in an ever-changing state of development. In our day, for instance, it is thought that the right and opportunity to participate in the political process is an essential ingredient of general well-being. Does a government that represses or denies such participation thereby fail in its God-ordained function and therefore throw into question its legitimacy?

The questions could be multiplied readily. Christian social thought still has much work to do if it is to make its full contribution to contemporary theory and practice. Issues dealing with governmental legitimacy, the limits of obedience, the right to revolution, and the role of conscience are not new, but they are posed for us in ways significantly different from those encountered in the first, the fourth or the sixteenth centuries. We would neither be indifferent to, nor would we absolutize, the modern world's understanding of democratic government. But it must be admitted that Christian social thought in the past has sinned more on the side of indifference.

In practical terms, there is no question but that Christian citizenship can be exercised within the social order that prevails in the United States. The Christian has not only a valid place but can pursue a divine vocation in government and other institutions of the social order. For example, whether in a military career or in political resistance to military influence, he sees himself as called by God. Nothing he or she does is secular in the sense of being outside the purview of Christian existence. In a democratic social order, "obedience" does not mean docility or passive compliance but a heightened exercise of individual and communal responsibility. Indeed, if we are to be "subject to the governing authority" in a democratic social order, mere docility must be viewed as disobedience.

For the Christian community, the church and its role in our kind of society is fraught with ambiguities. As in times past, the church's proper task is to proclaim the gospel, administer the sacraments, nurture the faith, and insist that the civil realm be subject to the law of God. Inherent in, and not incidental to, this task are such enterprises as education, social welfare, and witness on public policy. In short, loving service is inseparable from the church's authentic existence. As is evident in numerous conflicts, the church inevitably finds itself in very complex and frequently confusing relations with other institutions in the social order, including the government. Difficulties are compounded by the fact that the church is not only a religious community but also a corporate legal entity, a voluntary association, and, whether it wishes to be or not, an economic and political force. The church is one of the countervailing forces which comprise a democratic social order. As the individual citizen holds, in the precise sense, a "public office" and is himself a "magistrate," so the church lays claim to the rights and responsibilities that attach to being one of the "governing authorities" in a democratic social order.

All power is from God. But in a creation in which "principalities and powers" still protest the rule of the Creator, the exercise of power must be measured by the law of God. Power that is exercised in fact (regardless of the motives of those exercising it) in accord with the legitimate functions prescribed in, for example, Romans 13 is possessed of the authority "given by God." In a society of democratic pluralism that authority is exercised in diverse ways through myriad institutions, economic, political and social. Of all these institutions in the social order there are three that Christian theology has posited as necessary and permanent, short of the final coming of the kingdom: the church, the family, and the state (government). As we have seen, the institutional forms that each of these may take are subject to dramatic change and, in each instance, Christians should be captive to no one form.

The institutional form of the church has varied and may vary widely indeed. But some institutional form will always be required since Christianity is not simply the sum of individuals who believe Christian things but a community gathered around the Word in order to carry out God-given tasks such as proclamation and loving service. That gathering may be furtive and intermittent, as for example in times of persecution, but even if it is an underground network the church must by definition seek institutional form appropriate to its historical situation, whether hostile or benign. Against this church, this communal event of gospel proclaimed and celebrated, even "the gates of hell will not prevail."

While, as we noted, some have frequently spoken of "the state" in a way that encompassed the whole social order apart from the explicit tasks of the church, a special place has almost consistently been accorded the family in the "orders of creation." Today some theologians suggest that the "nuclear family" (parents and children comprising a household as the primary social unit), together with sexual roles, have undergone and are undergoing such vast changes that it is no longer possible to give the family the theological status it had in the past. Certainly the centuries have witnessed dramatic developments in our concepts of family, childhood, parental authority, sex roles, and such. Yet one cannot help but be struck at least equally with the core continuity in the institution we call the family. To abandon, for example, the arguments for the primary authority of parents over children would seem to invite the encroachment of competing authorities, especially that of the state. It is possible, of course, that some changes in social arrangements, combined with developing technology of procreation apart from present patterns of parentage, may one day eliminate or make unrecognizable what we now call the family. Such possibilities are not as remote as some may think, but we do not view them as hopes to be realized. As the policy discussions in this study make clear, we are very much committed to protecting and strengthening the family. That commitment is reinforced by the belief that the family is an inherent part of God's created order. As such, it lays claim to rights and responsibilities that must be respected by the other institutions of society. The continued evolution of family-related behavior and structure has a particular claim upon the attention of the church.

State and Church

The most problematic cluster of policy issues arises in the relationship of the modern state to other social institutions, including the church. It is not true that Christians posit a purely negative view of the governmental task, namely, that government is exclusively the product of sin and necessary only to restrain evil. We do not deny but readily affirm that government is a legitimate arena of Christian vocation and can be an agency for much positive good, especially in advancing our ever-expanding notion of the society's general welfare. At the same time, however, we make no apology for our profoundly sober estimate of the limitations of governmental power—both the limitations that must be placed on the self-aggrandizing propensities of the modern state, and the limitations on what, in a sinful creation, can be improved by the exercise of governmental power.

Because the church has said "yes" to the coming kingdom of God and has pledged itself to settle for nothing less, the church will frequently find itself saying "no" to the state when the latter presumes to exercise power in areas or in ways beyond its God-given authority. The church must say "no" to authoritarian states that would deny the God-given political, social and religious rights of its people. Most especially the church must say "no" to totalitarian states that deny there is any area or means beyond the state's authority. While saying "no," the church may nonetheless stop short of the revolutionary alternative of denying legitimacy to a particular government (although "justified revolution" is an option for Christians under carefully circumscribed conditions). While saying "no," the church may have no choice but to accommodate itself to what it views as governmental injustice. This is the case not only under authoritarian or totalitarian regimes, but also in a democratic order such as the United States aspires to be. The difference of course—and it is a very big difference— is that in a democratic order the church can, while temporarily accommodating itself, work strenuously and legally to correct the injustice. Indeed, if it is to be "subject to the governing authority" in a democratic order, it must work for such things.

The approach suggested here touches on a host of questions which fall into the category of "church-state relations." While these questions must be viewed also from a legal perspective, as that perspective is defined especially by the Supreme Court, the church's primary perspective must be theological. Too often the churches have been guilty of docility before "the law of the land" as defined by the courts, and not insistent enough that in a constitutional democracy all the instruments of government are to be responsive to the will of the people under the law of God. It will later be argued in connection with specific policy issues that, at present, the legal perspective on church-state relations is seriously skewed and frequently self-contradictory.

This does not mean that a geometrically precise formula for church-state relations can be proposed. To the contrary, in a world marred by sin and still yearning for its completion, such a formula is not available before the final coming of the kingdom, and then it will not be needed. While reasonably precise distinctions can be made, no exact line can be drawn between the institutional purview of the church and that of the state. However, that line can be drawn with greater care, common sense, consistency, and respect for the historical experience and general well-being of the American people.

The locus of legal controversy is, of course, the First and Fourteenth Amendments to the Constitution. For various reasons, including theological reasons, the churches in America should, and at least formally do, affirm the concept of non-establishment. The prospect of the churches, or of a church, taking over the government is today so remote as to be nearly inconceivable. The danger against which the non-establishment clause of the First Amendment was adopted has today been effectively precluded. The very real danger today is that the twin guarantee of free exercise of religion is being increasingly compromised, especially in the public realm, by the courts' tendency to place inordinate, sometimes exclusive, emphasis on the non-establishment clause. That tendency is both foreign to the original intention of the First Amendment and injurious to the well-being of our society. To the extent that it does indeed infringe unnecessarily upon the exercise of religious freedom, it is also contrary to the will of God.

The church should not be discouraged by the complexity and confusion that mark its role in the society. Such complexity and confusion are to be expected short of the coming of the kingdom in its fullness. The church must resist its own temptation to achieve preeminent power, as it must resist the efforts of any other institution to exercise absolute authority reinforced by Christian or other religious claims, including the religion of secularism.

If indeed the "two kingdoms" concept is a creative restatement of the biblical concept of the "two ages," then the nexus between Christian faith and public policy must be marked by the modesty, the courage and the yearning of the Holy Spirit that is reflected in the continuing prayer of the church, "Maranatha! Even so, come Lord Jesus!"

2

Relating Christian Faith
to Public Policy: Ways and Means

There are at least nine reasonably discrete ways in which the church can be instrumental in relating Christian faith to public policy. While there is nothing precise in that number, this approach may suggest some strategic possibilities that are often neglected and clarify others that are frequently misunderstood. The nine are: (1) prayer and proclamation; (2) the cultivation of civil virtue and piety; (3) the internal politics of Christian community; (4) individual Christian vocations; (5) research and education; (6) advocacy by groups and individuals; (7) corporate statements; (8) official leadership; and (9) political implementation.

Some of these are localized strategies to be pursued by congregations and individuals. Others relate to what is done by church bodies or agencies. Thus "the churches" will frequently be used rather than "the church." The use of "the church," however, intends also to underscore the ecumenical nature of the task described. Sometimes there are sound theological and strategic reasons for having a denominational label on particular approaches to public policy issues. Not only does this advance the common concern for Christian unity, but it also has the strategic advantage of giving greater public plausibility to the claim that there is a distinctively Christian faith perspective on some issues of public policy.

Prayer and Proclamation

Concern for public policy must be clearly rooted in and nurtured by the central event of the church's life, namely the community gathered around the proclaimed and celebrated Word. If such concern is perceived as an incidental addendum to, or even an intrusion upon, the core event of Christian existence, theological and political distortions are inevitable. The result is a theology and piety that denies the rule of God over the whole of the world, thus separating creation from redemption, secular from sacred, and private salvation from public hope.

Our liturgies include prayer for civil authority. The importance and meaning of such prayer should be regularly emphasized in the congregation. The very existence of such prayer is an unequivocal statement of belief that the social order is included in God's will for his world. At the same time, those responsible for the liturgical life of the churches should re-examine the prayers now used to see if they accurately reflect our understanding of the relation between Christian faith and public policy. Is obedience, for example, understood in terms of citizenship responsibilities in a democratic society?

While affirmative of civil order as such, prayer and preaching can be both critical and supportive regarding any particular order or policy question. Great pastoral care must be exercised of course in reference to policy specifics. Pastoral care, however, should not be confused with pandering to majority sentiment. Although there is a danger of manipulating sacred symbols for partisan purposes, the much more common temptation is the evasion of the controversial or the use of sacred symbols to reinforce the legitimacy of the status quo. The affirmation of civil order as such must always be accompanied by the clear understanding that any given order is always under judgment and is marked by intolerable injustices that must be protested. Again, at every level the church's most frequent witness of public policy will be "no" to particular injustices rather than "yes" to specific policy remedies which are proposed.

Most especially, prayer and proclamation must be keenly attuned to the perceptions and needs of the poor, the outcast, and the victims of existing policies and practices. In this respect, the more deeply immersed one is in the biblical and classic Christian tradition, the more profoundly radical is the critique of the social order. Such radicalism is not identical with, and may at times be opposed to, the various radicalisms in the general culture which claim to espouse the cause of the poor. Neither should such witness suggest indifference or hostility to the legitimate interests and sentiments of people who are not poor or alienated. For example, generating compassion for the poor and protesting the injustices that may keep them poor should not be confused with creating false guilt feelings among those whose placement in society is more fortunate. At the same time, legitimate sentiments such as patriotism and a sense of community within this social order should not be generated at the price of concern for the wretched of the earth in other countries, who may perceive America as the enemy.

As concern for public policy is more firmly rooted in and issues from prayer and proclamation, the conventional dichotomies between comfort and challenge, between priestly and prophetic, can be largely overcome. Even the most "prophetic" call to repentance and commitment must be viewed as an exercise of love. The word of judgment must be spoken within the bond of concern and trust in the Christian congregation. Pastors must be cautioned not to equate a "prophetic" stance with an adversarial posture toward their people. While selfishness, greed, and indifference are surely present in a community of sinners, the call to new life assumes also that there is, by God's grace, the capacity for repentance and self-giving love.

A lively interaction between the prophetic and the priestly, the comfort and the challenge, must be nurtured within the community's gathering around preached and sacramental Word. It is probably not true empirically, and it is certainly false theologically, that commitment to the "spiritual" dimensions of Christian existence must be purchased at the price of diminished concern for social justice. The great majority of Christians in America believes that they and their churches should be addressing issues of public policy. They are equally insistent, however, that the churches not neglect the distinctive institutional functions that make the churches different from other institutions which are also concerned for public policy. It is not enough for the churches to be "with the action." They must demonstrate that they are with the action in a distinctively Christian way. That distinctiveness may surface in the motive, the rationale, or in the actual positions taken.

In its opposition and advocacy, what is distinctively Christian in the church's witness may not always be self-evident. In terms of specific policy direction, the church's position may sometimes be identical with that of other groups. But by exercising critical and independent judgment, the church will not permit itself to be taken captive to any one approach to public policy, whether conservative or liberal, revolutionist or reactionary. The distinctiveness of the church's *rationale* for engagement in public policy must be constantly highlighted. Against some, the church makes clear its protest against injustice and its pursuit of justice are premised upon its belief in the purposefulness of obedience to God in the arena of historical change. Thus the church defies the notion that the struggle for change is futile and history finally absurd. Against others, the church makes clear that its engagement is premised upon a sober assessment of human sinfulness and of the limitations of politics. Thus the church's engagement is liberated from the illusion that the whole of life is political or that society is perfectible short of the kingdom of God.

These are among the themes that must be accented in relating prayer and proclamation to questions of public policy. They must be accented because they are true and because they are crucial to healing the all too common divorce between Christian piety and political responsibility.

The above considerations should be kept in mind as we examine other "ways and means" of relating Christian faith to public policy.

Cultivated Civic Virtue and Piety

Because he affirms civil order, the Christian understands that action in the public realm can be a pleasing service rendered to God. He recognizes that many non-Christians exercise a "civic righteousness" sometimes morally superior to the behavior of Christians. The Christian views this as evidence of the Creator's loving disposition to his creation and accepts it as a provocation to stir up the special gifts of grace that are his as a Christian.

The church most deliberately cultivates among its members the virtues and attitudes appropriate to a humane society. In short, the church supports what is called "civility." Civility implies a positive disposition toward the tasks of social relations in the *civitas,* or city of man. It also implies a certain restraint regarding the passions that attend such relations. The Christian exercises restraint because he knows that, no matter how enthusiastically espoused, all positions are provisional. There is no particular policy proposal upon which the coming of the kingdom is dependent. The church's ultimate hope and

passion is directed toward the kingdom. We also exercise restraint
because we recognize in even the most unscrupulous opponent an ultimate worth and sacred personhood. On questions of public policy
Christians seek neither the last word nor the destruction of opponents.

There are those who disparage civility as a pallid virtue, but it is
essential if we are to prevent power and passion from conspiring to
dehumanize our common life. Civility is more than an aesthetically
pleasing politeness; it is a marriage of commitment and deference that
is based on the Christian understanding of reality. While not neglecting the deference, we of course recognize that it is the widespread
absence of commitment that must often be of prime concern to the
church.

In democracy's sometimes raucous interaction of counter-vailing
forces, civility is regularly put to the test. The Christian, and sometimes the church, enters the fray with the full intent of prevailing, but
prevailing within the limits noted above. The Christian does not seek
the humiliation of those who may be allies on another issue of another
day. While the Christian knows that his own person cannot be separated from his vocation, he is careful to advance not himself but the
course to which he is called. And because no conflict is final, he readily
forgives as he is himself so freely forgiven.

In cultivating the virtues of civility, the church affirms both the provisional character of the political task and the religious urgency with
which that task is to be pursued. That means the Christian knows that
absolute or perfect justice is not available short of the kingdom; that,
in a world in which we are all sinners, retribution should not be
pressed too relentlessly; that there are times for amnesty, for deliberate
overlooking of insoluble problems, in order to start over again together; that there are few public policy issues not marked by high
moral ambiguity; that the political experience is filled with irony, both
tragic and comic; that in politics one has no permanent enemies, only
opponents who may be tomorrow's allies; that God alone has the
last word.

To many in our time, as in all times, this Christian sense of the provisionality of politics is an intolerable check upon wholehearted and
passionate devotion to the political process. Many seek in politics the
experience of salvation which Christians know will only be fully at-
tained in the kingdom of God and can now be anticipated through

that new life revealed in Jesus the Christ. Christian civil virtue is based upon firm resistance to the ever-present temptation to make an idol of the political process.

At the same time, Christians can engage in politics with an intense, even religious, sense of urgency. Their engagement is theologically motivated by the knowledge of human solidarity under the rule of God. That means the idea of the human family, and the consequent obligation to bear one another's burdens, is not simply poetic sentiment but revealed truth. The political task can be undertaken with religious seriousness not because it promises salvation but because it is seen as obedience to God's call and participation in his work. More particularly, the Christian views injustice and evil in the world as sinful defiance of the Creator and therefore combats them for the sake of the glory of God. It is this mix of provisionality and urgency, of modesty and devotion, that should mark the Christian's participation in the political process.

The cultivation of civic virtue and piety touches on "civil religion." In brief, we affirm the nurturing of the bonds of sentiment and obligation that are associated with patriotism and the communal sense of promise-making and promise-keeping. Ours is not a historically abstracted view of Christian civil responsibility. American Christians are to fulfill their vocations in this particular society in this particular moment in time. If by "civil religion," however, is meant a kind of narrow nationalism that is incompatible with our obligations to the whole of the human family, then "civil religion" must be rigorously opposed. Equally important, if it means the establishment of a "religion of the republic" in which the American social order would be proclaimed as self-legitimating, with no appeal to a transcendent point of reference, the church would have no choice but to condemn such a development as false religion and idolatry. Again, the church's determined resistance to secularism in the public realm is premised upon its understanding that the avowed exclusion of religion is in fact an invitation to false religion. "Under God" means the social order is under judgment, and the church has a particular responsibility to sustain that understanding.

The political virtue described above may seem peculiarly attuned to our American social situation, and it is appropriate that it should be. Yet it has more universal application to Christian responsibility in any social order. We are painfully aware that the great majority of human-kind, and of the church, lives under regimes in which the exercise of such responsibility is much more repressed than it is in North America. In situations requiring revolution, it may be that Christian vocation in the political realm cannot be exercised within the established order but only against it. In other situations it may be that Christian exis-tence is truncated by the virtual exclusion of any legitimate role in the public realm. Ours is a minority and privileged situation. Further, we should be keenly aware of the insecurity of the freedoms we enjoy, threatened not only by external enemies but perhaps even more by our failure to cultivate and exercise the political virtues appropriate to democratic government. It is not a foolish national pride but an enor-mous sense of responsibility that should move us to acknowledge the degree to which a universal hope may be attached to the American social experiment and to the church's ability to contribute to that experiment's success.

The Internal Politics of Christian Community

In relating Christian faith to public policy, the church's own life is itself a potent force in the public realm. There is great wisdom in the assertion that the church's mission is "to be the church." The church not only proclaims the presence and coming of the rule of God but should also signal what it proclaims. Or, to put it another way, the church's life is part of the proclamation, for better and for worse.

The possibilities for ordering human relations that should be evident in the Christian community may signal alternatives that are possible also in the larger social order. In the civil realm they are possible not by virtue of saving grace but by virtue of the natural goodness and righteousness that is part of the creative order. In this sense the life of the Christian community can be viewed as a political experiment; in biblical language, the life of the community is judgment, light and salt to the world outside that community.

This does not mean, however, that the social order can be modeled upon the politics of Christian community. That would constitute an impossible confusion of the "two kingdoms," of the Now and the Not Yet. Indeed, precisely by the difference between the church and the larger social order—a difference centered in the church's radical obedience to, and celebration of, the saving presence of God in Christ—the civil order is reminded of that transcendent Other to whom all are accountable. Thus when the church attends to such politically "irrelevant" business as the worship of Almighty God, it is in fact making an important contribution to the public welfare.

The plausibility of the church's witness is enhanced and possibilities are signalled for the civil realm when the Christian community demonstrates, for example, the bridging of the gaps that so sadly divide the human community. Especially is this true as the church by its word and example underscores the universals that bring people together across racial, class, and ideological divides. The church does not deny that in the political realm relations often are and must be conflictual in nature. But by drawing together political opponents in a holy communion the church can highlight—although too often does not—the common humanity and potential for divine healing that are greater than what people have in conflict. Again, this witness underscores both the restraints that must be exercised in the political process and points to new possibilities within that process. In American life this witness is especially important in racial and ethnic relations and in bringing together rich and poor.

The transnational character of the politics of the Christian community needs to be emphasized much more than has been done in the past. The one, holy, catholic, and apostolic church can provide an international linkage of peoples of a character quite different from that provided by intergovernmental and other institutions. If we have indeed witnessed the end of the "great missionary era," it must not be permitted to mean that the transnational character of Christian life and mission will be neglected. To the contrary, the end of patterns of dependency on "foreign missionaries" can mean the emergence of a much livelier and more mutual sharing of the gifts God has bestowed. upon the whole of his church.

This sharing and interaction should not be merely on the level of national churches but must be systematically and intensively geared to local congregations. Exchange programs and programs of mutual assistance using the church's vast resources for volunteerism should be given determined support. It is possible, for example, that two or more years of international service under Christian auspices, voluntarily supported, could come to be viewed as a normal part of Christian formation. In any such approach, of course, it is imperative to underscore our need, as American Christians, for the service and perspectives of Christians from other countries and cultures. It reflects poorly upon the American churches that the idea of the Peace Corps and similar projects struck so many Americans as exciting in their novelty. Had the church on all levels taken itself more seriously as a transnational community such programs of cross-cultural interdependence would have been more familiar to, and firmly rooted in, American church life, and therefore less vulnerable to the fluctuations of the political climate.

A new programmatic emphasis on global interdependence offers a number of important benefits. First is the service rendered to the American and other churches. Second is the growth in understanding and discipleship it brings to volunteers involved and to those congregations and individuals supporting them. Directly related to public policy, it can give large numbers of Christians a perspective on international affairs that is relatively independent of the viewpoints promulgated by governments and by the media. Such perspective and the personal bonds formed across political and ideological lines can be particularly important in times of international stress. The American churches would thus be better equipped to speak to international public policy because they are supported by both the resources and credibility of a large church constituency with broad and intense international experience.

The transnational character of the politics of Christian community is manifest also in various international associations of churches. Whether these are confessionally or ecumenically based, they should be viewed as inherent and not incidental to the church's life and mission. The great power of America in the world means that American Christians have a particular responsibility to let their view of the world be tempered and informed by the many millions who are affected by, but have no say in, the ways in which American power is used. The churches in this country have a unique opportunity to serve as a kind of lobby for the legitimate interests of those who have no franchise in the determination of American public policy. We have hardly begun to realize the potential of this role.

The various international councils and federations that would manifest the universality of the church have been handicapped in several ways. The absence of determined programs to relate the transnational dimension to local congregations has made such international associations seem, in the view of most American Christians, remote and even esoteric. This obviously has a bearing on the degree of grass roots support for such associations. In addition, many American Christians have little confidence in the public policy statements and postures emanating from these associations. Frequently they seem excessively anti-American in their analysis of world affairs and selective in their outrage against the injustices the church must protest.

In a world in which the freedom of public protest is very unevenly distributed, such international associations have tortuous difficulties in being both representative of the whole Christian community and honest in addressing the evils which oppress the human and Christian families. The depressing fact is that in the World Council of Churches, for example, the majority of members feel that continued membership in the Council precludes addressing a prophetic word to their own societies or governments. There are similar, if not quite so glaring, problems in confessional associations such as the Lutheran World Federation. We will return to some of these problems. Here it is enough to note that the enthusiasm of American Christians will not be enlisted for organizations that too often seem to make a scapegoat of the United States, thus exercising a mendacity that denies the universality of the sin in which the universal church is called to speak the Word of judgment and of hope.

The church must strive to demonstrate at all times that it is not captive to the ideological and political alignments that falsely divide the human community. In its internal politics this means strengthening the bond of solidarity with fellow Christians who are the victims of oppression, especially of religious oppression, whether in South Korea or Estonia, in South Africa or China, in Chile or Cuba. The whole of creation is under God and the rights appropriate to the sacredness of human life are as universal as his rule. Again, such a bond of solidarity places the church's witness in a minority and truly prophetic posture over against all other political alignments, and can only have real meaning if that bond is firmly linked with the life of local congregations.

Individual Christian Vocation

As we need always to be reminded, the church does not decide whether or not to become involved in the civil realm; it is deeply and inescapably involved. The church is, in the precise sense, the Christian people living and acting in the whole world. They are "in but not of the world," rendering their service in the left and right hands, the now and the not yet, of God's rule. Whether and how Christian faith is related to public policy depends for the most part upon individual Christians who, supported and nurtured by the believing community, fulfill their vocation as citizens.

We have spoken already of the cultivation of the virtues appropriate to citizenship in general. More careful attention should be given to the recruitment and support of Christians who pursue a full-time vocation in the public realm, whether in electoral politics or in government and non-governmental service. Support for such vocations is both affirmative and critical. That is, service in the public realm is an honorable vocation. At the same time, because it is vocation, the Christian is always accountable to God. Before he is a public servant he is a servant of God, and at those points where the two may be incompatible the Christian has his priorities straight. In a healthy society, the voice of the people and of civil authority may sometimes be in accord with the voice of God but is never to be confused with the voice of God.

The church has a great interest in combating the cynicism about politics and politicians that from time to time assails all societies. While Christians should maintain a healthy skepticism about the frequently inflated claims made for the political process, as mentioned earlier, they honor the calling exercised by those in the public realm. Nor is that honor extended only to Christians in public life. Indeed the civic righteousness of nonbelievers is frequently a judgment upon "the children of light," and the church should not hesitate to praise virtue even when it reflects unfavorably upon its own members in public office. This means the churches should resist the common temptation to obsequiousness toward their members who achieve a degree of public importance. Similarly, Lutherans should not vote for Lutherans because they are Lutheran, nor should Christians vote only for Christians. Our understanding of the integrity of the civil realm means we should support those who are best equipped to exercise the governing authority that belongs to all of us. One hopes, of course, that being a Christian might contribute to such ability, but we have no illusions about the certainty of that.

Research and Education

In relating Christian faith to public policy, we cannot overlook the importance of research and education. (Here "education" is used in the broad sense; specific issues posed by church-related educational institutions will be considered later.) Much has already been said that is pertinent also to this facet of the church's public responsibility.

The churches in this country have a mixed record when it comes to research on public policy questions. Some have almost no programmatic provisions for sustained work in this area, others have strong staffs and, in addition, a well-established practice of utilizing theological and other expertise in seminaries, colleges, parishes and public life. These disparities suggest it might be useful for Christians to think through together especially the role of research in relating Christian faith to public policy.

Research in public policy has two chief aims. The first is to provide guidance to Christians, whether as citizen generalists or as full-time public officeholders. The second is to help the churches in formulating their collective positions on public policy, when that is appropriate. Research is simply one way of trying to assure that when Christians speak to public policy, whether individually or collectively, they know what they are talking about. It also helps to expose alternatives and nuances, so that church resolutions, for example, will represent more than mere majority opinion at the moment or casual assent to the productions of ad hoc committee compromise.

Such sustained and programmatic research will, of course, use all the resources relevant to the issue studied. Christians have no special revelations or other privileged knowledge about which is the best public policy. Christians do have some special questions to ask and values to emphasize that might otherwise be neglected. In particular, Christians will examine the operative assumptions that are present in all policy questions, but that examination will be particularly intense when the assumptions have to do with the values by which a society lives. Careful research helps assure that "moral statements" cannot be dismissed as mere expressions of subjective emotion or of "secular" proposals. Such research also helps policy-makers be aware that they are choosing between values and not simply between rationally calculated facts. In encouraging such research, the churches make no secret of their hope that the choices will be in accord with the Christian construction of reality.

Research is important then, if Christian witness on public policy is to have greater credibility in the public arena. It must be combined with sustained education of the church's own membership. This education is aimed at sensitizing and informing Christians, of course, but perhaps even more important, at enabling them to be more reflective and disciplined in their own thinking about the meaning of Christian faith for public policy. Sad to say, many ethicists today, including Christian ethicists, live in a world of language and concern far removed from the everyday reality of most Christians.

If resources for ethical and theological reflection are to be made more accessible to church members in the exercise of their political office, church leadership will have to find better ways to educate not only about the policy positions themselves but about how such positions are reached. The role of publications, teaching material and other media are, of course, important in this connection. More important is the education of pastors and teachers to equip people to do their own thinking about the meaning of Christian faith and public policy. And that, obviously, has to do with the questions raised in the first section concerning the rooting of public policy in prayer and proclamation. New techniques and programs are no doubt required. Crucial to such a renewal of concern, however, is the theological securing of the political as an integral part of Christian piety and obedience.

Advocacy by Groups and Individuals

Advocacy is any individual or group action aimed at changing specific public policy. In this section we include protest as a form of advocacy.

It is usual and altogether fitting that, before a church body takes a formal position on an issue, the issue is picked up by individuals and smaller groups within the church. Indeed in many instances this will be the chief way in which the church body relates to a public policy question. This is especially the case when an issue may be so ambiguous that it does not lend itself to corporate pronouncement, or when church membership is so polarized on a question that any meaningful corporate statement can be produced only at the price of excessive divisiveness, or when an issue is being advocated so effectively by some group within the church that the church body needs only to give a tacit assent to the direction being urged. As we shall see, there is a continuing need for public policy statements by church bodies. The point here, however, is to underscore another, and often neglected, means by which Christian faith may be related to public policy.

Although the records of the churches differ on this score, there is frequently an excessive anxiety on the part of church officialdom about "the use of the church's name," in the public arena. When there is a serious likelihood that the position of an individual or group will be confused with that of the church body, the church can dissociate without disowning the individual or group. Except in the rare circumstances mentioned below, it is important that the official church not discourage the multiplicity of advocacies which the gospel can generate. To do so is to imply a from-the-top-down view of the Christian community, which is contrary to our understanding of the church. Such discouragement also squelches the very vocational diversity described in the section on "Individual Christian Vocation" above and, in addition, runs the danger of marginalizing groups and persons in a way that can be destructive of Christian unity. By a more positive and pastoral approach to such individuals and groups, church leadership can play an important role in keeping divergent perspectives in conversation and in restraining the excesses to which political passions are prone.

There are several legitimate reasons why groups may press for public policy change in the name and from the base of a church community. First, the rationale of the group's position may have emerged from, for example, Methodist life and thought. Second, the group may wisely choose to limit its decision-making in a way that is guided by the parameters of a particular denominational tradition. Third, the group may desire the denominational identification for reasons of public credibility and communication. Finally, a religiously-specific group can appeal to that church constituency that may feel less comfortable with a more generally-based organization. All these reasons can become problematic, but none is in itself illegitimate.

There are situations in which the church body can and must disown advocacy groups. This is not warranted when it is simply a question of such a group disagreeing with what may be the "official" position of the body. Indeed, if we believe in the value of dissent, the church body will be eager to keep the conversation going in such cases. But individuals or groups must be disowned when, by the most charitable and sober judgment, they advocate positions that constitute false doctrine or heresy. Admittedly the notion of public policy heresies seems somewhat curious theologically. But it might well arise in instances where policy proposals are explicitly, or implicitly but clearly, premised upon ideas contrary to Christian teaching. Such instance might be the advocacy of slavery, of racial segregation, of anti-Semitism, of a "triage"—type solution to world population problems, or of enhancing our quality of life by the elimination of the socially undesirable or "useless." (Triage proposals, sometimes also called "lifeboat ethics," suggest that the rich of the world should, as a matter of deliberate policy, conspire in eliminating large numbers of people in order to alleviate the global pressures of overpopulation.)

These positions, it is suggested, would be utterly incompatible with being a Christian, and, insofar as they can, the churches should make that incompatibility clear. In this connection, Christians need to rethink, perhaps to revive, the idea of churchly discipline. As a rule of thumb, the churches should not disown or discourage any public policy group unless its activities and positions are occasion for church discipline and affect the good standing of its member within the Christian community. An exception would be a group whose alleged association with the church is clearly fraudulent, that is, not based upon the legitimate reasons for church identification mentioned above. While the above speaks primarily about groups, the same approach would apply to individuals, although in practice the problem usually only arises in connection with individual clergy.

We have focused on some difficulties posed by the church-related identity of groups and individuals in the public arena. What follows, however, accents the positive. Were Christians more faithful in exercising their public vocation, there would no doubt be many more groups pressing vigorously, and in diverse directions, on public policy issues. Many devout church members are uncomfortable with the democratic process and the emphasis it places on individual citizen responsibility. They want to know what the official position of their church is so that they can know what they are to think about this question or that. Church leadership should not pander to this abdication of citizen responsibility. To the contrary, the role of leadership is primarily to stir up the gifts of reflection, reason, and public concern among the membership so that the many perspectives on public policy that Christian faith might generate will be manifest in as lively a fashion as possible. The prospect of the churches having an official position on every public policy issue is not only not desirable, it would be disastrous. The unity of the church does not depend upon agreement on such questions but upon a common commitment to God's will in the whole of his world, fully aware that our knowledge of his will is at best partial. In short, the church must nurture in its own life the pluralism which it espouses for society.

Corporate Statements

Now we finally come to the topic with which many would begin a discussion of "ways and means of relating Christian faith to public policy." It should be obvious by now that this ordering of ways and means is not accidental. Corporate statements by church bodies have two chief purposes. The first is to facilitate and reinforce all the ways and means described above. The second, and more exceptional, is to specify the outer limits within which public policy can be compatible with Christian faith.

Corporate statements refer primarily to the pronouncements of the highest body in a church, such as convention resolutions. The positions taken by other councils, department or agencies are, it is assumed, subordinate to the church body in convention. (Different churches have different polities, but the principles sketched here would be widely applicable.) Where a unit, such as a national church council, is empowered to act between conventions with the authority of the convention, corporate statements on public policy can be made. While such statements may have the formal authority of convention resolutions, they are obviously on a different level both of process and of plausibility. In general, they cannot depart too far from what, in the prudential judgment of leadership, are the prevailing attitudes in the constituency, and, therefore, from what a convention would likely do if confronted by the same question.

While departments, agencies, and the such are subordinate, we are well aware they play an important, sometimes decisive, role in shaping the official positions to which they are subordinate. More problematic, such agencies can and do exercise some selectivity as to which positions will be interpreted and how. The curious mix which determines both the formation and fate of corporate statements on public policy defies both canon law and systems analysis. That is hardly surprising. It is rather what should be expected in a communal enterprise marked by mutual trust and respect, and by a very inegalitarian distribution of individual talent and initiative.

(Here it is also appropriate to say something about the peculiar character of corporate statements by inter-church agencies. Whether it be the Lutheran Council in the USA or the National Council of the Churches of Christ in the USA, councils are more removed both from the process and from the authority implicit in the "ways and means" described here. This does not mean, however, that they are unimportant. On issues where the member churches are truly of one mind, the council can credibly "speak for" the member churches, especially in relating to government and other institutions. At the same time, they help to coordinate, inform, and shape the corporate positions of member churches. The Lutheran Council in the USA, for example, is an agency, even a creature, of the member church bodies. It would be a relatively useless and lifeless creature, however, if it did not also challenge and influence the member bodies. The various ecumenical ways of relating Christian faith to public policy are also dimensions of the "internal politics of the Christian community" described in the section by that title above. Although the present focus is on corporate statements made by the churches, it should be emphasized that the conciliar dimension is an important and integral part of the subject at hand.)

In facilitating and reinforcing the ways and means of relating Christian faith to public policy, corporate statements emerge from the Christian community's consultation with itself under the guidance of the Spirit. Not all such statements are position-taking statements. When the community discovers or is led to a consensus on some policy issue, however, it is altogether appropriate that the consensus should be formally articulated. The resulting statement provides a valuable point of reference in the ongoing conversation and consultation that is the life of the church.

While we should not blanch at the fact that politics is an inescapable part of the life of the church, corporate statements should not ordinarily be adopted by the brute exercise of majority power. Where views on public policy are closely divided, Christians should restrain themselves from the temptation to capture the collective voice in order to put the church body "on record" in support of a position for which they have a few more votes than "the other side." It may be better in such a situation for the corporate statement to reflect candidly the division of opinions and to give the reasoning of alternative views short of a consensus. The churches should also refrain from the all too common practice of adopting resolutions so severely compromised that they say very little, confuse the issues, and generally degrade the level of Christian reflection on public policy. A candid statement of differences is honest and open-ended, placing the question on the church's continuing agenda. Statements that are so compromised as to be meaningless merely foster the delusion that the church body has "dealt with" an issue and make religious witness on public policy look publicly ludicrous.

Obviously consensus is not to be confused with unanimity. Unanimity on many issues of this nature is impossible of achievement. There is a point, however, at which "the sense of the meeting" can be divined. Even then, it is important that dissenting views be publicly expressed and acknowledged and that the agenda be kept open for the church's continuing search for greater wisdom. In all this, it is obvious that the politics of the Christian community, under the rule of the gospel, is quite different from the politics appropriate to the civil realm. As candid as we should be about church politics, church conventions are not simply legislative assemblies nor is the church itself a constitutional democracy. It is to be feared that, in relation to modern democracy, the churches have frequently appropriated the most inappropriate aspects of the latter while at the same time neglecting democracy's challenge and opportunity for the church to play its proper role in society.

Corporate statements of consensus are valuable to the extent they reflect an *informed* consensus. Here the importance of what was said earlier under "Research and Education" should be underscored again. It is hoped that this present project will be a contribution to the goals espoused there.

The focus here has been on the role of corporate statements within the church body. Such statements are, however, also addressed to other churches in order to enrich and strengthen the whole of Christian witness in our society. In some instances one might even strive for unanimity in the Christian witness. But we do not have a word from the Lord on whether the hungry children of the poor should be fed through a food stamp program or through a guaranteed annual income. We do have a word from the Lord against a system that allows them to go hungry.

Some social policies are and always have been incompatible with Christian faith. The utter incompatibility of others—such as slavery, racial discrimination and anti-Semitism—have only become apparent to the church through long and, in these instances, painful experience. Christians of other times did not recognize these evils or, if they recognized them, saw no available remedy. The change is not in God's will for his world but in our understanding of God's will. Frequently, as in the instance of anti-Semitism, our understanding had to be illuminated by enormous horror. Given the sinful condition of the world and of the church, further illumination may have to be purchased at even greater cost than humankind has paid in the past.

The church should try to anticipate the time in which it might condemn in the name of the Lord the public policies that result in the starvation and malnutrition of millions of human beings, in hundreds of thousands of political prisoners, in the blighting of lives through war and terror, and in a world held ransom to the threat of nuclear holocaust. If we knew now with certainty which specific policies created such horrors, the church could condemn them with an unequivocal "Thus saith the Lord." But we do not know, or at least we are not agreed, and we are not prepared to exclude from the Christian community those with whom we disagree. For the church to speak on public policy in the name of the Lord is an awesome responsibility. Acknowledging the tragic that is so much part of human history, we expect that in the decades or centuries to come the outer limits will be defined more clearly by human suffering caused by policies that now should be, and then will be, condemned in the name of the Lord.

Official Leadership

Leadership includes especially pastors and bishops but also others who have some official leadership role in the churches. They are in a key position to set an example of faithful exercise of Christian citizenship. Unfortunately, this opportunity is often missed. Ironically, the impression often given is that engagement in the life of the church inhibits the very public concern that the church exhorts its members to exercise.

Church leadership is not limited to speaking and acting publicly only on those issues and in those ways for which the church has given explicit mandate. Indeed the example and direction given by leadership should be viewed as an important factor in shaping corporate consciousness and position-taking. Which is to say that leaders should lead. Frequently they may "represent" the churches best by representing the diversity of viewpoints within the churches.

As officers of the corporation they may ordinarily be expected to promote the official positions of the body. As leaders of the community they should, above all, be expected to offer the community their gifts of wisdom and conscience. Before they are elected, they are called. They are not called to be bureaucrats or simply elected representatives but to be shepherds and teachers of the flock. In the civil realm, office-holders have a conscience clause to which they can appeal when orders conflict with their sense of the right. In the church, office-holders have no conscience clause; the office itself is based on a covenant of conscience.

If, for example, a church body has an official position in favor of public policy X, the bishop (or, in the case of a congregation, the pastor) should be free not only to dissent but to publicly advocate the opposite position. Thus the conversation within the community is kept open and it may even happen that the official position is reconsidered and changed. Of course if such public disagreements were so extensive and so persistent as to throw into question the leader's sensitivity to "the mind of the meeting," the meeting might choose for itself another leader. In truth, much leadership talk about not disturbing the church reflects an excessive concern for the leaders' security of position and a blindness to the need for the church to be creatively disturbed. The obsession with avoiding controversy and the confusion of unity with uniformity reveal the churches' lack of trust in the Spirit's community-building power to enrich us through his diverse gifts. In the task of helping Christians relate their faith to public policy, the example of church leaders is, with exceptions, a major debilitating factor. On issues of major import for Christian witness, pastors and bishops in particular should not keep secret their own convictions about public policy or cravenly conform to majority opinion. To do so is a betrayal of their office and an implicit denial of what Christians believe about the honor and imperative of the citizen's vocation.

There are others who are in more clearly "staff" positions. They are called less to be shepherds and teachers than to be instrumental to the function of carrying out officially mandated directions. A particular policy having been determined by whatever authority is prescribed in the organization, they are to implement it. Even here, however, the "internal politics of the church" (see above) demands respect, even reverence, for conscience and the diversity of gifts and viewpoints. Reassignments are often possible. More frequently resignations for reasons of conscience would probably be healthy. Conditioned, to be sure, by Christian love, staff people are nonetheless hired and can be dismissed. Lutheran theology at least has not been prepared to say the same about the pastoral office.

In addition to offering an example, the role of official leadership is, of course, to facilitate all the "ways and means" described here. Especially pertinent on the parish, district and national levels are the considerations offered in the first section above, "Prayer and Proclamation." The role of official leadership needs much more attention than it has received to date. If the cry of the orphan and the widow goes unheeded, it is in large part because their cry is not magnified by the voice of leadership.

Political Implementation

All along we have been touching upon facets of political implementation. This last section is to mention specifically additional steps and programs by which the churches can relate Christian faith to public policy. Given a membership actively exercising their citizenship, given churches providing lively guidance, example and leadership, given a plethora of groups in pursuit of specific goals and in energetic conversation with one another, what else can the churches do to affect public policy?

Public witness and communication is crucial to creating the public climate within which policy options become politically viable. The churches should, individually and in concert with one another, utilize the mass media to change that climate. This means breaking out of the "go to the church of your choice"—type of public advertising, which understandably strikes most people as both banal and self-serving. On issues where a corporate position is both urgent and theologically well grounded, the church should not hesitate to be specific in its protest and advocacy.

Especially on television, the most politically potent medium in our society, the churches must continue to challenge their confinement to the "Sunday morning ghetto." (It would help if the churches could effectively get together on revising "equal time" provisions that make media managers nervous about presenting "sectarian views".) Also in other areas, such as book publishing, the churches could do more to insinuate Christian values into public discourse. It is an unhappy fact that most of the intellectual discourse relevant to public policy in our society is devoid of any explicitly Christian presence. There are no doubt many reasons for this. To say it is the process of secularization is simply to say the same thing in different words. Surely one reason is that the churches have not encouraged or exercised an aggressive approach to public policy that engages the serious attention of the society's intellectual leadership.

On selected issues there is no reason why the churches should not encourage their members to write to Congress and the President or to engage in other political action. Whether this is done by the churches or by groups within the churches, as discussed above, will vary from issue to issue. In connection with such political action, the churches should steadfastly resist the government's efforts to define or restrict what constitutes "religious activity." The church does not receive its mandate from Caesar. (More later on how this relates to tax policy.) In addition, on those issues connected with the policies of business corporations, the churches can use their investment power to effect change.

The churches also give testimony before congressional and other legislative committees. As mentioned above, some of this activity should be understood as assistance to legislators in the form of policy expertise and lifting up the sometimes hidden moral and religious implications in policy decisions. A large part of such testimony is also a matter of persuading and pressuring, that is, lobbying. It is a perfectly honorable enterprise and, on selected issues and in appropriate circumstances, the churches should not be embarrassed about it. As the largest associational network in the society, the churches should not feel government is doing them a favor when it takes their views into account.

The churches should be vigorously and unapologetically engaged in litigation before the courts. Litigation is an increasingly important means in forming public policy. While one might have misgivings about the growing role of the courts in the political process, their importance cannot be denied. Christians should both initiate and support litigation affecting the church's mission and vital issues of human welfare.

It is conceivable, although almost certainly ill-advised, that the churches as such become directly involved in electoral politics, including endorsing and supporting people for office. The churches have almost without exception declined to take this step in American public life, and for sound reasons. Such activity would be viewed as un-American by a large part of American society, and the experience of churches engaging in such activities in other societies, notably European societies, is not encouraging. The idea, sometimes proposed, of a "Christian" political party (or a Baptist or a Lutheran one!) is fraught with so many problems, ideological and practical, that one hopes it will remain as unlikely as it now seems. There is no compelling theological reason, however, why the churches, as institutional participants in the society, could not engage directly in electoral politics. There are very compelling pastoral and political reasons why it should not be in the context of American society.

Having now sketched briefly the theological considerations which mandate Christian engagement in the civil realm, and having discussed the ways and means by which that engagement can be pursued, we turn to the third section of this first part: "Testing for Decision." The first chapter dealt with the theology of our concern and engagement in the political task. The second dealt with the Christian resources for that engagement. We cannot, however, simply leap from the theological affirmation to policy decisions. A bridge is required. That bridge is built by what is commonly called social ethical considerations.

It is false to think that Christians must have an explicit theological or scriptural warrant for every decision they make about public policy. Such a view violates the classical Christian respect for the role of reason in the civil realm. Ethics is the discipline of rational and systematic reflection on the value choices facing all of us, Christian and non-Christian alike. While the next chapter does not presume to offer an ethical system, it does suggest some of the presuppositions and principles that can help us discuss with one another and with others the choices facing us in common. "Testing for Decision" will help prepare us for the actual exercises in decision making which compose the second major part of this study.

3

Testings for Decision:
Ethical Principles and Intuitions

The purpose of this section is to state briefly some of the "testings" by which public policy decisions might be reached. Others can debate as to which school of social ethics, if any, the following guidelines belong. They are consistent with, indeed often emerge from, the theological assertions in the first chapter, are amenable to the "ways and means" outlined in the second chapter, and serve as an ethical bridge to the exercises in policy decision which make up the second major part of this study.

No apology is made for the brevity with which these testings are asserted here. Their significance should become apparent as they are applied in the later policy exercises. What follows, then, is a statement of approach, of presuppositions, of intuitions; in short, a statement of bias informed by one understanding of Christian faith and public policy.

The Political Task

1. The political task is one form of partnership with God in the right ordering of human relations within his creation. Since the final right order is a matter of divine promise rather than human design, all political achievements are at best proximate achievements.

2. Optimally the political task is participation, through anticipation, in God's will for this world. Usually, participation through anticipation takes the form of opposing behavior and policy that opposes what we believe to be God's will.

3. Good public policy is limited public policy. Public policy is

self-limiting also in that it recognizes the difference between pursuing "public happiness" and trying to satisfy all possible discontents.

4. The vision of public policy is not that of salvation but of a better society in a far from the best of all possible worlds. In Christ we participate in an eternal life that transcends what is usually meant by the political task of history. This transcendence can be, but need not be, a distraction from the political task. Rather, we take the human enterprise and its politics more seriously because we recognize the eternal significance human life has been given by God.

5. Judgments on public policy are to be shaped by the ethics of responsibilities rather than the ethics of absolutes. The Absolute who is God and his New Order radically relativizes all political aspirants to absoluteness.

6. The primacy of the political task should be affirmed in the ordering of society. Economic, biological, military, social and other factors, while of great importance, are not, singly or together, finally determinative. To allow the contrary is to consign the political task to ultimate futility and to preclude the need or even the possibility of ethical judgment.

7. Politics is a function of culture and culture is, at its heart, formed by religion. The culture provides the resources by which political choices are, consciously or unconsciously, made. Religion, broadly understood, provides the "meaning systems" by which the culture understands itself.

8. Power in society is the ability to change and control situations and to get others to do what you want. Politics is concerned with the distribution and exercise of power. The goal is not to get beyond politics and the use of power but to make them as apparent, as accessible and as just as possible.

9. Public policy should therefore not be manipulatively hidden in purpose but openly stated. The process by which it is determined should be as accessible as possible to all who are affected by it. It should be fair also to those who cannot or will not participate in that process.

10. The political task is essentially public in purpose. This assumes the existence of a private realm within which persons give concrete expression to freedom by shaping their lives in relative indifference to

political purpose. Politics should resist the temptation to encroach upon, and indeed to subsume, the private realm.

11. Politics should not succumb to a mechanistic management mentality, whether of socialism or laissez faire capitalism. That is, society is not a piece of machinery requiring only more "rational" management, but a communal experiment demanding constant definition of purpose, ethical judgment, and the art of conflict resolution. A just society is not the product of a natural or historically determined order, but is constructed—and that always proximately—by human enterprise.

12. Public policy should always be conditioned by a "postulate of ignorance." That is, the precise connections between causes and effects in society elude discovery and, even more, prediction. Therefore public policy should not be irreversible but kept open to future correction.

13. In politics, truth must not be subservient to tactics or strategy, no matter how honorable or compelling the goal. Such subservience demeans public discourse, destroys the possibility of conversation between parties in conflict, and thus forecloses the hope for correction by future decision.

14. Governance in a society should be widely dispersed. In democratic society the authority to govern is not bestowed by the central state but emerges from the people and the institutions which they create and which mediate their relationship to the mega-structures of the social order. In order to insure the rights belonging to all citizens, the state must sometimes intervene in the function of such mediating institutions. It should be the aim of public policy, however, that such intervention is aimed at strengthening mediating institutions to govern justly, not at displacing such institutions. Dispersed or decentralized governance is not necessarily the same thing as democratic governance. Tyrannies may be highly localized. Therefore we must maintain a dual concern for dispersion and for democratic control, with the former reinforcing, but by no means guaranteeing, the latter.

15. Public policy should be measured by whether it restrains or encourages the dynamics of self-aggrandizement in the modern state which constitutes one of the chief dangers of politics in our century.

16. A number of modern ideas about the state have led to the tyrannies, both left and right, of our time and must be firmly resisted. Such ideas affirm: (a) that the state is the voice of the people, or

represents the general will of the nation, or reflects the natural order of society, thus requiring the subordination of differences to the general welfare as defined by the state; (b) that the society is to be viewed as a family, leading to cultivation of a spirit of fraternity in response to state leadership established by charismatic force, natural right, or by destiny; (c) that the state should create consensus or even unanimity through political education and mobilization of the people; and (d) that the authority of the state should penetrate every area of society in order to bend all forces to a common social purpose. Against these myths of the modern state we contend that the state does not embody the will of the people but is at best an instrument of self-limiting and democratically determined policies, always under the judgment of God.

17. In order to maintain the instrumental character of state power, opposition must be institutionalized and there must be structural provisions for the peaceful transfer of the exercise of power. Those who dissent from the ruling consensus will exercise mutually agreed upon restraints in order to assure the stability of the state, but the expression of differences in speech and political action will be guaranteed by the state. In a sound society, conflict and the interaction of countervailing forces will be recognized as signs of vitality. Far from being a family or a reflection of the natural order, the nation and its government are human artifices subject to human modification and to serve human purposes. The state is one instrument of governance among others and is superior to others only in protecting individual and communal rights which are otherwise imperiled. In a free society the state exercises only those powers that have been assigned to it by democratic decision. In such a society, among the chief national purposes is to sustain a pluralism of purposes, some of which are pursued by those who temporarily exercise state power subject to further political notice.

18. In our time it is important to distinguish between two types of tyrannies, authoritarian and totalitarian. Authoritarian regimes, whether of left or right, are to be viewed as a lesser evil than totalitarian regimes. While repressive of rights and intolerant of opposition, authoritarian regimes do not aspire to encompass, mobilize and control the whole of society. That is by both definition and admission the aspiration of totalitarian regimes, although, to be sure, an elite

pursues that goal in the name of "the people." In authoritarian societies, dissenters are "enemies of the state." In totalitarian societies, they are "enemies of the people." In free societies they are the loyal opposition and potential government. The ominous character of totalitarianism in our time is that, while authoritarian regimes have been overthrown, totalitarianism has to date proved irreversible.

19. The widespread assumption that authoritarian or totalitarian methods are more socially efficient is, on the evidence, highly doubtful. In addition, efficiency is not the most important political value. In public policy the bias should be toward freedom, pluralism, and openness to the future. We should therefore demonstrate the liveliest skepticism about declared crises and emergencies which presumably warrant the compromise of these values.

20. When it is truly the last resort and when other considerations which may justify violence are met, we affirm the right to violent revolution. The potential for revolution requires that some centers of political, economic and social power remain free from control by the state.

21. Realistic as we are about the temptations attending the political enterprise, it nonetheless offers the chance and the call to participate with God in the building of the earth. The Christian makes his vital contribution to the political process by encouraging the ongoing change required to rectify injustice, by holding politics accountable to that which transcends the political process, and by refusing to despair of the vision of a better society to which public policy can make a modest but crucial contribution.

The Church and the Political Task

22. The church's role in the political task is both direct and indirect, one of both action and influence. As a public institution, the church speaks primarily to protest patent injustice and to broaden, deepen and elevate the quality of public discourse.

23. The church and the truth claims it asserts cannot be confined to the private realm. The Word by which the church lives encompasses, calls to judgment and transforms the whole of creation.

24. In ascertaining the relevant data and in calculating policy consequences, the church is as dependent as any other institution on

the worldly or secular wisdom. Its chief contribution is in pressing the questions and values which emerge from the Christian understanding of human nature and historical destiny in the light of God's revealed purpose and promise.

25. If the church is true to its mission its public witness will not be conformed to any existing party or school of thought. The church's witness should be perceived as *politically radical* because it provides an independent place to stand, shaped by a distinctive understanding of human nature and destiny; because it is devoted to an Absolute Future by which all existing political designs are relativized; and because it is concerned with the misery of the poor, the marginal and those often deemed unimportant to the political process. The church's witness should be perceived as *politically liberal* because it distrusts the hubris by which people seek to control other people; because it believes in maximizing people's freedom over their own lives; and because it is committed to keeping the political process open to future development and correction. The church's witness should be perceived as *politically conservative* because it recognizes human sinfulness and therefore the fragility of humane social order; because it values tradition, custom and communal ethos, and is suspicious of designs that disregard the same; and because it insists upon the limited character of all political programs short of the kingdom of God.

26. Finally, the church and its members will not be excessively concerned about how they are perceived in terms of shifting definitions of radical, liberal, conservative, or whatever. In obedience to its Lord, the church will manifest its confidence in the purpose and promise that both illumine and empower the whole human enterprise.

Values in Public Policy

Social Order

27. Social order, the freedom from the chaos of terror and arbitrariness, is a good in itself. A higher good is good order, which is defined by values other than order itself. Good order is always an approximate achievement to which existing order should not be sacrificed without a careful counting of the costs. The point at which change threatens a degree of disorder that invites chaos will be variously perceived, no doubt depending as much upon personal temperament as upon factual

analysis. Acknowledging both the horrors of which people are capable and the promise of God's engagement in the human project, Christians will make their political decision with a mix of realism and confidence, reflecting their understanding of the fragility and hope which mark the social enterprise.

28. Society itself depends upon promise-making and promise-keeping. Thus public policy should aim at strengthening covenantal relations among individuals and groups, and toward the transcendent referent, that is, God, to whom the social enterprise is dedicated.

29. Law and morality are inseparably bound together. Law is, at its best, the articulation of the developing vision of the good order to which a society aspires. Law should therefore be formulated not only in accord with the logic of legal precedent but in lively conversation with the society's understanding of the good. All law—whether natural, constitutional, living or positive law—is proximate in relation to the will of God.

30. In addition to restraining evil, the law witnesses to the moral vision from which the law itself emerges. Thus law has a pedagogical function. It is a continuing question of prudential judgment as to when a particular law advances good behavior by pointing toward the good and when such law is so far removed from popular belief and behavior that it is entirely unenforceable and brings law itself into disrepute. In general, however, law should be supportive of the vision of the good order and not merely conformed to the order as it presently exists.

Justice

31. Although moral excellence is variously and confusingly defined, the idea of justice is inescapably linked to the idea of moral excellence. Justice is doing the right thing, and a just society is one whose structures encourage, although they cannot guarantee, the doing of the right thing. In this sense, justice is closely connected with the biblical understanding of righteousness. Short of the consummation of God's rule, justice is always approximate and provisional.

32. Distributive justice refers to the fair distribution of social goods, such as wealth, power and status. Logically connected to distributive justice is retributive justice which aims at fair punishments and re-

wards in support of doing the right thing. The Christian does not understand justice to be rooted in a natural order by which conflicting interests can be rationally harmonized. Nor does the Christian understand justice as a mere human convention to be modified by rational calculation of interests. Justice is, at its heart, obedience to the will of God, and the will of God is one of love for and within the creation. Justice may therefore be understood as the provisional form that love takes in a world not yet conformed to the will of God.

33. Public policy which reflects a vision of justice that is exhausted by the division of social goods is therefore truncated and dangerous. The vision of justice transcends the distribution of social goods. Public policy should respect and nurture the human capacity for self-transcending altruism in order that the vision of justice not be trivialized and consumed by envy and greed. As a matter of practice, that policy will be accepted as just which best combines commitment to transcendent value and perceived self interest.

Liberty

34. Liberty or freedom is the power of individuals and groups to control their own lives in a manner consonant with the basic rights of others and the survival of the society. Any vision of justice which denies or restricts such liberty is, to that extent, unjust. Respect for the liberty of others is love's response to the mystery of God's being in human beings.

35. Liberty and justice (especially when the latter is defined primarily as equality) should not be set against one another. Liberty is demanded by justice. In addition, experience suggests that those societies that have set justice against and above liberty have done worse by both liberty and justice than have those societies for which liberty is an indispensable component of justice.

36. Public policy should, in general, not be framed monothematically, even if the theme is liberty. That is, in practical decision-making we should speak of liberties (as of equalities, rights, duties, etc.) in the plural rather than the singular. Guided by an over-arching idea of liberty or freedom, decisions must be made about specific liberties or freedoms.

37. Great care must be exercised in speaking of communal liberties

as distinct from personal liberties. Almost every denial of individual human rights, from the most trivial to the Holocaust, has been perpetrated in the name of the community's freedom to secure a higher good. It is not anti-social individualism but Christian truth that insists the social order is to serve persons, not the other way around. Public policy that is attuned to "society" abstracted from the concrete lives and beliefs of persons in society is therefore bad public policy. The Christian will be guided in decision-making by the criterion of the concrete.

38. There is an intimate connection between liberty and property. The right to personal property is not absolute but it is essential. Property is one means by which the individual has leverage to exercise, and thereby make real, his liberty in society. Property is always "in society," however, and its use is therefore subject to the limitations mentioned above and by the society's idea of justice. That justice requires liberty and that liberty requires property does not lead to the conclusion that the right to property is unrestricted. Rather, it underscores again that ours is a world in which conflicts are not definitively resolved but are provisionally balanced. Christians understand property not in terms of possession but of stewardship. What is legally guaranteed as possession is therefore to be used as a trust in loving service to the neighbor.

39. The modern communications media, together with other techniques of manipulation and surveillance, pose very real dangers to liberty in our society. As the same time such media have been invaluable in protecting liberty by highlighting its violation and abuse, especially by the state. The great danger is in collusion between the state and the communications media, usually with the latter subordinate to the former. The presumption that the society needs to be educated to its own welfare or needs to be protected from itself should be met with strongest skepticism. Public policy should be biased on the side of personal liberty, even at the expense of foregoing some real or alleged higher social good. The state has the responsibility to educate the populace to the rules by which we have constitutionally agreed to conduct our public life, and to enforce those rules. It does not have the right to propagandize for its interpretation of those rules nor to inhibit advocacy for changing those rules.

40. Personal liberty is exercised in a society that is, in turn, com-

posed of many communities. Liberty does not mean simply that individuals have the right to speak and act in certain ways but that such speech and action is institutionally secured in communities. Thus liberty requires the institutions of pluralism. Public policy should reflect what might be called cognitive respect for communities in which and through which liberty is exercised. That is, what communities believe and how they organize their life together is not the business of public policy except to prevent such communities from denying a like liberty to others.

Equality

41. The egalitarian impulse is characteristic of, and may be necessary to, modern democratic society. In view of the many dynamics making for inequalities, it is important that public policy nurture the value of equality, especially political equality and equality before the law. In these realms, the principle that each person counts as one and no more than one is, although incapable of literal application in all instances, worthy of support.

42. In specific decision-making it is important to speak of equalities in the plural. That is, we should distinguish equality before the law, political equality, equality of social status, equality of wealth, and equality of power. Absolute equality describes neither the present state of affairs nor a realizable social policy. Equality as an overarching ideal is rooted in the acknowledgement of the *potential* in each human being which is, in turn, dependent upon eschatological promise. For the Christian, the idea of equality emerges from the knowledge that all persons are equal before God. To try to establish absolute equality now through public policy is an act of hubris in violation of the "not yetness" of our present moment in history. On the other hand, to act politically in resistance to that idea of equality by closing off the further realization of potential is to oppose the promise of God's working within the historical process.

43. Inequality is not therefore in itself an evil. Those things which most contribute to the public good are rare and therefore unequally distributed. Short of the kingdom to come, there is always a scarcity of excellence, whether it be honor, genius, heroism or distinguished achievement. Any egalitarianism that discourages excellence in the

way it distributes the social goods of wealth, power or status is a misbegotten egalitarianism and should be resisted.

44. The definition of excellence should as much as possible be left to individuals and mediating communities. The state should in no way dominate or monopolize the continuing process in which excellence is defined and rewarded.

45. Enlightened egalitarianism focuses on the realization of potential rather than on the levelling of social condition.

46. In highly complex industrialized societies the cause-effect connections within economic and other inequalities are extremely elusive. While inequality is in part the cause of poverty, it is certain that poverty causes and perpetuates inequality. The focus of public policy therefore should be on poverty. In such policy, urgent and massive attention should be given to equalizing opportunities for the realization of potential. Some redistribution of the wealth which is one consequence of past realization of potential may be necessary, but such redistribution should be undertaken in a way that enhances rather than discourages the pursuit of excellence.

47. While not enslaving the economic factor to political decision, neither should public policy assume that economic reward is dictated by market factors alone. It should be public policy to emphasize rewards other than economic, such as the celebration of distinction in public service.

48. Public policy should reflect an awareness of the pervasive sentiments of envy and resentment. It should as much as possible resist the force of such sentiments in public life. It must at times accommodate such sentiments, especially when inequalities provoke widespread and politically potent comparisons of an invidious nature. It should never legitimate such sentiments as principles of political life.

49. Not all wealth is gained at the expense of the poor. Inequalities of wealth are innocent until proven guilty. Those inequalities should be corrected by public policy which demonstrably perpetuate the poverty of the poor and are sustained by patently unfair competition. The terms "demonstrably" and "patently" are admittedly subject to changing factual analysis and changing social sensibilities. It is increasingly realized, for example, that real equality of opportunity requires significant changes in the competitive patterns of American society.

50. Volatile definitional debates about equality can to some extent be ameliorated by focusing public policy on absolute poverty rather than relative poverty. Human misery rather than inequality is the enemy. A level of human decency, in both present fact and in the chance to realize potential, rather than egalitarianism is the goal.

51. The principle of equality before the law should not be so rigidly interpreted as to preclude mercy or the consideration of special circumstances, especially when the law relates to the poor and those of limited competence. In distributing both rewards and punishments, the law should operate in a way that respects the circumstances of individuals and groups within a highly differentiated society, always sensible to the sound egalitarian impulse of a nation that would nurture excellence.

Calculating Costs and Benefits

52. Almost all public policy decisions involve an element of risk and should involve a calculation of costs and benefits. In making such calculations we should neither fear the future nor too readily sacrifice the present to designs which may turn out not to be the future. Fear of the future leads to a perpetuation of injustices in order to sustain the present modicum of good. Enlightened conservatism acknowledges the need for accommodation and change in order to preserve the measure of good already achieved. On the other hand, those (whether of left or of right) who would sacrifice the present in order to achieve an alleged new social order frequently betray a lack of understanding both of the provisionality of our historical moment and of the human propensity for wickedness and stupidity. In calculating the connection between ends and means, public policy should (with reluctant exceptions such as war and revolution) reflect the principle that the end is the means in process of becoming. Thus public policy will be marked by a hopeful modesty that is more devoted to the every day than to the grandiose and salvific. Again, decision should me normed by the criteria of the concrete.

53. Public policy calculations should be informed by an understanding of the unity of misery and the diversity of happiness. That is, people can more readily agree on what constitutes human misery than on what constitutes human happiness. Miseries—such as terror,

dehumanizing poverty, sickness, etc.—can be calculated while happiness is subject to infinite variations of definition and vision. Public policy should therefore be aimed at alleviating misery more than achieving happiness. The alleviation of misery, insofar as this can be achieved through public policy, is a vision of excellence which includes tasks enough to occupy our society and most societies for some time to come.

54. Costs do not include only social goods of wealth, power and status, but also costs in "meaning." That is, public policy that is sensitive to the values of pluralism will not deprive or inhibit individuals and communities that have a distinctive way of "putting the world together." The cultural costs of policy decisions should be calculated with the same respect shown economic or other costs.

55. In any calculation of costs, the impact upon the poor will be given priority consideration. That is, a society should be measured more along its fault lines than along its success lines. Policy should be framed in sensitivity to the injustices visited upon the poor more than to the discontents of the successful. In our time, as in biblical times, the plight of the poor signals the changes demanded by justice. Given the propensity of all people, including the rich, to look out for their own interests, this insight must be skillfully applied in policies that balance self-interest with the desire for righteousness.

56. A calculation of policy costs must include the factor of global interdependence. Especially for an imperial power such as the United States, the line between domestic and international policy is frequently blurred. The "quality of life" in our society should not be advanced at the expense of how people live elsewhere. Accountability to the One God places severe strictures upon notions of national sovereignty.

57. Finally, a calculation of policy costs must include the impact upon the natural world. While humankind is both the focus and the voice of God's redemptive purpose, that purpose encompasses the whole of creation.

These, then, are some of the testings, presuppositions and intuitions which shape our approach to public policy issues. The next part of this study moves on to exercises in "testing" specific public policy issues facing our country and our world, and calling for decisions by individual Christians and, in some cases, by the churches. Those issues will frequently be referred back to the "testings" of this chapter.

PART II

DIRECTIONS FOR PUBLIC POLICY

Introduction

The world is one and interdependent. The idea of the human family is not one of poetic sentiment; it is grounded in the creative and redemptive love of the God of us all. Every policy, whether domestic or international in name, must be measured by its impact upon the whole of humanity. This is especially true of the policies of the United States of America which have such singular influence—militarily, politically, economically and culturally—upon the rest of humankind.

Global unity and interdependence is the fact. The task is to devise policies and structures appropriate to that fact, in the knowledge that the unity of humankind will not be fully realized politically or socially short of the kingdom of God. Until then, our task is chiefly one of minimizing the hurt human beings do one another and of seeking a greater, although always provisional, measure of justice.

The "shrinking" of Planet Earth in the course of this century has been much remarked. Technology, especially in communications, has brought people closer together. The "global village" and similar concepts should not be exaggerated, however. With regard to communications, we remember the great events that were largely hidden from the world community, such as the Nazi Holocaust, the Stalinist purges, and, to this day, the conditions of the one quarter of the human family that is in China. Nor do we assume that greater proximity and interaction necessarily make for peace. Indeed they may create or exacerbate conflicts that distance might prevent.

Yet today we witness in our society a heightened awareness of the global community, and we would encourage that awareness. The common destiny of humankind is forcefully underscored by strains in the links of an increasingly interdependent economic system. Likewise, there is increasing understanding of the environmental perils which confront the whole human community. Most urgently and dramatically, our common destiny is manifest in a universal vulnerability to nuclear war or accident. While resisting the widespread temptation to exaggerate the discontinuities in the modern world, we acknowledge that these three developments in particular are unprecedented in human history. They pose unprecedented challenges to international policy.

Because God's world is one and interdependent, it is sometimes difficult to draw the line between international and domestic policies. This is true not only because America is still a unique experiment in which much of the world thinks, rightly or wrongly, that it perceives the future of all advanced industrial societies. It is also true because American domestic decisions, notably in the economic realm, frequently have enormous impact upon the well-being of the rest of the world.

We should not exaggerate the novelty of the American experiment. American society and power are subject to the ailments and sins which have afflicted all social orders from the beginning of history. At the same time, there are, in both theory and practice, genuinely new factors at work in the American social order. We are still engaged in a great struggle "testing whether that nation or any nation so conceived and so dedicated can long endure." God's purposes in history are not dependent upon the endurance of the United States of America. Yet there is little doubt that, for both better and worse, the modern world has a great stake in what happens in and to America. Regardless of its newness or oldness, its importance or dispensability, the United States is that part of the world for which we as Americans are chiefly responsible. As stewards called by God, we must take the decisions regarding its future with religious seriousness.

It would be disappointing were Christian thinking about public policy in America to be easily categorized as liberal or conservative, radical or reactionary. Indeed we should question the careless use of these categories in public discourse and encourage the constant re-examination of all conventional "schools" of political, economic and social thought. However we identify our viewpoint, Christians can share a common commitment to making the American experiment "work" in terms of God's revealed will for the well-being of all his children.

In the following policy reflections which relate especially to the more traditional domestic concerns, the reader will note three recurring themes: 1) a commitment to examine policy in terms of its impact upon the poor, the marginal, and the outcast; 2) a devotion to a more fully democratic process of decision-making; and 3) a high enthusiasm for the pluralistic character of American society.

On the last score especially, but closely related to the other two, the importance of what might be called "mediating institutions" in our society needs to be understood. Our society seems increasingly dominated by impersonal mega-structures, notable the state, big business, big unions, and some professional establishments. Between the individual, in the relative isolation of his or her private life, and the mega-structures stand the mediating institutions such as neighborhood, ethnic group, extended family, church and voluntary associations. Public policy should be aimed at strengthening rather than undermining, deliberately or inadvertently, these mediating institutions.

We should not oppose "bigness" as such. In a modern technological society such as ours there can be no return to romantic efforts to dismantle the mega-structures. Because we are a big society, intricately interconnected on many levels, some things must be done in a big way. But social policy should not be abstracted from the particularities of ties and associations that, in a radically pluralistic way, give distinctiveness and meaning to the everyday lives of millions of Americans. Collective and governmental responsibility for social problems has greatly expanded in recent decades, and that is good. That responsibility, however, is best exercised in a personal and pluralistic manner that strengthens rather than weakens the mediating institutions in American society. That is the course that is best for the poor, best for the political process, and best for the advancement of the American experiment in pluralistic democracy. This perspective on American social policy pervades all that is said below, but is especially pertinent to areas such as education, social welfare, and the roles of racial and ethnic minorities.

A word about the order in which these "exercises in decision making" appear: Chapter Four starts out with a discussion of the international order, taking up several controverted questions of foreign affairs, including the future of international order itself. Chapter Five moves on to the pressing issue of relations between poor and rich nations and what might be done to attain greater justice in a hungry world. With Chapter Six, "Human Rights and Freedoms," the transition is made from more universal concerns to what are usually perceived as domestic issues, namely, what kind of society do we hope America might become. "Advancing the Common Good," Chapter Seven, is something of a blockbuster and deals with many of the concerns that are, in government parlance, under the umbrella of "Health, Education and Welfare." "Law and Criminal Justice," Chapter Eight, addresses the problems posed by those who criminally dissent from the society's definition of "the common good." Chapter Nine, "Economics for People," treats the connection between all these political and social decisions and economic structure, a connection that has too often been neglected in the past. Although "church-state relations" has been our concern from the very first chapter on, a final chapter summarizes some of our conclusions in this area and suggests directions for such specifics as tax exemption for churches and other institutions.

Again, the reader should keep in mind that these are "exercises in decision-making"; they are neither formal pronouncements nor exhaustive analyses of all the issues facing us in public policy. Throughout, these exercises make use of the theological, ethical and practical considerations of Part I. It would be tedious and an unnecessary burden upon the reader to constantly hark back to specific statements in Part I in order to show their relevance to Part II. That will not be done for the same reason that Part I was not laced with strings of citations to the Scriptures and other authorities. Such lacework usually demonstrates little more than that the author knows how to use a concordance. Rather, the reader is assured that, as Part I is written with the history of Christian thought very much in mind, so the exercises of Part II assume the concepts and principles of Part I, thus forming a unified whole. Sometimes the linkages between the two parts are made explicit, more often they will be evident to the thoughtful reader. Most important, what is done here will provoke the reader—whether in classroom, parish study group, or church agency office—to make one's own linkages and conduct one's own exercises in decision, for that, finally, is the only way Christian faith will be related effectively to public policy.

4

International Order

The Nation-State

Clearly the development of the modern state has brought great good, as well as much evil, to humankind. Just as clearly, it is not the last word in the political organization of the human community. Its sovereignty will likely be checked increasingly by the demands of global interdependence. Most people depend on the state for their scurity and well-being. Because of the global nature of nuclear and other threats, no state is able to provide security and well-being to the degree that some have in the past. Many people are severely oppressed by the structure of particular states. In short, the state as an instrument of power is as morally ambiguous as is power itself.

We witness today the perduring and perhaps increasing force of nationalism. There are no clear guidelines as to what constitutes peoplehood or how peoplehood should find political expression as a nation. Many states today are nation-states in the precise sense of the term. Others are subnation-states, yet others are in fact multination-states. Africa, for example, offers many painful case studies in the problems of relating nations to states. Simultaneous with a growing global awareness, our world is marked by a widespread passion for various separatisms and "liberations" from existing nation-states. A Christian perspective does not imply an absolute and uncritical commitment to self-determination, but if a group identifies itself as a people, is economically and otherwise viable as a nation, and is prepared to fight and die for its distinct nationhood, its claims must be considered by a purely prudential measure. The goal is not the largest political unit possible but the protection of diverse communal identities within a network of responsibility that minimizes conflict.

No nation is sovereign in the precise sense of that term. Each is accountable to God and to the whole of the human family. Nonetheless, the concept of national interest is a legitimate tool in the making of policy. Indeed the predictability and reliability that are inherent in a rational calculation of national interest is crucial to world order. Christians should be involved in strengthening *and in defining* the national interest. At the same time, people are not always rational, nor is the universe so harmoniously complete as to accommodate all rationally calculated national interests. National interest must therefore be checked by responsibility within the larger human community. Again, this is especially true of nations whose policies have a great impact on others.

Equality between nation-states, except in the limited political sense of equality of sovereignty, is not a moral goal. As there are inevitably great inequalities among people within a nation or of different nations, so there are inequalities among the states that represent people. Neither domestically nor internationally can status, power or wealth be, in any meaningful sense, distributed equally. A sense of fairness should be cultivated and as much as possible codified in laws and structures, in the full knowledge that fairness is an elusive and ever-changing concept. No state should be humiliated or denied the degree of self-determination that is feasible and is appropriate to its collective human dignity.

Our concern for the people who live within states takes priority over our concern for nation-states as such. That is, today many, perhaps a majority, of states cannot make plausible claim to representing the express will or even the well-being of their people. While, as noted earlier, the legitimacy of all state power is always under challenge, some states are of more doubtful legitimacy than others. This is true whether legitimacy be measured by democratic political theory or by the functions ascribed to government in biblical thought, as, for example, in Romans 13. The result is that in programs of cooperation, development assistance, humanitarian aid and the such, it is sometimes necessary to minimize the role of the state or even to bypass the state in order to reach the people. In this respect non-governmental international networks, notably the church, become crucially important.

International Law and Organizations

Social and political structures have evolved or emerged from revolutionary change in the past and it is reasonable to expect further transformations in the future. There is no automatic progress in history that makes necessary the development from various tribal and feudal orders to a world order befitting an interdependent human family. Nor would some form of world government necessarily benefit the peoples of the world in terms of the values we cherish and which we believe are universal in their import. Yet, for the limited purposes of minimizing conflict and cooperating on those issues requiring global collaboration, we favor those policies which would secure and advance networks of international accountability.

The basis of international law is the same as the basis of domestic, or municipal, law. It is the recognition of the moral importance of law as law, insofar as it creates the possibility of society. The effective means of enforcement does not yet exist in the sphere of international law. The power of enforcement cannot be based upon some contrived notion of "equality among states," but must rather take into account the enormous disparities in size, needs, responsibilities and power among the nations of the world. The development of such an international agency or scheme of enforcement may yet be a long way off. The churches should be committed to such a development, however, and encourage the study of alternative formulas by which it might be realized. Most important, the churches should now urgently underscore the moral weight of international law and capitalize upon the human desire of nations to obey such law in order to enhance self-esteem and secure the good opinion of humankind.

The churches should combat the widespread cynicism regarding international law. The facile manner in which it can be ignored or defied, by nations large and small, does not detract from its inherent moral significance. If there can be no absolute commitment to the sovereignty of the nation-state, then the process from which international law emerges is one with the process by which law itself is developed and sustained. Indifference to international law undermines the rule of law everywhere. The legitimacy of international law as part of "the governing authorities" we revere is connected with the biblical functions and universal values which lend legitimacy to all law. Admittedly, this may be seen as an ethnocentric or historically conditioned view of international law, but it is the experience, largely shaped by the Judeo-Christian tradition, from which international law has emerged to date. Were the process of international law-making to become captive to ideologies hostile to these functions and values, international law would have no moral claim upon our obedience. That is, the legitimacy of law and government in the international sphere is the same as in the domestic sphere (see previous section on "The Nation-State").

International law limits the independent freedom of action exercised by nation-states. In addition to binding states, it is in some crucial respects a "law of mankind" under which organizations and individuals have rights and duties. An important and often neglected dimension of international law is that developed in connection with international organizations which cooperate and regulate in areas as diverse as postal regulations and fishing rights. The growth of multinational corporations also has, as we shall see, important implications for the development of world order. The notion of the sovereign nation-state has already been accommodated in large part to the need for global cooperation. Further accommodation is favored, not because a world government is a good in itself but insofar as such accommodation will help protect against the dangers and advance the hopes shared by all humankind.

Some see the current process of regionalization leading away from the rigidities of national sovereignty and toward the strengthening of international law. Regional courts for the adjudication of disputes between nations in a given area would indeed seem to strengthen international law. This is not so clear in the cases of political, military and economic "regionalization." The history of geopolitical power-balancing is not a happy one. It is not certain there is, in a world such as ours, an alternative to it. But it is certain we should strive to change the world so that such alliances and balances of power are tempered by greater accountability to the global commonwealth. This is more than pious sentiment. It means we must repudiate any vision of world order that disregards the commonalities of human need and hope as articulated in, for example, international law.

Because a more stable and just world order is so important, Christians must be aware of the naivete that is reflected in much discussion of world government. The universe is not harmonious, nor are human beings by nature peace-loving, generous and just, only needing global institutions to give expression to their virtue. All thinking about world order should reflect a healthy respect for the provisionality, diversity and perversity of the human condition, as is made clear in the earlier chapter, "Testings for Decision." With sober urgency, however, the churches should encourage the exploration of new international means to fend off the terror and to realize the more hopeful prospects that face all the inhabitants of spaceship earth.

The United Nations

Because of its great importance in our thinking about global interdependence, we must be concerned that the American people appear to be increasingly disenchanted with the United Nations Organization. The reasons are no doubt complex and related to dramatic changes in popular understanding of America's place in the world, changes largely forced by the United States debacle in Indochina. Among the reasons for disenchantment is the role increasingly played by the General Assembly. Blocs comprising a majority of the more than 130 member nations gain an attention that is sometimes disproportionate to their power and responsibilities, if not to their population. Outrage against injustices is sometimes expressed on a ludicrously selective basis, much of it having anti-Americanism as its common theme and the harassing of American interests as its common purpose. American popular disillusionment with the U.N. is therefore understandable. The churches should play a part in helping to keep such disillusionment under control.

The U.N. remains an important symbol and agency of world order. Whatever its faults, the potential consequences of its collapse are ominous indeed. It would undoubtedly confirm in many minds the suspicion that the quest for a more rational world order is hopeless. The formal or de facto withdrawal of the U.S. would likely result in the effective end of the U.N. The precedent offered by the death of the former League of Nations should give pause for thought to even the most determined critic of the United Nations.

Through its various humanitarian and educational programs, as well as through the work of the international organizations connected with it, the U.N. continues to fulfill important functions. As a forum in which potential belligerents can gain time to discuss and negotiate, the U.N. has probably facilitated the avoidance of some conflicts (which is not to deny that interaction at the U.N. may have exacerbated other conflicts). As a symbol of world order, however, the U.N. is most important. Despite the fact that it is flagrantly violated by most member nations, the Universal Declaration of Human Rights, for example, represents the symbolic importance of the U.N. It has been said that hypocrisy is the tribute that vice pays to virtue. It may happen, of course, that hypocrisy is so gross and persistent as to undermine belief in virtue. However, that has not yet happened with the U.N.

In addition, the U.N. provides important forums for the poor of the world who, often with justice, feel they have been unfairly exploited. To be sure, some member states do not adequately or honestly represent the grievances of their people. Yet there is no better political forum available. As a transnational community, the church can and should temper and correct the representation of the grievances, needs and hopes of the poor in all lands. But the church's forums, such as the Vatican, the World Council of Churches, or the Lutheran World Federation cannot replace the U.N. in a world where policy-making power rests primarily with nation-states.

One therefore hopes for an intensified and more enlightened U.S. engagement in the United Nations. The U.S. should not hesitate to press its case, and the case of those whose interests are aligned with America, in this international forum. Further, it should be more manifestly U.S. policy to nurture whatever elements of international law and cooperation can be fostered in connection with the United Nations.

Ideological Conflict

Ideology, simply stated, is any systematic scheme by which reality is described in the service of a sociopolitical program. Many Americans seem to be unaware of the ideological component in their opposition to "ideologies." It is a commonplace, but a commonplace unfortunately rooted in fact, that U.S. foreign policy has been excessively, even obsessively, preoccupied with anti-Communism. One consequence of this obsession is America's frequent support for dictatorial regimes that have no affinity with American ideology other than a vaguely defined posture of "anti-Communism." We must take most seriously that Communist tyranny is either a present fact or an impending threat for many millions. This does not mean, however, that anti-Communism is an adequate rationale for U.S. foreign policy.

"Detente" has marked U.S. relations with various Communist states in recent years. It should be remembered, however, that detente is not the same thing as peace. The appearance of relaxed tensions between nations should not be purchased at the price of ignoring the plight of millions trapped under various tyrannies. The chief value of detente is its apparent contribution to lessening the likelihood of nuclear confrontation. At this time it is still too early to make a final judgment about the other costs and benefits of detente. Clearly a "secure structure of world peace" has not yet been achieved. Just as clearly, humankind will for the foreseeable future face contradictory and even conflicting alternatives as to how society and the world should be organized. That is, ideological confrontation will continue, and perhaps even intensify.

In the past, and still too much today, an anti-Communist obsession has tended to obscure for Americans the many varieties of Marxism and socialism in today's world. In addition, it has given a dominantly negative cast to America's role in the world and inhibited the expression of the positive values which America professes to represent. In today's world most nations describe themselves as being in some sense "socialist." The compelling attraction of what is called socialism is no doubt related to its emphasis upon the communal solidarity and collective planning that are seen, rightly or wrongly, as essential to social, political and economic development. Especially in the Third World countries, however, the term socialist frequently has little or no relation to what we have known as Communism as, for example, in the Soviet Union. The usefulness of the idea of "the free world versus the Communist world" as the inclusive model for understanding international affairs has long since expired. In relating to other countries, U.S. policy should be deliberately indifferent to ideological labels. Nations should rather be measured by their treatment of their own people in terms of respect for the rights, values, and needs by which we would measure America itself.

U.S. policy toward the poor nations of the world will be considered later. Here it is enough to say that an end to obsessive anti-Communism and its replacement by a positive statement of hope for U.S. policy in the world are essential if the American people are to be engaged in a new and democratic determination of the direction of U.S. influence. The churches have a most particular responsibility for nurturing and helping to shape that democratic determination.

Multinational Corporations

Although multinational corporations have been around since the turn of the century, the cluster of multinational (or transnational) corporations that has developed since World War II poses a genuinely new phenomenon in international affairs. Such corporations—most of the largest being "based" in the United States—offer unprecedented technological and capital resources for global development. The larger of them wield economic power far in excess of that possessed even by many middle-sized nations. Because their myriad influences and decision-making processes appear nearly inscrutable, they are understandably the object of great suspicion as instruments of "capitalist imperialism."

The value or faults of multinational corporations should be measured in terms of what they do to and for people, not in terms of political ideology. That they clearly signal the emergence of a new force or sovereignty in the international community is not in itself bad since, as we have indicated, our commitment to the nation-state is neither an exclusive nor an absolute commitment. Poor nations have significant leverage in dealing with multinationals through controls and expropriation. U.S. public policy should resist the temptation to reduce that leverage, no matter how unwise U.S. government and business may think its exercise to be. The powers of national self-determination should be protected as much as possible. The costs and benefits of working with multinationals must be calculated by those with the right to decide. What a developing nation views as opportunity we should not condemn as exploitation.

At the same time, U.S. foreign policy should never be captive to the interests of multinational corporations. It is by no means self-evident that the political and other interests of the U.S. are always congruent with those of multinational corporations. Further, it is intolerable that the wielding of such enormous power as that possessed by multinationals should be unchecked by any structural accountability of a political nature to the people whose lives are affected by the decisions of multinationals. In saying this, one should be aware that international finance in general is checked by only the most fragile and partial structures of political accountability. A degree of independence of action is no doubt essential to doing business profitably. But unless multinational business and finance is more believably checked by home and host countries, as well as by international and regional interests, multinational corporations will continue to exacerbate international resentments and misunderstandings and will continue to be viewed by many as the masters rather than the partners of U.S. foreign policy.

Only in recent years have the implications of multinational business gained popular attention. Yet more recently has serious thought been given to the moral limits and responsibilities of multinationals. The churches have a very special responsibility in helping to think through the ethics relevant to this new power configuration. This can more effectively be done as the churches exploit the full resources inherent in the trans-national character of the Christian community. At the same time, the churches in America especially should more vigorously use moral suasion, political influence and the power of their investment portfolios in those cases, such as Southern Africa, where American-based multinationals perpetuate grave injustices. In pursuing this course the churches should resist the temptation to self-righteousness. It is by no means obvious that shareholders or, alas, church members are less racist or more devoted to freedom than are corporate executives. Indeed sometimes the church's greatest contribution is in encouraging and strengthening the hand of those within the corporate structure who would direct its policies toward greater justice.

War, Arms and Disarmament

The criteria of "justified war" as variously elaborated in classic Christian moral theology are still indispensable. (In saying this, one must recognize that what is meant by "war" has changed dramatically over the centuries, and especially in our own time of nuclear terror.) The absolute pacifist witness is an invaluable contribution in posing peaceful alternatives and sharpening Christian and civil conscience;

but to depend upon pacifist assumptions in the civil realm constitutes a dangerous confusion of law and gospel. Or, at least, so most Christians believe. Taking seriously the criteria of justified war may not have prevented past wars, but it can do so. It can certainly determine Christian participation in or resistance to wars. A justified war is not a good war; war remains always among the greatest manifestations of human sinfulness and the Christian can only engage in war with the greatest reluctance and with unremitting reliance upon God's correction and forgiveness. In times of war and heightened patriotic passions, the church must be especially jealous of its sacred and moral symbols lest any nation pretend to be waging a holy war.

The church must also be unequivocal in its support of conscientious objection to all war or to a particular war. Those classical Christian traditions that operate on non-pacifist assumptions offer clear support for what is called selective conscientious objection. In this connection public policy must take risks on the side of conscience, knowing that we cannot search the hearts of men as to purity of motive. If and when conscientious objection becomes so widespread as to limit a nation in waging war, the roots of the problem should be sought in the society or in the justifications for the particular war being waged. It is neither right nor safe to try to "remedy" the problem by violating the rights of conscience.

A healthy society will be uninhibited in exhibiting its profound bias toward peace and against war. While it is true that peace is not just the absence of war but also the presence of justice, justice in our kind of world is an always provisional state and the absence of war is in itself a great good. A justified war is a war of last resort, and one in which the means used are in proportion to the end for which the war is fought. In addition, there are absolute limits imposed on the conduct of war. In this connection international law must be strengthened and obeyed.

There is no way in which a full-scale nuclear war, such as the U.S. and the U.S.S.R. are equipped to wage, can be a justified war. The horrifying dilemma in which we are caught, one hopes temporarily, is that of feeling compelled to threaten what can in no way be justified. Within the existing balance of terror, changes are possible. The churches have a special responsibility to challenge the climate of fear or complacency that prevents a popular thinking through of alternatives to the unthinkable. It is, for example, morally intolerable that strategic planning should persist along assumptions of "mutual assured destruction." To kill 100 million innocent human beings because another nation has killed 100 million innocent human beings is an obscene prospect to which we must not permit ourselves to become accustomed. Yet the credibility of that prospect is now at the heart of the strategic thinking that undergirds the balance of terror. Whatever may be the achievements of our era, the existence of the nuclear equivalent of 15 tons of TNT for every man, woman and child on the globe and the declared preparedness to use it stand in grotesque judgment upon the stupidity of our times.

The enormity of this evil, actual and potential, should not paralyze us but impel us to a more urgent search for alternatives. We do not need to know the alternative in order to know that the threatened destruction at the heart of present planning constitutes a bizarre betrayal of human stewardship, a gross failure of wisdom, and a blasphemy against creation's Lord. The churches must persistently, boldly and uncompromisingly say "no" to the morally intolerable assumptions of present strategic planning. We say "no" in the hope of a "yes" leading to a better way.

At the same time, however, the sober fact is that the U.S. will continue to need its own independently strong military force. The employment of an international force, as through the United Nations, can be an effective symbol of international cooperation. In the event of conflict between great powers, however, such a force would in all probability either be inoperable or would destroy the U.N. An inoperable military force in such a situation may at first seem to be an inviting prospect. It would likely lead, however, either to violent chaos or to the triumph of injustice which the judicious use of force might prevent, or to both. While an international force is important, although of limited utility at present, Christians should vigorously oppose the beginnings of a policy whereby the U.S. government "contracts" military and quasi-military operations to independent agencies, sometimes connected with multi-national corporations. This presages a course of deceit and potential entanglements that can only further poison American public life. Decisions about war and peace must be made through the legitimate processes of the body politic. In this connection, the revitalization of the role of Congress in matters of national security should be welcomed. The "balance" between congressional and executive power in shaping foreign policy changes from time to time. In the mid-1970s it was widely thought that the Congress must assert itself against an "imperial" Presidency. At other times the same critics call for a "strong and decisive President" who can override the "bickerings" of a fractious Congress. Once again we are reminded, as emphasized in the "principles and intuitions" of Chapter Three, that politics is more art than science and that there is no one way of striking a structural balance of power that will serve all needs of all times.

While the U.S. must have an independently strong military force, reasonable people may disagree about whether the present defense establishment is proportionate to that need. A profound suspicion of the military and of militarism is healthy in a democratic society. Christians should be urgent in protesting the numerous instances of military waste and deceit in the use of public monies. The churches should be actively engaged in the ongoing task of rethinking national priorities. Certainly military preparedness that is premised on anticipating every "worst possible case" prospect is a logical absurdity and a formula for social disaster. It is neither necessary nor desirable that U.S. military power be superior to the power of all other nations. It should be appropriate to the nation's ability to maintain itself, to the changing articulation of national priorities, and to the responsibilities and practicabilities of U.S. influence in the world. In a most elementary sense, America's military strategy at present, as that of other nations, must be deemed a failure in that it does not assure the society's security against destruction by external forces.

The alternative to the intolerable balance of terror is disarmament. In an improved international climate of recognized mutual interests, disarmament may be achieved by negotiations. Except for the qualified instance of biological warfare, there has been no disarmament since World War II. To the contrary, we persist in an ever-escalating arms race. While agreement on certain "ceilings" in the arms race may in some respects be welcome, it further reinforces the assumption of mutual assured destruction which we must reject. To be sure, nuclear disarmament may lead to greater reliance on "conventional" warfare, which could entail both greater financial expenditure and greater likelihood of war between great powers. We are today a very long way from having to deal with that problem. In addition, the speculative increase in the risks of conventional warfare does not compare with the holocaust threatened by nuclear warfare in present strategic thinking.

The chances for disarmament depend chiefly upon an improved international climate and consequent negotiation. At the same time U.S. policy should not hesitate to "take risks for peace." Unilateral steps can be taken, both in refusing to escalate and in disarming, especially where these steps are readily detectable by potential enemies. The churches need regularly to remind their members and the public that the Soviet Union, for example, is as suspicious of our intentions as we are of theirs, perhaps more so. Unilateral steps can reduce the climate of fear without imperiling the nation's security any more than it is imperiled, together with the security of all humankind, by present policies.

The widespread readiness to rely indefinitely upon the balance of terror betrays a proud and foolish confidence in human rationality and restraint and in altogether too fallible technology. Whether by design, madness or technological accident, the chances of a nuclear holocaust in no way warrant the present complacency about strategic planning and disarmament. The situation is made the more perilous by the certain proliferation of nuclear technology among other nations and even among private interests. An irony may be that stemming such proliferation may require that the great powers give more definite guarantees to protect others under their respective "nuclear shields," which in turn assumes a continuation of the balance of terror. This section began by saying that the problems of war, especially of nuclear war, pose excruciating dilemmas. One should not expect any easy solutions. There is little confidence, however, that our government or others concerned are working toward alternatives to the morally intolerable assumption of mutual assured destruction. The search for such alternatives is not now, as it must be, an urgent part of the public discourse regarding the future of America and the world.

America is increasingly becoming the arms supplier to the world. Billions of dollars of weaponry is being sold more out of consideration for U.S. balance of payments than for the security of the world. The extent of the armaments sold will probably do more to increase than discourage the chances for conflict in other parts of the world. It is not adequate to say that if the U. S. did not sell these arms other nations would. The dope pusher makes the same argument. In addition, an increasing sector of U.S. industry is becoming dependent upon arms production and the lines of accountability between governmental and business decision-making become increasingly confused, to the further detriment of the democratic process in our society. One recognizes that in some instances arms sales may be a legitimate means of gaining and maintaining influence with other nations. For the reasons mentioned above, however, the U. S. is at present relying much too heavily on this means of international leverage.

Again, we should welcome the reduction in the climate of fear, suspicion and isolation promised by the present detente in U. S. relations with the Soviet Union and China. A genuine and mutual relaxation of tensions is clearly in the interest of peace. We should take seriously the criticism that the benefits of detente may be unfairly distributed, and that the legitimate interests and values of the U. S. and its allies may have been shortchanged to date. As noted earlier, international cooperation does not replace the exercises of enlightened national interest. Similarly, we can be sensitive to the appeal that detente should be used as leverage to advance change, especially in the area of human rights, in the societies that are benefiting from such relaxation of tensions. The extent to which this can be achieved is a matter of prudential judgment, but it should be explored to the furthest extent possible without seriously endangering the course signalled by detente. In view of the strategic and other considerations discussed above, any deliberate return to a U. S. policy of confrontation between great powers would be morally reprehensible.

America's Peace-keeping Responsibilities

Not all war is nuclear war, although any war involving conflict between the Great Powers may become a nuclear war. Nor are all alliances in which the United States is involved primarily military alliances. Indeed we appear to be seeing in our time an ascendency of economic, as distinct from military or political, power in international affairs. For now and for the foreseeable future, the United States will be a great, if not the greatest, power—economically, politically, culturally and militarily. In itself, Christians need neither endorse nor oppose this fact; we simply acknowledge it. American power is as morally ambiguous as is all power. In addition to acknowledging the fact, we should accept the responsibility to play a part in shaping an ethic appropriate to the American *imperium,* and where necessary in challenging that *imperium.* This requires that the churches provide a steadiness and clarity of witness that is not blown about by changing public moods, whether of militant globalism or of world-weary isolationism.

It may well be, as many contend, that the U. S. has greatly over-extended itself through its numerous alliances. Certainly a retraction of its geo-political "sphere of influence" does not necessarily mean a weakening of America. Indeed by advancing its own domestic experiment and by relying less upon military alliances, America may be internally strengthened and its influence in the world greatly enhanced. We cannot yet, however, dispense with alliances, including military alliances.

Earlier mention was made of guarantees given through U. S. membership in the United Nations. In addition, Americans must continue to be responsive to the anxiety of millions in Western Europe who perceive a very real threat from the East. The U. S. is also responsible for the security of a large, if retracting, area of Asia, notably Australia, Japan, Indonesia and the Philippines. In situations such as South Korea and parts of Latin America where American principles are severely compromised by the support of dictatorial regimes, the U.S. should press for democratization without undermining the basic dependability of its treaties and other legal commitments. The churches should persist in protesting the evils perpetrated by such regimes. Where, unlike the Soviet Union or China, some dissent is permitted under these regimes, the American churches should amplify here especially the protest of fellow Christians against injustice in other countries. While moral purity tests have no place in our thinking about such alliances, the United States government should be more energetic in advancing among allies the political values which give such alliances their moral rationale. After the tragedy of America's war in Indochina it seems to many almost inconceivable that American power should again be directly involved in waging war on foreign soil. We must be prepared, however, for quite possible scenarios in which the U. S. might be so engaged in the defense of, for example, Western Europe, Japan, Australia, and the Middle East.

The U. S. has a signal responsibility to Israel. The churches may and should protest specific policies of Israel, deplore the injustices by which the State of Israel came into being, and plead the plight of Palestinians and others who have been treated with great injustice by Israelis and Arabs alike. Yet the steadiness and dependability of U.S. commitment to Israel's survival as a state must never be permitted to be thrown into question. We can hope that commitment will increasingly be shared by other powers, but if necessary the United States must stand alone with Israel.

This thinking about Israel is singularly affected by the relationship between living Judaism and the church, a relationship which remains a great mystery and is marked by a most tortured history. In this relationship God has exercised judgment beginning with the household of faith. Lutheran Christians have particular reason to be aware of that judgment in view of the European Holocaust. It is necessary to distinguish, but it is not now possible to separate, Israel from Judaism. Many people, both Christians and Jews, believe that upon the survival of the State of Israel may well depend the survival of living Judaism. Some Christians may strongly disagree with that evaluation, but we cannot gamble with the prospect of its turning out to be accurate.

We have yet to adjust our thinking, not to mention our policies, to the new and important emergence of the Arab nations in international affairs. While some versions of an "even handedness" between Arab nations and Israel that would compromise the statement above should not be accepted, we can warmly welcome new policy initiatives aimed at establishing friendlier relations with the Arab states. Wisely handled, such relations can contribute to the security of Israel and of the whole world.

Beyond the potentially great contribution to world stability, Christians have a special reason for welcoming closer relations with the Arab countries. In addition to the many Arab Christians, Islam is one of the three great religions emerging from the common trunk of biblical tradition. In recent years, under the earthshaking impact of the Nazi holocaust, there has been extensive exploration of the great mystery that is the relationship between the church and living Judaism. The mutual exploration still has a long way to go. At the same time, however, dialogue with Islam has been almost nonexistent for many centuries. Surely with Muslims, who also claim to be children of Abraham, Christians have much to discuss and much to learn. It may well be that, in the mysterious ways of God, a new era of religious history— as well as of political and economic history—began with the assertion of Arab oil power in the fall of 1973. Opportunities that may be implicit in this development should not be lost upon the churches.

We have noted the apparent ascendancy of economic power in international relations. The strategy of the oil producers is likely a portent of an increasing use of economic force in order to achieve purposes which were in the past advanced by military force. The question now arises, and will no doubt arise in the future, as to when economic force might be viewed as an act of war warranting military retaliation. It is exceedingly difficult to conceive of a situation in which such use of military force would be morally justified. Discomfort to Americans or even severe economic strictures caused by the manipulation of scarce resources would not constitute a "last resort" situation justifying war. At the same time, prudence dictates that the U.S. cultivate more secure relations with suppliers of scarce resources while also energetically developing greater independence from such suppliers, both through exploiting its own abundant resources and through developing synthetic substitutes for vital commodities.

Peace that is based on the just harmonization of all legitimate interests is an eschatological hope. But it is a hope that impels us to earnestly seek and secure the provisional forms of peace that are attainable now.

5

Resources and Global Development

The Care of the Environment

Christians should welcome the new awareness in recent years of the dangers posed regarding the environmental envelope by which life is sustained on Planet Earth. That awareness must be further refined, especially as it touches on the ethical and public policy aspects of ecological strategy.

God's creation is not one of scarcity but of abundance. Where there are real problems of scarcity, the fault lies with human planning and behavior, not with the gift of creation. The various environmental problems do not discredit the biblical view of the relation between nature and humanity. The biblical mandate is not one of unlimited dominion and exploitation. To the contrary, the Judeo-Christian tradition underscores human accountability to God and understands the Divine mandate to be one of stewardship and caretaking of the creation. Thus environmental problems confirm the biblical view, illuminating only our failure to act in accord with it. Nor need one accept the notion that nature is harmonious and innocent while only man is vile. All policies premised upon pitting humankind against nature are profoundly suspect. People and nature are together part of a sinful and incomplete creation groaning for its fulfillment in the kingdom of God. Human history is the arena and the interpretive center for what God is doing in and for his creation. Extra-human nature is to be respected but not worshiped. It is to be gratefully used and cherished to the glory of the Creator who has, in Jesus the Christ, positioned himself at the human center.

While highlighting the very real dangers of environmental damage, the churches must caution against the excessive crisis-consciousness that would reduce public policy to the issue of survival. Survival is not in itself a normative moral value. There are conceivable worlds on which Christians would not wish to survive, but would rather struggle to the death in resisting. Such a world, for example, would be one on which the survival of the rich in their privileges is premised upon the elimination of the poor. The churches must warn against the tendency, endemic among the rich of the world, to define survival in terms of the survival of privilege based upon gross injustice. Policy proposals associated with "life boat ethics" or "triage" solutions to the environmental problems posed by the poor of the world are, as mentioned previously, (cf. Chapter Two) thoroughly odious and contrary to Christian faith. We should affirm the biblical command to compassionately bear one another's burdens, recognizing the whole world as neighborhood and all people as neighbors to whom we owe the ultimate duty of love. Our obedience to the command of other-regarding love is not based upon any proof we possess that it will be successful, but relies upon the promise of a gracious God.

Christians should welcome the role of the United Nations and other international organizations in trying to more effectively coordinate human care of the enrivonment. Especially important is the monitoring of environmental damage and dangers on a global scale. At the same time, and against the advocates of policies of "no growth," the poor nations of the world are surely right in saying that a measure of environmental "pollution" may be necessary to their development. Not all change in the state of nature is pollution. Indeed, most of the desirable achievements of society, modern or primitive, require dramatic change in the natural environment. There is always a cost-benefit factor in any use of nature, and we now know we must make that calculation more carefully than we sometimes have in the past. The state of nature is not the measure of all things. God's will is the measure of all things and man is the measurer. It is God's will that nature be used to the benefit of humankind, including humankind's need and desire to live in communion with extra-human nature. Humankind's benefit today requires the development whereby the majority of people who are poor can obtain greater security, health and freedom. Policies which the rich would impose in a self-serving appeal for environmental protection and which might lock the poor into their present misery must be resisted by the churches. As in most matters of public policy, (See Chapter Three, # 12 et al.) environmental policy should be set by prudential judgment on a case-by-case basis, with those most directly affected having the greater say.

Resources and Technology

In the present stage of environmental consciousness, it is necessary that the churches press for greater clarity and honesty in policy-related public debate. It seems evident, for example, that the much discussed "energy crisis" is little understood. There is widespread and understandable suspicion that it is a contrived crisis, in view particularly of the benefits it has produced for multinational oil companies. Rationing and other proposed policies of austerity should be publicly accepted only when people are confident that the relevant facts are known and that alternatives have been rigorously explored. The ascetic stream within Christian piety, which should be valued highly, should not be invoked in a way that invites its exploitation by those who have an interest in creating artificial crises. More affluent Christians are free to choose the spiritual values which come from living more simply. The virtues of asceticism, voluntary poverty and freedom from consumerism should not be confused with public policy, however. In order to avoid that confusion it is necessary always to view such proposals through the eyes of the poor, both in this country and the world, whose chief problem is definitely not that they are sated by the accumulation of a "consumption mad" affluent society.

Like all human creations, indeed like civilization itself, modern technology has been bought with a price, including an environmental price. The benefits of modern technology, however, far outweigh its cost. As to the resources necessary to sustain and advance technology, U.S. policy should be aimed at more fair arrangements with suppliers (more on that below) and at the development of alternative resources, synthetic or natural. God has abundantly supplied the earth with sources of energy: oil, coal, geothermal, tidal, solar, nuclear and no doubt others of which we are not aware. Resources are not a static entity, but become resources as the technology develops that makes them resources. In view of the already known but unexplored energy sources, it is possible that we are today at a very primitive level of technological development.

Not everything that we can do technologically should be done. There are today grave and well-founded misgivings about the rapid expansion of nuclear energy sources. Some are related to the problems of proliferation mentioned earlier, others to operational safety. This too is a question of prudential judgment about the seriousness of the risks involved. We should reject the proud and foolish confidence in technology that believes that anything that can be done should be done. At the same time, we should reject the assumption that we should pursue only no-risk policies. There is no technological change, nor for that matter, social change, that does not entail risk. Nothing can be "proven" safe. We can only determine what seems to us reasonable probabilities. Proof is in the future and is known only to God. We can never be certain; we should always be responsible. This sense of responsibility most emphatically includes responsibility to future generations. While the immediate welfare of those now living should not be sacrificed to an unpredictable future, neither is it tolerable that the satisfaction of unlimited present desires preclude the meeting of future needs. It is a sound axiom that the creation can accommodate the needs but not the greeds of all.

Due to efforts made in recent decades, most of our cities and industrial areas are far cleaner, in terms of air and water pollution, for example, than they were 40 or 75 years ago. As encouraging a sign of human stewardship as this is, there is much more to be done. There is no rational purpose in aiming at absolute "purity" in air and water. Indeed such a goal could have devastating economic and social consequences. Neither, however, is there cause for complacency. Both government and industry must be pressed constantly to preserve the environmental values necessary to human life. Business and industry must continue to be pushed to count environmental costs and their repair into production and pricing. Above all, public policy must be aimed at attacking the most egregious environmental pollution, which is the slum housing, sickness and poverty that blight both urban and rural America.

There is a growing call today for a redirection toward a no-growth economy. Growth is, in itself, not a virtue. Indeed the question the churches must persistently raise is, "Growth of what and for what?" As we have noted, however, much no-growth advocacy has about it an elitist and self-serving flavor and portends ominous consequences for the world's and the nation's poor. In addition, a no-growth policy would raise, in a way that they have never been raised in our society, a host of problems in connection with the ethics of distributionism. Some moral theorists and political ideologists might welcome the opportunity to deal with the problems of distributive justice which have been attentuated, if not avoided, by economic growth in the past. The Christian faith, however, supplies neither a formula for, nor does it mandate, distributive justice, as that term is variously understood in secular moral theories (see Chapter Three, "Testings for Decision"). There is no reason to welcome the class and other conflicts such a struggle over distributive justice would bring to our society. Injustices presently perpetrated upon the poor can be rectified, as they sometimes have been in the past, without recourse to policies of state-directed economic equalitarianism. We should not choose a course of no-growth economy. If it is forced upon us, the churches will have an increased and difficult responsibility to participate in the evolving public definition of justice. Meanwhile, Christians must continue to influence, in a way that reverences individual freedom and is respectful of corporate freedom, the *direction and limitation* of growth in both the private and public sectors of the economy.

On a global scale, important decisions may soon be made regarding the presumed wealth of the seabeds. It is argued by some that the wealth of the seas should be designated as international property. Certainly this has exciting implications for the development of international law and organizations. At the same time, it is far from clear that the wealth of the seas should be the property, in effect, of the United Nations. The U.N. in addition to its other difficulties noted earlier, has not the means to turn potential resources into actual resources. The moral argument that, because ownership has not heretofore been designated, the seas belong to everyone is, at best, weak. First, there is no political structure effectively representative of "everyone." Second, the argument ignores the ways in which previously unclaimed territory has in fact, and *presumably* with moral right, been claimed throughout history. The current debate about ownership and law of the seas raises difficult and fundamental questions about the nature of property.

We should in principle favor those policies which would make the wealth of the seas most accessible to the whole of the human community. Wealth, in order to be real wealth, must be exploited. The financial, distributive and technological means to realize this wealth for humanity lies largely with multinational corporations and a few advanced industrialized states.

In this, as in other areas of economic development, those who can sow sow because they expect to reap. That is, there must be a plausible cost-benefit expectation. The alternative is that incentive will be undermined or that those with the means of exploitation will reap hastily and wastefully because of an uncertain future. The latter possibility would constitute a great loss of opportunity, and perhaps danger, for the whole world.

So long as the nation-state remains the linchpin of the international order, the wealth can be more equitably shared through a generous expansion of off-shore rights. The arrangements, then, for the exploitation and distribution of wealth from the seas can be made between the country that has ownership and the corporation or other country that has the means to transform ownership into resources. As is evident in our discussion both of the multinational corporation and of the nation-state, this is not an entirely satisfactory policy. Few policies are. It may be that such a policy should include a mandatory transference to the control of a more viable instrument of international order, if and when that is developed. Meanwhile, it is far from clear that the wealth of the seas should be under the control of the United Nations, and it is grossly unfair and short-sighted that such wealth should be completely open to exploitation by whoever can get there the first with the most. Finally, any international agreement on territorial limits and exploitation rights should take into account the needs of the many land-locked nations which should not be excluded from the benefits of such exploitation.

World Hunger

The right to food is an elementary human right. In relating to the hungry of the world, our own human wholeness no less than theirs is at stake. A nutritionally adequate diet is available for all people and it is a severe judgment upon our humanly constructed world order that all people do not have access to such a diet.

Today hundreds of millions suffer from acute hunger. Increased governmental action is also needed, working both between nations and, as much as possible, reinforcing church and voluntary programs. The churches and other voluntary agencies also must greatly increase their efforts to alleviate that hunger.

In addition to emergency aid, long-range strategies are required in dealing with the causes of hunger. These include poverty, illiteracy, lack of health services, technical inadequacy, rapid population growth and unemployment. If and when, God willing, the present crisis created by massive famine and human stupidity is past, the churches must strive to sustain an earnest and long-term commitment to development on the part of the general public.

The relatively rich of the world, among whom are to be found almost all American Christians, share a measure of responsibility for perpetuating the poverty of others. Americans must be prepared, for example, to pay higher prices in some cases for goods produced by landless peasants who are forced to work for a few cents an hour. (How the benefits of higher prices might actually get to the peasants in question is largely determined by internal arrangements in other countries. On the limitations of the U.S. affecting such internal arrangements, see the prior discussion of "International Order.") The U.S. especially, with its extraordinary wealth relative to the rest of the world, has a great responsibility as a nation. That sense of responsibility is not necessarily based upon guilt, for it is not true that the prosperity of some is always bought at the price of poverty for others. For Christians that sense of responsibility is rather grounded in our understanding of the unity of the human family and of the truth that from those to whom much is given much is required.

United States food policy should be committed to world food security and to rural development, as proposed by the World Food Conference of 1974. The U.S. controls most of the world's grain exports. U.S. commercial farm export earnings in 1974, for example, were double the amount of our entire development assistance to other countries. At the same time, U.S. food assistance has declined sharply. The churches have a particular duty to liberate the general public from the myth of America's "extravagant giveaway programs." We must again stir up the public capacity for generosity and altruism that have sometimes marked American policy in the past.

The U.S. should participate in a world food reserve program. Reserves should be under national control and, wherever possible, distributed through voluntary agencies. U.S. food assistance, especially the grant portion, should be greatly increased, at least to a level of a tithe (10 percent) of our food exports. Food should not be used, as some have suggested it be used, as a "weapon in the U.S. armory." Food aid should be given on a humanitarian rather than political basis and channeled through, or in cooperation with, international agencies, including non-governmental agencies.

Policy should provide for a fair return to the U.S. farmer, with curbs against windfall profits. In addition, the U.S. should participate fully in the International Fund for Agricultural Development and should devote itself more generously to research and development aimed at food production in hungry lands.

World Poverty and Development

The U.S. ranks near the bottom of developed nations in the percentage of GNP devoted to development assistance (.21 of GNP in 1974). Americans can and must do better than that. One percent of GNP devoted to such assistance would be a worthy national goal. The quality of assistance is also important. It should develop self-reliance rather than dependency on the part of receiving nations. Assistance programs should be designed with sensitivity to the cultural impact of innovations, should be aimed at low or medium level technology and should be labor-intensive rather than capital-intensive.

There should be a more honest accounting of U.S. assistance. Loans, for example, should be counted as loans. Assistance should be "untied" from requirements that it be spent on American goods. (Not infrequently the U.S. net income from such assistance now exceeds the assistance itself.) While there are strong arguments for assistance going through international and transnational agencies, the expansion of bilateral assistance should not be precluded.

In the world as it is and, sad to say, will probably be for some time, some hard decisions are necessary in the distribution of assistance.

While any criteria are exceedingly difficult to apply in practice, the criteria to be adopted as policy should be, in order: (1) need, (2) evidence of development taking place among the poor, (3) respect for human rights, (4) leadership initiative to undertake basic reforms, such as land reform, tax reform, and anticorruption measures, and (5) the absence of wasteful military spending. In all this it is assumed that many poor nations will adopt political and economic systems different from our own. Once again discretion must be shown in responding to the various "socialist" approaches that others might proclaim or implement. As underscored in Chapter Three, decisions should be made by the "criteria of the concrete" rather than by ideological labeling, the latter still being too much the propensity in American opinion and policy.

U.S. trade policy is as important, perhaps more important, than U.S. aid policy. In this regard, Americans must re-examine trade policies which perpetuate poverty in other countries. While suppliers of raw materials, such as the oil producers, are beginning to reorganize in order to exert greater leverage, it is still largely true that poor countries must sell materials at bargain prices while importing high-priced manufactured products. While it is not necessarily true that the terms of trade are worsening for poor countries, it is unhappily the case that many countries have very little to trade. Recent rises in food, fertilizer and oil prices have placed the 40 poorest countries (the so-called Fourth World), which include a billion people, in an increasingly desperate situation. While some, notably the oil producers, should more generously share their newly created wealth, the U.S. is in a weak moral position to make its own action contingent upon what others may be prepared to do.

The U.S. should lower trade barriers, such as tariffs and quotas, especially on semiprocessed and finished products. (Such a step would also save the American consumer a great deal of money.) The U.S. should also expand and strengthen trade preferences for the poorest countries, regardless of their ideological or political alignment. Development is severely hindered if such countries do not have access to markets for their products. The U.S. worker should not be pitted against the interests of the poor, nor made to bear an unfair burden in alleviating their misery. Therefore, the U.S. should immediately undertake an aggressive policy of economic conversion here in order to move domestic production into the many areas which are not sharply competitive with the productive capacity of poor countries.

The churches should resist the perennial temptation to blame world poverty on population growth. The rich have always found it comfortable to believe that the chief cause of poverty is too many poor people. Population growth will not be effectively curbed if it is dealt with in isolation from total development needs. Hungry people show eminent logic in having large families in order to have surviving children to care for them in their old age. Experience demonstrates that where social and economic gains include the poor, and where the infant mortality rate begins to approximate that of the affluent nations, people then feel secure enough to have smaller families.

U.S. policy must clearly eschew all proposals for coercive population control. Effective and morally acceptable approaches to the real problems of rapid population growth are forms of assistance that enable poor people to work their way out of poverty; expanded health programs aimed at reducing infant mortality and increasing health security; additional research to develop and disseminate family planning methods that increase individual freedom and are dependable, inexpensive, simple, and morally acceptable to the user.

These then are some, not all, of the international policy issues which have an urgent claim upon the church's attention now and in the years ahead. This attempt has been to point directions which are congruent with our belief that this is indeed God's world, one and interdependent, and that we are the stewards of it.

6

Human Rights and Freedoms

Human Rights

Christians affirm the utterly singular and sacred status of the human person. Our relationship with God himself is reflected in the manner of our relating to other persons. The rights possessed by human beings are to be revered, Christians assert, because they are ontologically based, they are a gift rooted in the very Being of the Creator. Human rights are not privileges that can be bestowed or withdrawn by any human agency, including the state. Society can and must limit the exercise of certain rights, but only for the most compelling reasons that must always be subject to examination. Rights can only be limited for the sake of other rights, when, as happens, rights appear to be in conflict. The freedom to exercise God-given rights is the greatest achievement and highest goal of civil society. The goal is never realized completely. In a sinful and uncompleted creation, there can be no once-and-for-all rationally calculated determination of the balance between, for example, individual and communal rights. The art of politics itself is the pursuit of that balance at particular moments and on particular issues in accord with proximate justice.

The recognition of a balance between individual and communal rights, of course, underscores that rights should not be understood in an exclusively individualistic way. The individual is part of a community, or, more accurately in a pluralistic society, part of several communities. Chapter Three, "Testings for Decision," and elsewhere cautions against the idea that the nation is the primary or only community and that rights are to be interpreted as subject to the "general will" expressed by the state. The state is one actor, but by no means the only actor, in the public realm. To forget this is to invite a fatalist view of society that is hostile to all our democratic and pluralistic values. The alternative does not mean, however, that the individual is left in complete isolation without any sense of belonging or of community. He is a member of several communities—what we have called mediating institutions, such as family, church, neighborhood, ethnic group—which have rights that should be respected by all. The choice, then, is not between collective totalitarianism and individualistic libertarianism. The hope, rather, is for a society in which the individual has maximal freedom in relating to a pluralism of communities—with their distinctive life styles and belief systems—which have rights that must be respected in public policy. Again, politics is in large part the art of brokering rights in conflict.

Rights, both individual and communal, should not be viewed as antithetical to responsibilities. That is, rights are secured only by the exercise of responsibility on the part both of those who claim a right and those who see that claim in conflict with other rights. The state in particular has the responsibility of securing and protecting the individual and communal rights that make democratic society possible. This does not mean the state is a mere referee in the ongoing contentions of other parties. The state itself acts on behalf of the national community (as ambiguous as that term may be) and has rights to assert in connection with, for example, national security. But the state is not to act as the agent of the supreme community to which other communities and their values are to be conformed. The responsibility of the state is to secure and enhance the fullest interplay of individual and communal rights, and, when necessary, to establish and sustain the greatest possible degree of fairness between conflicting rights. It is the responsibility of each individual and community to assist the state in this its proper role.

There is much more that could be said about the relation between individual and communal rights and between rights and responsibilities as duties. But any such discussion must begin and conclude affirming "the utterly singular and sacred status of the human person." This is not simply an ideological bias but a biblically grounded insight that has been and continues to be crucial to the understanding of human rights. Any concept of human rights that violates the truth of this insight must be condemned by Christians as contrary to the will of God.

The Universal Declaration of Human Rights adopted by the U.N.

General Assembly in 1948 is a useful and important summary of human rights. As recognized above, these understandings of human rights have historically emerged from and are sustained by a particular religious and moral tradition within the whole of the human family. Reflecting as they do our understanding of God's creation, they are in the fullest sense universal. It may be that their observance depends upon widespread adherence to the tradition from which they emerge. Most Christians do not seek, nor would they welcome, the "Westernization" of the world. One might fervently hope, however, that some values, notably the understanding of human rights, might be shared by all within a pluralism of cultural, political and religious traditions.

The Universal Declaration of Human Rights (and the Bill of Rights of the U.S. Constitution) should be "disseminated, displayed, read and expounded" (U.N. Declaration) as widely as possible. The churches should take care to make clear that these documents reflect not merely political agreements but theologically grounded perspectives on man and society.

It is to be deplored that these rights are not more universally observed, either in the U.S. or in other countries. It is notoriously unacceptable that some nations have used Article 29 of the Universal Declaration as an escape clause, thereby systematically violating almost all the rights previously affirmed. ("In the exercise of his rights and freedoms, everyone shall be subject only to such limitations as are determined by law solely for the purpose of securing . . . the just requirements of morality, public order and general welfare in a democratic society.") We should repudiate as odious and tyrannical the notion that the general welfare or the general will can be determined by an elite in power without reference to the freely expressed opinion of the people affected. This notion makes the concept of human rights meaningless and attributes to the state a dangerous and potentially idolatrous power. Also in its respect for human rights the state acknowledges its accountability to a judgment which transcends its own.

Because they involve questions clearly related to God's will for his human family, the church should be especially assiduous in protesting the violation of human rights. As noted earlier, Christians should insist on the exposure of hypocrisies practiced by both this country and others, and the churches in their international forums should be scrupulously honest, without regard to political or ideological alignments, in their statements regarding human rights.

Rights in law can only become rights in fact if people are free to exercise such rights. In our society too little attention has been given the economic rights without which the exercise of civil and political rights is inhibited or even precluded. This point also is taken up in connection with world poverty and domestic welfare. Here it is enough to say that we should reject two common approaches to this problem. First we should reject a radical egalitarianism that is premised upon a false anthropology. A complete equalization of economic wealth is neither desirable nor realizable. Experience demonstrates that efforts toward that end invite a totalitarian negation of human rights, often including economic rights. Second, and more relevant to our own society, we should reject a radically laissez-faire devotion to liberty without reference to equality. Such an approach is also based upon a false understanding of human nature and has led to unjust social orders in which extravagant wealth coexists with massive and humanly degrading poverty. Christians need not have, and indeed do not have, a precise formula in order to repudiate the false assumptions on which other formulas may be premised. Again, the art of public policy in this excruciatingly difficult area is the pursuit of a balance in accord with proximate justice.

Minorities and Civil Rights

The discussion of many of the domestic policy questions that might well come under this section is scattered throughout the succeeding chapters. It is not necessary to repeat here what is stated about race relations or sexual rights under the sections on "Education" and "Personal and Family Life," respectively, in Chapter Seven, or about sexual rights in Chapter Eight, or about the free exercise of religion throughout. The attempt here is to focus on selected policy issues which have not suggested themselves for treatment in some other connection.

America is a nation of minorities. The current awareness of minority rights emerged largely from the tortured history of black-white relations in America. Many of the metaphors, legal rulings and social policies relevant to that particular history are now, sometimes carelessly, applied to the relationship between other minorities and the larger

society. The singular character of the struggle for racial justice in
America needs to be emphasized throughout. We should be skeptical
of the tendency to analyze other social problems in terms of that struggle. The current propensity of so many white groups in American
society for claiming victim status as the "niggers" of America should
be resisted. Of course many persons and groups have been "victimized" by this and other societies. In America, however, the *public
policy* of slavery and its continuing aftermath are without parallel.
Clear thinking and the cause of justice require that this historical fact
not be fudged by indiscriminate, although often well intended, application of the slavery model to other injustices.

The proscription of discrimination against black Americans must be
rigorously enforced. While in general it may seem both virtuous and
socially desirable to eliminate other forms of discrimination on the
basis of race, sex, religion, country of origin or previous condition of
servitude, such elimination must be qualified if we are to preserve a
pluralistic and democratic society. It is important to be discriminating
about discrimination, recognizing the differences between just and
unjust discrimination, between the violation of rights and freedom of
association, between the public and private spheres of behavior. If
these distinctions are not made, it would result in a society in which
not only unjust discrimination is *pro*scribed but in which the presumably "just" and "equal" distribution of people, power and privileges
would be largely *pre*scribed. A society of enforced prescription is quite
the opposite of the society we desire.

It may be doubtful whether there is any need for further race-
specific legislation or public policy. That is, the primary racial problem
in America, aside from personal attitudes of a racist nature, is economic. The goal must be to protect vigorously the civil rights already
secured and to address with new commitment and creativity the
scandal of poverty that so heavily afflicts the black community in particular, although not the black community alone. In the years ahead
public policy must increasingly address the problems of Hispanic
peoples who—counting citizens and both legal and illegal aliens—may
soon be as numerous as American blacks.

Women are not, properly speaking, a minority. Because of many
individual and social injustices in the past, however, they understand-

ably reflect a "minority consciousness" in many respects. We believe that the drive for women's rights is not a passing phenomenon but portends major changes in social relations, some of which are relevant to public policy decisions. Some of the legal aspects of women's rights have already been addressed. Policy changes with regard to rights relevant to marriage, divorce and family life should be made with caution and on a case-by-case basis. Rights regarding alimony and property, for examples, should be defined in a functionally-specific rather than sex-specific manner. Except for equal rights before the law, we should not seek a unisexual society, but rather celebrate the God-ordained diversity within the human condition. The goal of policy in this and other areas should be to maximize freedom of decision. Thus neither law nor education nor any other public activity should tend to preclude the choices of occupation or life styles for women or for men.

Indian Americans pose a very special claim upon the conscience of our society. As complex as the legal and moral status of past promises may be, there is no doubt that, through treaty violations and other betrayals, America has not kept faith with our Indian brothers and sisters. Native Americans are, as a group, the most impoverished of Americans, the most plagued by bad health, and the least upwardly mobile. Policies aimed at opening educational and economic opportunity should be designed with high sensibility to the history and culture of Indian Americans. It is by no means clear who "speaks for" Indian Americans. It is also unclear whether the long-range goal sought by Indian Americans is some form of cultural, economic, and national separatism or assimilation into the larger society. Except that their civil rights should be scrupulously respected, and that compensatory programs aimed at equal opportunity should be intensified, and that Indian Americans have a peculiar choice regarding their future status as a nation-people, the churches have no special wisdom to offer in this area. It is likely that the great changes presently convulsing the Native American communities have not yet reached a point where public policy can be effectively responsive to their needs and desires as they perceive them. If and when that point is reached, it will be the moral responsibility of public policy to be responsive, insofar as is possible, to the American Indian's own decision regarding his future. The danger against which Christians must struggle is that, after the present turmoil is past, Americans will once again be relieved to forget about the plight of their Indian brothers and sisters. The cause of Native Americans must be given a permanent place of high priority on our public agenda.

Immigration

America is a nation of minorities because it is a nation of immigrants. The era of immigration is, one hopes, not at an end. Indeed immigration from Third World countries, especially from Latin America and the Caribbean, is and will continue to be at an all-time high. The churches should contend vigorously for a generous and open policy of immigration and should combat relentlessly every sign of a revival of what used to be called nativism. Nativist sentiment is morally repugnant and, in an immigrant nation, conceptually absurd. This great land is nowhere near being overpopulated. To be sure, it can be argued that the people coming to America might make a greater contribution to humanity by staying in their own countries. On one level, that is their personal decision. On another, it is a decision other countries can make by limiting emigration. As for our public policy, we should be as open and generous as possible. Nor is this purely a policy of altruism, although altruism in public policy should not be belittled. Immigrants have in the past, and will in the future, enrich our common life. As to immigration from Latin America in particular, which is now estimated to be at the rate of more than a million (legal and illegal) per year, we should welcome the prospect of America's becoming a more truly bilingual culture. Through amnesty and other measures, the illegal status of many immigrants can and should be rectified. Also "culture shock" can be minimized and our society enriched as we move away from a "melting pot" approach to immigrants and toward greater celebration of pluralism (see, for example, "Testings" No. 54).

A serious dilemma is posed by the exploitation of immigrants in migrant agricultural labor. The churches should strongly support the extension of labor protections to agricultural workers. This includes the necessary right to operate "closed union shops," although we need to recognize some of the individual injustices this may create.

Communication as a Freedom

Christians should affirm as absolutely essential to the society we cherish the freedom of the press and of the media. The confidentiality of news sources must be carefully protected. In the mass communications media, especially in television, there should be a greater manifestation of the pluralism of American life and opinion, especially as this relates to the religious expression of our common life. This need not mean the dismantling of the present network news and program systems of production and distribution. Rather the number of channels of television available can be expanded, an expansion which is now or may become technologically feasible. The possibilities of public, non-commercial, television should be explored more vigorously. The present and growing dependence of public television upon corporate subsidies is cause for concern. Through government and citizen funding, as well as through improved structures of accountability, care should be taken that public television remains genuinely public. Much of this concern can be met by multiplying the number of available and operating channels. The churches should play a livelier role in monitoring and, where necessary, challenging the operation and licensing of present stations, in accord with their commitment to free expression.

Some qualifications with regard to freedom of speech are discussed later in connection with "victimless crimes." We should unequivocally support the right of anyone to advance any view, no matter how odious, in writing or in public forums. We must oppose any ideological restriction upon the exercise of academic freedom. This is not to say that academic freedom is absolute. It is to say that restrictions should be based on judgments of competence and social interest regarding the subject to be taught or the research to be advanced. Institutions expressly designed to advance an ideological or religious viewpoint will of course consider ideology as a factor in defining competence.

There are many other ideas of rights and freedoms which we might treat. This chapter has tried to address those that seem especially pertinent to the making of public policy at this point in the American experiment if it is to be kept open to the critical judgment of the future.

7

Advancing the Common Good

Personal and Family Life

The state has a deep interest in the vitality of the family as an institution. The church has a special responsibility to cultivate the virtues that sustain the family. The covenantal relationship of promise-making and promise-keeping in the family is a model of the relationship that makes society itself possible.

Although marriage is usually also a legal contract, in the church's view covenantal marriage may exist without the legal contract, as the legal contract may be present without covenantal marriage. Public policy should be geared to regularizing the marriage relationship as much as possible in order to provide the legal, economic and social incentives against the relationship being lightly entered or lightly abandoned. This is especially the case when children are involved in the marriage. Since it is possible that today many more people, especially young people, are living together outside formal marriage, we need to reconsider the idea of common law marriage which is in some states being discarded. There may well be a growing need for legal protections of all parties in such unions.

The rights of individuals must be balanced against the social significance of the institution of marriage and family. Law in this area has a pedagogical function, illuminating the values by which the society would live, as well as a preventive function, guarding individuals against acting hastily on their own, frequently temporary, dissatisfactions with a marriage. Again, especially where children are involved, divorce laws should be properly inhibiting and should have a structured bias toward continuing the marriage relationship. In most of the states of the union, laws regarding marriage and divorce are seriously flawed in these respects.

The law correctly and most importantly recognizes the rights of parents regarding the care and training of their children. It is necessary to maintain the legal distinction, with all that implies regarding rights, between children and adults. At what age that line is drawn is a matter of prudential judgment in the context of changing cultural conditions. The state should intervene in the exercise of parental responsibility for children only under extraordinary circumstances, such as instances of child abuse and other criminal behavior. Families should be free, by themselves or in association with others, to inculcate the traditions and beliefs of their choice. One therefore welcomes, for example, the state's recognition of the Amish people's right to educate their children as they see fit, even though such education may, in the view of the larger society, be "unhealthy"or encourage "cultural deprivation." Freedom means the freedom to make what others view as mistakes. In most instances the only alternative to parental control in the rearing of children is one form or another of state control. With the exceptions mentioned above, the church should favor the family in instances of conflict between parental and state authority.

Public policy regarding marriage must be respectful of the difference between crime and sin. It is not the state's business to monitor and repress sin as such. Since this distinction is important to what is said later in other connections, one should try to have the distinction fairly clear in mind. Some would say that sin is the concern of the church while crime is the concern of the state, but that is somewhat too simple. Both crime and sin are manifestations of the rebellious and incomplete character of the creation. What the law may call a crime is not necessarily a sin. Indeed, in the instance of unjust laws, the Christian may be compelled to commit a "crime" in being disobedient. Neither is all sin a crime. Indeed some of the most serious sins— pride, envy, avarice, sloth—do not lend themselves to inclusion in any criminal code. *Sinful behavior may become criminal behavior when it has seriously negative social consequences, when it is within the proper purview of public concern, and when it is reasonably subject to public restraint and control.* How a society determines what behavior is criminal is a subject of ongoing public policy debate, as we shall see in connection with the current discussion of "victimless crimes." Here it is enough to note that, although there is an unbreakable connection between morality and law (with the latter derived from the former), the distinction between these two is vital in making public policy.

Many forms of behavior in marriage are sinful in terms of what is commonly called revealed or natural morality. But they are not all subject to public policy. In this and other connections, the distinction between public and private behavior is crucial. Our understanding of the limitations of civil authority requires the utmost respect for the private sphere. Good public policy is self-limiting public policy. (See Chapter Three, "Testing for Decision, # 3.) Thus laws which try to regulate private sexual relations between consenting adults are illegitimate and should be removed from the statute books. Exceptions would be relatively rare and bizarre instances in which "sexual relations" include assault and battery or sado-masochistic acts leading to severe injury or even death. In that case the law should, in principle, protect people from one another. In practice, however, the law should show the greatest possible tolerance of any sexual relations between genuinely consenting adults and should recognize its limitations in probing the psychic mysteries engaged in sexuality. In addition, except in divorce proceedings, the law has no legitimate role in concerning itself with sexual fidelity in marriage. In principle, some Christians may see nothing wrong with laws against, for example, adultery. In practice, however, they cannot be enforced without grievous violations of rights to privacy. In this instance, or in others, the pedagogical value of the law is not as weighty a consideration as the threatened expansion of state powers over individual freedom.

Both the church and the state should honor also the single estate. The church does this positively by affirming the virtues associated with celibacy and sexual continence. In addition, the church can contribute to a fuller ethical understanding of sexual relationships outside of marriage. The state honors the single estate by refraining from laws that have a discriminatory effect upon single people. This is especially important in the areas of tax law, employment, and housing regulations. The making of social policy through tax law is always problematic, and this has been notably true in income tax regulations which have variously had the effect of penalizing single people and now, it is widely claimed, of penalizing the married. Public policy, including tax policy, should as much as possible be biased neither toward the single nor the married estate. Where other requirements are met, single people should have the right to adopt children.

The state should legally recognize as marriage only the union between male and female. There is no compelling societal need for the legalization of homosexual "marriage," and steps toward such legalization may do considerable social mischief. In addition, the mimicry of heterosexual marriage would seem to discredit what some would claim is the inherent integrity of homosexual relationships. There is a great need to develop a more sympathetic public understanding of homosexual persons, especially as many are victimized by the isolation, rejection and promiscuity of the "gay world." While few of these problems are amenable to public policy solution, the churches can lead in creating a more understanding social climate (see "Ways and Means," Chapter Two, on the church's "social influence"). This does not mean moral indifference to homosexual acts or embracing the goal of social equality with heterosexual unions. It does mean building an informed and compassionate attitude less likely to pressure individuals into isolating or "ghettoizing" themselves. It does mean expanding and making more sensitive the church's understanding of its obligation to minister to all. In this and other areas, the fact that a social problem is largely outside the purview of public policy increases the responsibility of non-governmental institutions, including the churches.

Contraceptive devices should be legally available to both adults and minors. In instances of artificial insemination, legal rights and other conditions should approximate as closely as possible the situation resulting from conception by marital partners.

The age of consent for marriage should be the same for women as for men. Other legal rights and obligations relevant to marriage, divorce and family life should be examined on a case-by-case basis in order to assure the greatest possible legal equality between men and women. In general, and as we have emphasized elsewhere, good public policy is not sweeping and abstract but sensitively related to the particularities of society.

The current pressure for women's rights should be recognized as a force that could bring about changes of great historical moment. Although no one can predict all the changes implicit in that movement, and although the movement itself is internally diverse and sometimes contradictory, we warmly welcome it as a needed provocation to re-examine the meaning of both love and justice in all aspects of male-female relations. Again, Christians should respond to this movement not as a passing fad but as a salutary challenge toward a fuller and more humane social order for both women and men.

Abortion

Among all the issues connected with marriage, family life and sexuality, none is currently more controversial than that of abortion. It is obvious the issue has not been "settled" by the Supreme Court decision of 1973 which permits in effect, abortion on demand. ("Abortion on demand" or "abortion on request" means the absence of any legal restrictions which effectively prevent a woman from obtaining a legal abortion.) While most Christians probably agree that abortion is incompatible with Christian morality except under the most extreme circumstances, there is much less agreement as to what public policy ought to be regarding abortion. There are a number of concerns and observations which we can all share and which might be helpful in formulating a more just public policy. This is one of many areas in which there is little expectation that public policy can be absolutely just or satisfactory to all.

First, we should reject as spurious the contention that the current debate about abortion is created by one sector attempting to impose its "sectarian religious views" on the whole society. Abortion is not a "Roman Catholic issue" but most emphatically an issue confronting the whole society's understanding of the definitions, rights and obligations relevant to individual freedom and the protection of unborn life. As is obvious throughout this statement, the necessary interaction between religion and public ethics, between morality and law, is strongly affirmed. We should also affirm the competence (in the sense both of right and ability) of the democratic process to address issues of complex social policy, including the issue of abortion.

Christians are not in agreement as to exactly when human life begins. From a biological viewpoint, from at least the time of implantation in the womb through to death there is a continuum of human life. The abortion debate involves many issues, including women's rights, the relationship between law and politics, and the interaction between morality and public policy. Most awesomely, the abortion debate involves the definition of human life and the question of societal protection afforded that life. The first and overriding responsibility of the state is the protection of human life.

The present reading of the law provides no effective legal protection for the unborn children even after "viability" in the third trimester. That is, abortion can be prohibited in the third trimester except where it is necessary, in appropriate medical judgment, for the preservation of the life or health of the mother. Since "health" includes undefined and undefinable psychological criteria, effective legal protection for the unborn child is precluded. Before the third trimester, abortion is to be available without condition, except that appropriate medical procedures be observed.

The dangerously ambiguous language of the Supreme Court ruling is deeply troubling. It is not clear that the principles invoked to permit abortion do not also, *in principle,* permit infanticide or the elimination of other "non-viable" humanity both at the beginning and the end stages of human life. In noting this ominous flaw in principle, it is alarmist to contend that what is permitted in principle will in fact become a clear and present danger. However, already there are those who invoke the court decision on abortion in order to support arguments for the legalization of a variety of "mercy killings." Deeply troubling also is the Court's reasoning that, because there is no positive evidence that the constitutional writers included unborn life under the definition of "person," unborn life is therefore not entitled to the "due process" protection of the Constitution. In the last century, precisely the same reasoning was invoked by the Supreme Court to exclude slaves from constitutional protection. In principle, it is the course of social progress to expand rather than retract our public understanding of the human family and of the obligations due its members.

Moreover, it is both dangerous and presumptuous for the Court to venture an opinion on what constitutes "meaningful" human life. All human life, even insentient human life, is meaningful to the Creator and is to be reverenced by all. The state trespasses the limits of its competence when it presumes to make such differentiations within the mystery of human existence or to limit the diversity of ways in which meaning is structured and affirmed. We are all only "potential" or "developing" human life, growing toward the full humanity revealed in our Lord Jesus Christ. It is therefore perilous, at best, to try to define "full humanity" or "full personhood" by contemporary criteria drawn from psychology or other disciplines.

There is a further and serious concern that our society could become dominated by what some call an "abortion mentality." That is, public policy could be oriented in an increasingly anti-natalist direction. Then too, there is the danger of a superficially utilitarian approach to human life; that which is not useful is dispensable. Such an approach is utterly contrary to Christian faith. Our society and all societies are measured in terms of the concern we evidence for the weakest, the poorest, and the most despised.

There is widespread agreement that in cases of life *versus* life (the unborn child's *versus* the mother's), abortion should be legally available. When abortion is posed in terms of life *versus* the rights of the mother, the situation is not so clear, especially when "rights" includes the right to abort the unborn for reasons of mere convenience. In the statistically slight instances of rape or serious deformity of the unborn child, perhaps the choice of abortion should be legally available. However, the proposition that a woman should have complete freedom over her own body is misleading at best. Such a proposition ignores accountability both to God and to society; and it ignores the fact that in pregnancy another life must be taken into consideration. The proposition of complete freedom over the body would of course, also be wrong if applied to men, although in that case another life is not at stake.

The churches should encourage the deepest empathy for the woman who does not wish to carry her child to term. It is not indifference or chauvinism but obedience to the law of God and commitment to social justice that compel us to emphasize that obligations must be balanced against the exercise of rights and that society has a legitimate interest in the protection of all human life at all stages of development or the lack thereof.

The prevalence of abortion in America today is deeply disturbing. Especially alarming is its increasing use as a means of contraception. Some Christians believe the problem is intractable and can only be exacerbated by further public debate. Therefore, while the church should emphasize the moral unacceptability of abortion except in extreme circumstances, the decision of the Supreme Court should be permitted to stand as the law of the land, in the hope that improved contraceptive devices and changing attitudes might gradually reduce the incidence of abortion.

Other Christians strongly support public policy change reflected in the several proposed constitutional amendments which have in common that human life is entitled to due process of law from the moment of conception. Yet others would favor a constitutional amendment that would provide legal protection from implantation or from some later point in the development of the fetus.

Given these differences, public policy on abortion should have a clear and emphatic bias toward preserving the life of the unborn, and should involve the father and others with a legitimate and intimate concern in decisions affecting the unborn. How such a policy might be established, or even if it is possible, is the subject of continuing debate.

Public policy should advance research on and disseminate information about more effective means of contraception. Public policy should clearly forbid any government employee—notably welfare agents dealing with the poor—from overtly or subtly using coercion to encourage a woman to have an abortion. Public policy also should supply every form of support and medical help for women who choose to carry their children to term. This should include financial support where necessary and also legal protection of employment while away from the job. Centers for maternal care and support have at least as much claim upon public funding as do abortion clinics. In implementing such policies the state should work as much as possible in cooperation with church and other voluntary agencies.

Health Care

It is both unconscionable and unnecessary that any American should die or suffer acutely because of the unavailability of medical care. It is unconscionable because it is unnecessary. Today we are at an important point in public policy in which it seems likely we as a society are moving toward "health care for all Americans." This is a most encouraging direction.

The United States lags behind some other developed nations in both its health care system and in the actual health of its people, as measured by such basic statistics as infant mortality, life expectancy, and the such. This may be explained in part by the polyglot makeup of the American population which makes possible the pluralism we cherish. At the same time, the lag is no doubt also related to the absence of universal and adequate health care as a commitment of national policy. An additional factor is that health care has been almost exclusively limited to care of the sick rather than care of the healthy. This means much more attention must be given to preventive medicine.

Health care should be seen as a corollary to the right to life itself. A program of national health care should include the principles of universality, accessibility, comprehensiveness and accountability. Universality means it is offered everyone in the society, yet provides for maximum individual decision as to whether or how an individual or family chooses to participate. Accessibility touches on the distribution of health services, a distribution which is now largely out of line with the actual health needs of the population. It means accessibility to basic health care is guaranteed, not accessibility to "equal" health care. Unless we are prepared to assault in principle the social differentiations created by wealth, status and power, there will be inequalities in the style of health services; such inequalities often include items only peripherally related to the substance of health care. "Basic health care" is a slippery and ever changing concept, but it would seem to include those services that contribute directly toward prolonging life and alleviating illness and suffering. Basic health care should be equally accessible to all.

Such a national program should be comprehensive in intent. That is, it should include preventive, diagnostic, treatment and rehabilitative services. It should include regular check-ups, mental health programs, and continuing family and child health care. A particular emphasis should be placed upon screening systems in order to detect present and potential health problems. Such a program is premised upon what should be the self-evident assumption that the health of the people is an invaluable national asset.

And such a program should include the principle of accountability. This means accountability between the government and the network of agencies and communities in which services are delivered. It also means, as mentioned earlier, a structured guarantee of respect for the needs and desires of the patient and his family. In the last connection, there is a host of continuing problems about freedom of choice and the meaning of "informed consent" in medical care. The subject of "patient rights" has only recently come to the fore of public attention. The churches strongly support the further exploration of ways in which individuals and families can be protected from the depersonalizing effects of what is increasingly the mega-structure of modern medicine.

There is a variety of ways in which a national health program might be financed; by direct government program funding, through Social Security or a similar system, or by policy that assures universal access to private health insurance programs. There would seem to be no principled choice between these or other options, as long as the system meets the requirements outlined above and fosters the general directions previously indicated regarding public policy and the reinforcement of mediating institutions.

A national health program should not simply codify the present absurdities and injustices in American health care systems. The frequently inordinate costs, the maldistribution of resources, the obsession with often needless technological elaborations—these and other ills should not be uncritically funded and thereby reinforced by a national health program. While America can hardly substitute a Chinese "barefoot doctors" approach for its present health system, public policy should aim at seeking alternatives to the present operation of the medical establishment. This should include experimentation with immediate health technology and with a more "grass roots" and community-based approach to the delivery of services. Abbreviated medical training can equip many more people to do the work of general practitioners. The churches should foster a healthy popular skepticism toward the mystique presently enshrining the medical establishment and perpetuating its monopoly on decisions regarding the nation's health care.

At present many American children are not assured even one good meal a day. A major step toward improving the nation's health might be a program, similar to that in Japan, in which all school children are provided one good meal each day. Certainly existing food programs should cover at least all the children of the poor. At the same time, programs for assuring one good meal a day for the elderly should be expanded. Whether made available through agencies or in the homes of the aged, this type of program offers challenges and opportunities to the local church which should be more vigorously seized.

Medical Experimentation and Practice

Modern medicine has presented and will increasingly present excruciatingly difficult problems of ethical judgment. The churches should continue and strengthen their involvement in this area. Any claim that the medical profession is competent to police itself should be clearly rejected. In many instances the judgments involved are not merely medical but are moral and political, and it is noteworthy that this fact is increasingly recognized by the medical professions. The widest possible discussion of these issues can also serve the healthy purpose of demystifying the practice of medicine, illuminating the fact that the problems are indeed very human problems and not reserved to specialists or amenable to resolution by technological systems analysis.

Research for research's sake is not an acceptable assumption. There are some experiments that might be conducted, and that might even produce some scientifically useful knowledge, but which ought not be done. Medical science, as well as other sciences, must exercise greater self-limitation, which in turn must be reinforced by limitations imposed from outside the medical research establishment. Experimentation that is therapeutic in intent (that is, aimed at improving the health of the experiment's subject) is generally permissible when several conditions are met: when the danger to the patient is reasonably low or, in the case of greater danger, when the chances are carefully calculated in relation to the extremity of the patient's condition. It is also morally imperative that the patient's consent be truly informed, or, when that is not possible, that the consent of the family and others concerned be truly informed. This is especially the case when the subject's freedom is already compromised; for instance, prisoners or mental patients. Violations of these strictures must be urgently and publicly protested by individual Christians and by the churches.

Nontherapeutic experimentation, or experimentation that might injure the health of the subject, should be proscribed except when the most careful precautions assuring the subject's fully informed consent are provided. Since the fetus cannot give such consent, and since the mother who has sought an abortion is not competent to give such consent, nontherapeutic experimentation on a living fetus must be most narrowly restricted. In the case of the "viable" fetus, every effort must be made to sustain its life. In the statistically small instances of the births of enormities, even the doctor with the greatest reverence for life might feel compelled to act in sole reliance upon the forgiveness of God. Wherever possible, when it would not be grotesquely cruel in view of their personal and spiritual strengths, the mother and family should be consulted on such a decision. But this is one of many areas in which neither love nor justice can provide an absolutely satisfactory answer. We are grateful for the great advances in fetology which make such instances less frequent.

The current debate regarding the legal and medical definition of the moment of death also poses painful and complex decisions. One or more vital signs should not be sustained interminably simply because it is technologically possible to do so. While the bias must always be toward sustaining life, it is neither morally necessary nor desirable to use extraordinary means to sustain a vital sign that offers no hope of even marginal recovery and is sustained only at great suffering to the patient's loved ones. This is in no way intended to countenance the deliberate termination of life, even of insentient life. Human beings may be vegetable-like in their behavior, but they are never "vegetables;" they are always human beings living in relation to their Creator and participating in mysteries of life beyond our understanding.

In all these difficult areas of ethical judgment, public policy should scrupulously guarantee the rights of conscience of medical personnel. Church-related hospitals and clinics should set a particular example of sustained and disciplined moral reflection on medical practice.

While the subject of medical ethics is today largely focused on the kinds of questions discussed above, we would return to our opening statements on health care and underscore that the primary ethical concern about medical practices in America is the concern to make basic health care, which is correlate to the right to life itself, available to all Americans.

Responsibility for Social Welfare

"Social welfare" means the program and agencies that usually come under that heading, as well as welfare policy as it relates to sustaining the poor and reducing poverty itself. (Of course, "social welfare" could be so broadly defined as to include every dimension of politics and public policy. In our discussion it has a more precise definition.)

Historically the churches and voluntary associations in America assumed primary responsibility for a wide range of social welfare activities and, until relatively recently, shaped most of the assumptions and working designs for such activities. Now this is dramatically changed. Although, as has been stressed, the serving ministry is an inherent part of the church's mandate and mission, today the church is increasingly impotent to make the important decisions regarding its own programs of social ministry. The government can and does make these decisions through its power of funding and responsibility to license. We should affirm that responsibility, but we cannot help but be highly critical of the present trends in the exercise of that power.

Again, the rising sense in recent decades of what human problems constitute societal responsibilities is to be celebrated. But the growing assumption that the state is the primary or exclusive agency for the exercise of those responsibilities is to be opposed. The churches are in large part responsible for the trends that should be opposed. In addition to the faults in the quantity and quality of social ministry, the churches also developed a strategic rationale for the veritable handover of its responsibilities to the state. For whatever reasons, the churches lost the confidence, theological and strategic, which once supported their role in social welfare. One result has been the increasing power of depersonalizing mega-structures in social welfare, much to the detriment of democratic pluralism and to the hurt of the beneficiaries of such programs whose human need require more personal association through the mediating institutions that shape their lives and personal identities.

The churches' involvement in social welfare is not simply one of filling in gaps or conducting experimental programs until they are taken over by the state. The church has a *permanent, legitimate and necessary* involvement in social welfare, which is one corporate expression of its mandate to live in loving service to others. Many church agencies are inescapably deliverers of services to those in need. But the church agency should be more than that. It should be also an agent for social change (see "Ways and Means," Chapter 2). Church agencies should be more than incidentally church-related agencies. They should be enablers of the whole church, especially through congregations, in fulfilling the social service ministry which belongs to the whole church. The church agency, if it is true to itself, has no choice but to be prophetic, in the sense of social criticism, while at the same time delivering services. This necessity makes most urgent a re-examination of patterns of dependency and control in relation to the state.

In trying to change public policy on social welfare questions, the churches should coordinate their efforts as much as possible with other voluntary associations, including philanthropic organizations, voluntary health and hospital services, youth-oriented groups, and the more than three quarters of a million voluntary organizations supported by United Way efforts alone. Strenuous efforts should be made to sustain and expand the base of voluntary giving for such purposes in America. Church agencies should join in such efforts, but not at the expense of their own freedom to be innovative, and not at the expense of church-based giving which, in addition to funds raised, reinforces the ties between the social service activity and the whole Christian community.

Here again, related policy questions such as tax reform must be geared to these ends. It is not suggested that it is again possible for the church's social service ministry to be sustained without governmental support. The implications of that support, however, can be changed to reinforce rather than undermine the mediating structures of our society. That is also a clearly political task. It faces many obstacles. We do not know whether such a re-orientation can be achieved. We do know that the effort must be made and that the leadership of the churches is crucial to making it.

Volunteerism

Today volunteerism, an inestimably important factor in human services, is undergoing rapid change in our society. Church agencies are partially responsible for pressing "professionalism" in a way that tends to exclude the volunteer worker. We need professionalism—also professionalism in the important work of recruiting, training, and sustaining the morale of volunteers. Another factor in the decline of volunteerism is the notion, which should not be accepted, that voluntary work is by definition a form of unfair exploitation. To the contrary, volunteer work can be invaluable in meeting human need, in building and expressing our capacity for generous social behavior, and in providing satisfying activity for millions of people, men, and women, young and old. Voluntary work should also be recognized as job and educational "experience" in applying for private and government employment.

There are two current public policy directions on volunteerism which require the churches' attention. The first is the current, and perennial, proposal that there be some form of national service involving mandatory work by young people for a fixed period. While this proposal is in some respects attractive, it is inimical to the freedoms appropriate to our society and would probably have unforeseen and undesirable consequences for volunteerism in the society. It might distort the meaning of volunteerism itself, and foster the false notion that volunteerism is somehow peculiarly appropriate to youth. Grave misgivings are justified therefore about the wisdom of any program of mandatory national service. Of course, national service that is genuinely voluntary is quite another matter and can offer opportunity for services to people of all ages and diverse talents.

The second current policy direction is much more ominous. It is the increasing role of the government in pre-empting the traditional and highly decentralized focus of responsibility for volunteerism. On the face of it, it may seem innocent enough to attempt to "coordinate volunteerism on a national scale." The implications of such a proposal are wide ranging and dangerous. For many church and voluntary agencies, volunteers provide one of the last resources for a degree of independence from governmental control. In addition to having unforeseen effects on the nature of volunteerism, such expanded state control would seriously diminish the value of that resource.

A host of problems now appear on the horizon with the predictable growth of union organization in both public and voluntary social welfare institutions. In public agencies there is a new configuration, potentially awesome in its consequences, of the mega-structures of labor and governmental bureaucracy that may well pre-empt many decision-making powers traditionally located in the political arena. In voluntary agencies (to the extent that they are still distinguishable from public agencies) there could be a further limitation on policy and operational flexibility.

In this connection and others the churches should firmly support the right of workers to organize and bargain from a position of power. At its best, this is one of the most important of countervailing forces in our society. Support for labor should not be indiscriminate, however. Especially in the social welfare and educational fields, certain forms of highly centralized labor organizations are tending to, in collusion (perhaps inadvertent) with governmental structures, change the contest of interests by which social policy is made. The nature and consequence of this development are little understood. It is conceivable that some of the results will be beneficial. It is urgent that the churches give attention to what is happening and its possible effects both upon the society and upon the churches' ministry.

Church Agencies

In the area of social ministry, the churches should have clearer priorities. First of course must be the needs of the people for whom such ministry is designed. This requires a greater independence from the state on policy and operations. If a church agency is indistinguishable from a governmental agency, it does not mean the government should take over the activity; it does mean there is something seriously wrong with the church agency (which may of course be the result in part of governmental control). Second, the church agency should be concerned to enable the rest of the church in its social ministry and to cultivate volunteerism within the church. Third, the church agency should manifest humane treatment, including a concern for economic justice, in relating to all its employees, especially to those workers whose relation to the agency is not motivated by quasi-voluntary or church-specific reasons.

There are many areas in which public policy must be changed to make possible more independent and genuinely pluralistic programs of social welfare. It is intolerable that church agencies decide which needs to respond to and how to respond to them on the basis of what government funds are available. These and other temptations are powerful. They must be powerfully resisted. All the "ways and means" available to the Christian community must be marshalled for that resistance for, we hope, a major change in the direction of public policy.

Another related and troubling problem is that of discrimination. We believe there is nothing reprehensible in an old Italian Catholic lady wanting to be in a nursing home with other Italian Catholics. Indeed such a desire is both understandable and healthy. Public policy should facilitate rather than frustrate that desire. In at least some cases, if church agencies are to be more meaningfully part of the mediating institutions from which they emerge, we must change legal and regulatory attitudes toward discrimination. There should be no question but that church agencies, for example, can employ people who share the religious intention of the agency, especially in positions relevant to establishing the tone and substance of programs. A new approach to discrimination must and can be designed in a way that fully preserves the determination to combat racism. Racism is the specific evil the attempted remedy of which produced our society's general confusion about discrimination. Discrimination is another word for discretion, and discretion is the soul of voluntarism, without which democratic pluralism is not possible.

Where it is appropriate, denominational agencies should make no apology for focusing on service to members of that denomination. At the same time, it is our mission as Christians to respond to human need wherever it is to be found. This is true not because of government regulation but because of gospel imperative. In responding to need, church social agencies should respond to the whole person, including their spiritual needs. Any exercise of governmental control that limits the Christian distinctiveness of that response is evil, is to be resisted, and, if possible, changed.

Among the factors that should be distinctive in church agencies is the degree of respect shown the person being helped. This means that, as much as possible, the effective participation of the client in decisions affecting his or her welfare should be structured into the design of the agency. That is an important part of an agency's not being a captive to an impersonal mega-structure.

Social Welfare Policy

We now turn to social welfare policy as it relates to sustaining the poor and reducing poverty. The elimination of poverty is not an appropriate national goal. It is not even an ideal toward which to struggle. It is a pretension based on dangerous and false assumptions about human freedom and sinfulness and about the limits of public policy. It invites only frustration, or worse.

It *should be* public policy to sustain the poor in dignity and to reduce poverty. The elimination of enforced poverty is an appropriate national goal. Nobody should be locked into poverty, without hope for themselves or their children. Nobody should be forced to live at a level that is degrading of human dignity and is unnecessary in view of the wealth of the society. We should welcome the fact that our society's understanding of what is appropriate to human dignity is constantly rising. The wealth of the society and its political will make possible public policies congruent with that understanding.

Poverty has many causes. Most of them are related to profound social injustices both past and present. A person may be poor because of his own choice or his own failure. If a person is poor, however, it should not be by the failure of the society. Some people live in what others view as poverty by their own choice, about which we can make no moral judgment. Affluent and thoroughly acculturated Americans should resist the inclination to believe that nobody would by choice live differently from the way they do. Sober social policy acknowledges that a certain number of people in any society are not interested, for whatever reason, in sharing in all the presumed benefits of the society. Just social policy is aimed at keeping open the freedom to choose. Enforced poverty is an unjust limitation of choice and should therefore be eliminated. Such widespread poverty in America today is personally cruel, socially debilitating, and morally intolerable—and it is all these because it is in fact unnecessary.

Welfare reform should be aimed at breaking the pattern of dependency and denial of freedom fostered by present welfare programs. The state should intervene, and then only most carefully, when, as in the case of children, people are forced to suffer the consequences of decisions not their own. But welfare policy should have a structured bias toward respecting the decisions of the poor. The government does not know what is best for the poor. In general, the poor know what is best for the poor. Except for special problems, the resource which poor people need most is money. Public policy should therefore be directed at income maintenance rather than welfare services and should not, as it does now, link the two. Services, frequently of dubious value, should not be forced upon the poor any more than they should be forced upon the rest of the population. They should be available to the poor as they are available to the non-poor.

This does not mean that there should not be special services for victims of, for example, criminal neglect. There must be such services. But in terms of public policy, criminal neglect among the poor is the same as criminal neglect among the nonpoor. It is just that, for a variety of reasons, it occurs more frequently among the poor.

The best way to fight poverty is to give poor people money. We should therefore establish an absolute and generous "floor of economic decency" below which no person or family in America will be forced to live. Such a program might not break the cycle of poverty but it will desist from reinforcing it with the cycle of dependency.

At least in our culture most human beings are possessed of a strong desire to work and achieve. This belief is confirmed by evidence that a guaranteed income does not destroy that incentive. At the same time, a policy aimed at establishing a floor of economic decency should provide clear benefits also to the "working poor." This is required by justice and is essential to making such a program politically viable.

Until such a floor of decency is established, we should support such programs as food stamps and other income supplements, we should oppose the presumption of the state or other agencies in trying to manage the lives of recipients, we should have deep misgivings about programs of mandatory labor for recipients, but most of all the churches should work toward the establishment of a floor of economic decency.

In recent years there have been significant changes in the treatment of those with special problems, ranging from the mentally ill to the aged to those with various childhood disturbances. There is a new, but still too fragile, awareness of the need to protect the human rights or patients or clients in all these categories. In particular, the churches should keep under careful examination the provisions by which people are denied their rights because they are legally classified as mentally ill. No one ought to be confined against his will except it is justified by reference to criminal behavior, rather than by the need for "treatment." If a person indeed cannot care for himself, and his family is not able or willing to care for him, public policy should favor a custodial system, utilizing private and voluntary agencies where possible, that keeps the person in the liveliest possible interaction with his neighborhood and personal reference group and that respects fully his human rights and dignity in determining his own life style.

Another significant change now underway is the move away from large institutions of custodial, therapeutic and other care. The use of halfway houses and other decentralized facilities should be welcomed. Going further, public policy should direct itself to reinforcing the family and other mediating institutions by a system of reimbursement for those who take care of their own who have special problems. Thus the parents of retarded or emotionally disturbed children would receive a bonus which would make it possible for them to care for the child at home, with appropriate professional support systems, rather than handing him over to some agency, whether public or voluntary. The same policy could be applied with regard to care of the aged.

The present massive system of institutionalization is in large part made necessary because the adults in families feel they must be gainfully employed elsewhere and therefore cannot take care of their own. The policy direction proposed here would underscore society's recognition that caring for those with special problems is an occupation that should be honored and rewarded by society. Where such work cannot be carried out by the immediate family of the person concerned, policy should aim at enlisting relatives, neighbors and others within the network of the person's association. This approach would not preclude the need for professional workers of a wide variety, but their role would be changed from that of caring for the person to that of supporting and training those who are directly involved in the caring activity. In addition to the human and social values in such a redirection of social welfare policy, it would likely be less of a burden on the taxpayer than is the present maintenance of massive systems of institutional care. But that must be viewed, of course, as a secondary consideration.

Present abuses in the care of the old in run-for-profit "homes" are a national scandal. Some of the abuses are encouraged by policies that over-emphasize economy and efficiency in caring for as many as possible with the least personnel. As long as such run-for-profit enterprises continue, public funding should provide incentives for quality of care rather than for a very doubtful efficiency of operation. It may, for example, be operationally efficient to keep old people permanently tranquilized, but it is the very opposite of the kind of care that should be encouraged. Again, the direction urged here would deemphasize dependence upon such institutions for the aged, whether public or private.

Housing

Yet another policy issue that comes under the general rubric of social welfare is that of housing. Beginning in the 1930s massive programs were proposed for the demolition of slum housing in urban areas and the erection of public housing projects. Some of these have been remarkably successful in providing decent housing for people who would otherwise not have had access to such housing. Others have been disastrous exercises in creating new ghettos of isolation, frustration, and self-destruction. In the last decade, public policy experimentation was directed toward providing bonuses and other incentives for home ownership by the poor. Unfortunately, those experiments were plagued by charges of governmental corruption and exploitation by real estate interests. These unhappy experiences should not discourage public policy from continuing to move in the essentially correct direction of home ownership, rehabilitation of the existing housing stock, and maximum freedom of choice for the poor.

At the same time, loans and other incentives should be continued especially to middle-class would-be homeowners who move to better housing and thus make their present good housing available to the poor. There may still be cases in which massive demolition and the erection of public housing projects may be the only answer. But that should not be the chief thrust of public policy. Even in those cases, provision should be made for maximum community control and for encouraging various forms of apartment ownership and responsibility. Most intolerable would be the continuation of the mix of indifference and floundering that now marks public policy toward the problem of degrading and dehumanizing housing in both urban and rural America.

Education

In recent decades almost all the Supreme Court's decisions on the status of religion in our society have been made in connection with laws on education. Conceptually the court has gotten itself into a dreadful thicket. The schools are to promote moral and ethical values which clearly have a religious basis, both ideologically and sociologically, yet are in no way to promote religion, lest "the wall of separation" between church and state be violated. The court has also frequently acted on the false assumption that religion is purely a private phenomenon.

The results of this confusion are several. The most obvious result is to increase secularism in our public life. Others have responded to court rulings by teaching a kind of "morality in general" in the schools, divorced from its religious rootage and legitimation. It is also possible to teach explicitly religious ideas, so long as they do not come together in a way that is recognizable as a "brand name" denominational religion. The consequence is an increasing gap between the values of the family, which was primarily responsible for education, and the public school. In ruling after ruling on specific plans to aid nonpublic education, on the other hand, the Supreme Court has come increasingly close to declaring it illegal for public funds to contribute to any advancement of religion whatsoever, no matter how marginal religious instruction may be in the program for which such funds are used.

The court permits, even theoretically encourages, teaching *about* religion in the public schools. The churches should take fuller advantage of this provision, while at the same time frankly acknowledging that it is both difficult and undesirable to bifurcate religious subject matter from the beliefs of those teaching and being taught in the classroom. Other programs, such as released time, should be vigorously utilized. Church-related elementary schools can, under present legal strictures, explore programs such as dual enrollment and shared-time with public schools, and can obtain some indirect financial aid through textbook loans and other assistance.

Our concern should be both for the role of religion in the public schools and for the strengthening of the private and church-related schools which are important to the pluralistic character of our society. The recent direction of Supreme Court decisions is regrettable on both scores. It may be, as some have proposed, that a constitutional amendment is needed in order to assure the free exercise of religion in public education and to give parents an alternative, without severe financial sacrifice, to public schools. If that is necessary in order to achieve these goals, an amendment would be in order.

There are still some supporters of a constitutional amendment to permit voluntary corporate prayer as part of the public school program. The prayer decision of some years ago was a symbolically important step in the secularizing of public education. But such a constitutional amendment seems inadvisable since it touches on only one small part of a problem in need of more comprehensive remedy.

An educational system should maximize parental choice and provide stronger structures of accountability by the school to the parents. There is much to be said therefore in support of an approach such as voucher payments which can be redeemed in any state certified school. Although we can have little confidence in the Supreme Court's consistency on these issues, a voucher payments system would seem to be identical in legal theory with the constitutionally permitted GI Bill in vocational and higher education. Regrettably, the Court has excluded the state's reimbursement to parents of the money saved the state by children attending nonpublic schools. It would also seem the "French Plan" (more precisely the Debré plan of 1959) would be ruled out under present constitutional interpretations, although it might be construed to involve public aid only for "secular" education. (The core problem in our present situation is, of course, the court's confused distinctions between "religious" and "secular." While it may be that that confusion cannot be remedied short of constitutional amendment, the churches should seek every opportunity, including litigation, that might better inform the decisions of the courts.)

The concern for nonpublic schools, both religious and other, is aimed at giving the poor the same power that the more affluent now have, namely a choice in the kind of education they want for their children. There is a widespread assumption today that professional educators know better than parents the way in which children should be educated. While this may be true in certain instances, it should not be accepted as an assumption for making public policy. Instead of the schools becoming increasingly accountable to governmental and professional mega-structures, a development which has in many instances alienated parents from the education of their children, we should pursue policies designed to bring parents, mediating institutions and schools into closer cooperation. Especially among the urban poor, the alienation of the school from the real lives of both parents and children is in urgent need of correction. Unlike Supreme Court decisions, which increasingly operate with the model of a "national classroom" abstracted from the real communities in which people live, educational policy should be aimed at celebrating the cultural and other diversities that make America not a melting pot but a mosaic of constantly changing configurations.

The Brown decision of 1954 was correctly aimed at dismantling a dual school system that was deliberately and admittedly designed to maintain racial segregation. That decision remains a very bright and continuingly important act in America's often doleful history of race relations. The history of black-white relations in America is also unique. We must extrapolate only with great care from policies aimed at remedying specific racial injustices to general social policy. Racial discrimination in all public enterprises and publicly supported enterprises must be relentlessly proscribed. Racism is a sin which in its institutionalized manifestations constitutes a crime that is in no way to be countenanced. The condemnation of racial discrimination, emerging from the tortured history of black-white relations in America, must not, however, lead to a wholesale condemnation of discrimination as such. Again, the freedom of association and the future of every form of mediating institution depends upon the lively exercise of discriminations of many sorts. That freedom should not be denied by an artificial and abstracted mandate moving toward social homogenization.

As an instrument for effecting major social change, the public school is of limited utility. More important, the schools of the nation should be responsive to the perceived interests of parents rather than be viewed as tools of social policy. While racial discrimination in public and publicly supported schools should be rigorously *proscribed,* this does not mean that racial integration should be *prescribed.* The issue of busing for purposes for racial desegregation continues to be dangerously divisive in our society. It is clear beyond doubt that the great majority of both white and black parents do not share the courts' favorable disposition toward such busing. There is little or no empirical evidence that such racial integration is of educational benefit. There is unquestionable evidence of its divisiveness and destructive impact upon neighborhoods and upon our national life.

The major factors relevant to educational opportunity are class, community and, above all, family. Educational progress, especially for the poor, rests upon policies aimed at strengthening the economic, neighborhood, and family context in which children are reared. Busing for purposes of racial integration is a distraction from addressing these factors and we can hope that, as a matter of prudential judgment if not of court decision, it will be less emphasized than it has been in recent years. Whatever voluntary arrangements parents may choose in order to give their children an education in a more interracial or inter-class or inter-cultural setting should be encouraged. In all this, the focus should be on the most pressing question, namely, how to achieve quality education and especially how to do that in poor and changing communities.

It is regrettable that there are some for whom busing has become the test of commitment to racial justice. It is intolerably inaccurate and unfair to assert that all who oppose busing are acting out of racist motives; it is true that racism has become an important factor in some situations of conflict created by court-ordered busing. It is quite possible that the conflict produces racism much more than racism produces the conflict. The conflict itself is rooted in other concerns which need not be sinful and may well be sound and even essential. There is the negative concern that turns on the undeniably common-sensical understanding that there are "better" neighborhoods and "worse" neighborhoods, notable differences being in educational and economic achievement and, most important to parents, safety. There is a positive concern for preserving distinctive neighborhoods, associational patterns, and ties of accountability between school and home.

In education as in other areas major new policy commitments must be made to overcome the scandal of poverty and deprivation in rural and urban America. Beyond continuing to press for the effective proscription of racial discrimination, few if any of the needed policies are race-specific. That is, while blacks constitute a disproportionate number of the poor, policy should be directed toward the problem of poverty itself.

In pursuit of the goal of equal access to education, we should reject the notion that it is enough to rely upon a laissez-faire confidence in some form of meritocratic justice. To the contrary, it should be public policy of the highest priority to develop stronger programs of a positive and compensatory nature in order to help the poor compete on an equal footing. Such positive programs need not in any way threaten the merit basis of educational achievement, but can indeed strengthen it through sharpening the competition. Such programs should exclude any form of "quota system," however it may be disguised. A wise distribution, among both students and teachers, of sexual, racial, cultural, religious and other differences is no doubt desirable in some educational situations. Such diversity, however, should not be purchased at the price of educational quality, nor at the price of the other social diversities created by having diverse educational institutions such as all-girls schools or all-boys schools. Again, apart from institutions that inculcate blatantly anti-social or illegal behavior, parents (and in higher education, students) should have a free choice with regard to the education they desire. It should be the decision of the parents, rather than of the state, as to what kinds of diversity contribute to "educational quality." The one legally mandated proscription, made necessary by a singular history, is against racial discrimination.

In emphasizing pluralism, it is assumed that the "melting pot" rationale once invoked in support of a unitary public school system is no longer compelling. The "melting pot" was in any case largely a matter of assimilation to the cultural hegemony of the Anglo-American Protestant establishment. Today the culturally unifying function, once presumably served by "the little red school house," is served by the mass media, especially television. There are other unifying forces on a national scale, such as some voluntary networks, and a host of employment, business, professional and recreational patterns. A monolithic public school system is no longer essential, if it ever was essential, to "Americanizing" Americans. The accent today should be on diversity within the public school and on free choice alternatives to the public school.

Most of the above focuses on elementary education. We also face important policy decisions regarding secondary and higher education. Our society has hardly begun to undertake the many compensatory programs that are absolutely imperative if we are to move toward the goal of equality of educational opportunity according to merit. This does not mean it is social policy for everyone to have, for example, a college education. Indeed it would be foolish and wasteful to force every young person into such a uniform expectation. As the consequences of the post-war "baby boom" decline, and as more young people may freely choose not to attend college, there will be severe dislocations in our rapidly expanded systems of higher education. Public policy should be designed to encourage and facilitate adults to pursue higher education throughout their lives. Not only would this sustain employment in higher education, but it would no doubt enrich the larger society and create new freedoms of choice for the adult population.

Church-related colleges and universities, if they are truly distinctive in the education they offer and are of high academic quality, will continue to be very important. Fortunately, some of the church-state problems that afflict elementary education are not so rigorously imposed on higher education. Although they cannot be the major thrust of the church's educational mission, such colleges and universities contribute importantly to educational diversity in America. They can also be utilized more than they are at present in supplying the churches both with study and research resources and with training for new patterns in church vocations.

8

Law and Criminal Justice

Crime and the Purposes of Criminal Justice

As noted earlier, sin and crime are intricately connected. Crime manifests sin in behavior that is within the competence and responsibility of the state to control and punish. As platitudinous as it may sound, it is nonetheless both urgent and accurate to emphasize unceasingly the role of church, state, and other institutions in improving the "moral climate" in the society if we are effectively to address the problems of criminal behavior.

Crime and criminals do not reflect only the failure of the society. In even the most possibly perfect society there will be crime and criminals. The existence of meaningful social rules makes it inevitable that some will violate those rules. The notion that crime and criminals are entirely the fault of society reflects either a sentimentally naive view of human nature or a propensity toward totalitarian control of social behavior. At the same time we must underscore that there are unjust social conditions amenable to public policy change which contribute to producing crime and criminals. We must also be deeply concerned about policies and practices in the criminal justice system which are profoundly unjust and which both produce and perpetuate criminal behavior.

Our society today is seized by what is generally viewed as an alarming rise in crimes of violence against persons and property. Those who are concerned for social reform must take care not to belittle the legitimate public concern about such crime. Otherwise, popular confidence moves by default to the demogogues of "law and order" who demonstrate neither respect for human rights nor any thoughtful proposals for reducing crime and securing the safety of citizens.

It is important to have clear the basic purposes of criminal justice. They are, according to one judicial body, "to protect all members of society, including the offender himself, from seriously harmful and dangerous conduct." We would add that for Christians criminal justice systems are one manifestation of God's law in its political function contributing to the perservation of human life and liberty despite the destructive and enslaving effects of sin. Such a system must do several things: (1) identify and apprehend those who are accused of violating laws duly enacted by the body politic's representatives according to a rational and equitable system of justice based on the rights of all people to life, liberty, property, and the pursuit of happiness; (2) prosecute on behalf of the state and guarantee an adequate defense for those charged with criminal activities; and (3) implement sanctions against convicted criminals, such as fines, suspended sentences, compensation to victims, probation, imprisonment, and parole.

Punishment is a legitimate purpose of criminal justice. Every society reinforces its values and secures its very survival through sanctions, both positive and negative. Punishment, however, must never be based upon a vindictive intent or be drawn from an impersonally abstracted notion of retributive justice. At the most elementary level, criminal justice is society's way of restraining or temporarily removing those who constitute a proven danger to other people. Rehabilitation is also a crucial dimension of criminal justice. This is so because the society owes help to its every member, including the criminal. Rehabilitation is also in the society's direct self-interest since, as is too often forgotten, people who are imprisoned return to the society.

Finally, on the theory of criminal justice, there is a legitimate place for mercy. This is exercised through pardons, commutations of sentence, amnesties, and the like. Here criminal justice, like politics itself, is more art than science. That is, the magistrate is sometimes confronted with situations for the resolution of which there are no clear rules or precedents. Mercy is not pure altruism but is exercised in the interest of the society and must be related to a consensus regarding what is fair. Amnesty in particular is an admission that problems have become so compounded in the fair administration of laws that are themselves just that it is in the interest of the society and in accord with its mores to deliberately overlook offences. Amnesty means neither to forgive, which the state is not competent to do, nor to for-

get, which the society may not be able to do, but to deliberately overlook offenses, thus denying them any legal significance. Such an approach is especially relevant to crimes that can be defined as essentially political. Since we will not be returning to the subject of amnesty,
it should be said here that it would be in the public interest to enact
a complete and unconditional amnesty for all offenses committed in
connection with America's war in Indochina, and a complete and unconditional amnesty for all illegal immigrants who have been in the
country for a substantial period, perhaps three years or longer. It is
hoped the churches would work toward those goals.

Victimless Crimes

For a variety of reasons, there is today a widespread discussion of
what forms of behavior should be included in the criminal code. One
reason has to do with a rising sense of individual liberties and a rising
tolerance of social diversity. Another has to do with the desire to free
the criminal justice system to address itself to "more serious" crime.
A problem with the latter reasoning is that it might encourage the
notion that the most direct way to reduce the crime rate is simply to
reduce the number of forms of behavior we call crimes. In a completely anarchic society there would presumably be no crime whatsoever. That is not a very happy resolution of our present problems.

The serious discussion of "victimless crimes," as they are called,
raises problems deserving of careful consideration by the churches.
The phrase "victimless crimes" may not be an entirely happy one since
it seems to deny that people may be the victims of their own behavior.
To that objection it should be countered, however, that a liberal society, such as we cherish, should give the widest possible room for
individual decision-making, even when such decisions may be injurious
to the person.

Society should, however, continue to intervene legally in what might
appear to be perfectly private decisions. An example is laws against
suicide. First, such laws have a pedagogical function demonstrating
the society's reverence for human life. Second, many decisions to commit suicide are made in particular moments of despondency or distress
and society should protect people from taking such a definitive step
when, as experience amply demonstrates, many of them would not

take that step later under more normal circumstances. Third, people of ordinary competence who are genuinely determined to commit suicide will find the means to do so, and therefore no "right" is denied them by laws against suicide. That the law helps sustain a certain opprobrium around the act of suicide is perfectly appropriate.

The more usual topics in the victimless crime debate are public drunkenness, postitution, homosexual and other unconventional sexual acts, and gambling. As emphasized in other connections, good public policy favors a case-by-case approach to such questions rather than sweeping and abstract generalizations, especially when the generalization is so vague as "the removal of victimless crimes from the criminal code."

Public drunkenness, however lamentable, should not in itself be a crime. Certain forms of public behavior—such as disturbing the peace, molesting innocent citizens, and the such—are criminal and should be punished quite apart from whether the offender was drunk. This, the reader will note, is the same logic applied earlier in the case of the violation of law by the mentally ill.

Prostitution should not in itself be a crime. Here again the considerations mentioned in connection with public drunkenness should be noted. Of course prostitution is exploitative of all parties involved, but the pedagogical value of outlawing it would seem to be outweighed by the danger that such ineffectual prohibitions bring law itself into disrepute. Public solicitation should remain a crime, especially when it is flagrantly offensive to communal mores and civil peace. Similarly, the public promotion of pornography can and should be publicly regulated, although it would be a grave mistake to return to the censorship laws of the past that attempted to repress the availability of pornographic and other materials. It may well be wise to consider the system used in some European cities, where activities such as prostitution and pornographic promotion are confined to specific areas and kept under close governmental regulation. No one would be denied their rights and the satisfactions some people discover in such activities might be enhanced by the furtiveness with which these areas would be patronized. At present in America the libertarian and individualistic interpretation of legal rights in these respects has gone to an extreme that needs to be better balanced by concern for the rights of the larger community. As one's right to swing his fists stops where another's face begins, so the right to the public display of what is deemed grossly offensive behavior stops where the neighborhoods and communities begin in which citizens desire for themselves and their families a chosen "quality of life."

All laws relating to homosexuality, sodomy, or other private sexual behavior or preference should be removed from the criminal code. Any discrimination in the public sphere against people because of sexual orientation should be legally proscribed. People should be employed solely on the basis of their ability to do the job. Controversies over hiring homosexuals as firemen, soldiers or in other positions requiring intense and sustained interaction between members of the same sex are misplaced. Noxious behavior, if criminal on other grounds, can be restrained by law, but in most cases it is restrained by extralegal social sanctions. Homosexuals should not be barred from teaching in schools, a legal provision that is presently the source of widespread hypocrisy and anxiety. Those who, whether homosexual or heterosexual, teach children can be restrained from proselytizing for sexual behavior or attitudes that are offensive to the children's parents. In supporting the rights of people of diverse sexual orientations, the church does not endorse their behavior nor throw into question the primary status that chastity, marriage and family life should have in personal and public morality. Christians should cultivate greater sympathy and understanding for the problems encountered by homosexuals, as indeed this is already happening to some extent. The law violates the necessary line between the public and private when it concerns itself with sexual orientation or with sexual behavior, except when such behavior is criminal on other grounds clearly related to the public good.

It is not clear that gambling should be considered a victimless crime to be removed from the criminal code. Contrary to the seemingly plausible argument advanced by some, experience suggests that the decriminalization of gambling does not eliminate the criminal elements of society from gambling activities. Rather it seems to attract and intensify the criminal element, especially in connection with loan sharking, blackmail, and other criminal activities. Grave misgivings are also in order with regard to the tendency toward legalized and state-regulated gambling. Public funds should be raised as directly as possible through taxation in order to keep their use as accountable as possible to the citizenry. In addition, many believe it unseemly and inappropriate for the state to be engaged for profit in the exploitative aspects of gambling, especially as these affect the poor. While Christians are not agreed in opposing existing state lotteries, the state should not view such activities as a major source of public revenue. The wide-open decriminalization or legalization of gambling should be opposed, at least until the implications for the public good have been examined much more carefully than they have been to date.

One of the most difficult areas of criminal justice in our society today is that relating to the use of drugs. Public discourse on this subject is not helped by the high degree of emotionalism that surrounds it. Ours is a drug-oriented and, to a large extent, drug-addicted society, as is evident in the almost universal dependence upon prescription and brand-name narcotics, alcoholic beverages, and such. As most Americans oppose the legal prohibition of alcoholic beverages, so we should question the prohibition, often arbitrarily determined, of certain drugs today. Our present laws making the possession and use of certain drugs a criminal activity are of relatively recent vintage. It is quite possible that the laws themselves have to a large extent created our present "drug problem." The severe personal damage resulting from the use of certain drugs is not to be minimized, as the much more widespread tragedy of alcoholism is not to be belittled. The linkage between drug use and other criminal behavior, however, results largely from the exorbitant cost of maintaining an illegal habit. An approach should be followed in which addicts could be maintained through public or private clinics.

Evidence of the damage done by the use of marijuana is to date significantly less than evidence regarding the harmfulness of alcohol. Marijuana should be legalized and regulated in a manner similar to the sale of liquor. It is by no means clear that the incidence of drug dependency would be markedly increased by the legalization and regulation of these presently prohibited substances. Again, a free society is one in which people are free to make mistakes. Indeed some studies suggest that the incidence of severe dependency is increased by the present criminalization of drug possession and use. In any case, the churches should support a stronger and more effective network of services available to the drug dependent, purely as a matter of health care and devoid of criminal connotation. Such services should be premised upon the modesty-inducing knowledge that the "cure" of drug dependency is very largely a matter of individual decision and age. The question of public policy on drug use is in need of more careful and dispassionate study. The churches should continue to take an energetic role in that process.

Present public policy on drugs is grievously flawed in principle and ineffective in practice. By forcing people into criminal activity it contributes significantly to rising crime rates, especially in our cities. The implementation of present policy consumes an inordinate share of the law enforcement budget and energy. In addition, present laws, especially regarding the use and possession of marijuana, provide numerous temptations for the corruption of law enforcement and for the violation of citizen rights.

"Sabbath Laws," Children and the Law, and Gun Control

"Sabbath laws," as they are called, and legal holidays related to religious or other events are legitimate and important and should be left as much as possible to local discretion. Those who observe Saturday as the Lord's Day should have their rights respected, for example, and be permitted to close their business on Saturday rather than Sunday. Providing a day of rest for as many workers as possible serves the general good. In addition, it is important to any society to sustain its symbols and values through regular public holidays and other observances. Recent court decisions proscribing public holidays on dates of religious significance are absurdly abstracted in principle and dangerously secularizing in effect. In addition, a good case can be made for returning to the practice of observing national holidays on the actual date of the events celebrated, rather than the recently adopted non-observance of symbolically lost weekends. Especially in connection with religious holidays, the courts are tending toward a perilously individualistic view of rights in connection with the First and Fourteenth Amendments. It is not an individual right to be unaffected by the values, sentiments and symbols of the larger community of which the individual is part.

Yet another area of law in need of reexamination is that having to do with children. Forty percent of the children legally detained in the United States are detained for offenses which would not be violations of the law if committed by an adult. As indicated earlier, a legal distinction must be made, no matter how arbitrary it may seem, between children and adults. As also indicated, the churches should be particularly assiduous in asserting the primacy of family responsibility for children. It would seem that some laws regarding child behavior emerge from the state's excessive assertion of its parental role. Of the 100,000 children under eighteen annually—and with doubtful legality—jailed each year in the U.S., only about 4 percent are charged with committing "offenses against persons" such as assault or robbery for which custody might be justified on grounds of protecting society. Public policy should de-emphasize the custodial or parental roles of the state and be aimed at supporting family responsibility for child behavior. In instances of parental neglect or abuse, such as child battery, the law should act decisively against the parents and should aim at placing the child in as "natural" a community as possible. Again, rather than institutionalization, public policy should be designed to reimburse relatives of another family to care for such children. Where agencies must be employed, church agencies should demonstrate a greater willingness than they do at present to care for children from "multi-problem" backgrounds.

On another much controverted question of public policy, private firearms in American society should be prohibited, except in certified cases of recreational use or for extraordinary reasons of security. The argument for the constitutional right to bear arms is spurious. The constitutional provision was clearly related to the citizen's ability to resist internal or external tyranny and is not relevant to the military realities of the twentieth century. One might also hope for the day when, as in some other societies, law enforcement officers would not be armed except under extraordinary circumstances. While disarming our society might reduce crime, the climate that will make such a step politically possible might itself require a prior reduction in the crime rate. Toward the goal of a less lethally violent society, the churches, schools and mass media should energetically combat the male chauvinist mystique surrounding the gun in American life, both past and present. While we have here dealt primarily with crimes of violence, attention must also be given to so-called "white collar" crimes of embezzlement, fraud, and the such. The widespread attitude that these "respectable" crimes are less threatening to the society must be countered. This attitude inescapably breeds cynicism toward law and this contributes to a social climate in which every form of crime is more readily tolerated.

Reform of the Criminal Justice System

The seeming rise in criminality in our society is both produced by and reflected in our criminal justice system. While it is probably not true that there is more crime today than there was in the last century, especially in urban areas, it seems certain that more criminal acts are being committed now than, say, thirty years ago, and the rate of increase appears to be rising at a sharp pace, especially in connection with crimes of violence. The regressive politics of "law and order" (usually forgetting justice) would not be so potent were there not a popular sense of crisis to be exploited. The sense of crisis is, in turn, rooted in troubling realities.

While more crimes are reported, only a relatively small percentage of perpetrators are arrested and a ludicrously small percentage of those arrested are finally convicted and punished. It is agreed by almost all students of the subject that the greatest deterrent to crime is the likelihood of speedy and certain punishment. It is the certainty of punishment rather than the severity of punishment which deters criminal behavior. (It should be emphasized that most observance of law is positively motivated by the civic virtues discussed in an earlier section. In this section, however, we are dealing primarily with the behavior of people for whom such positive motivations seem largely ineffective.)

Today our criminal courts are grotesquely overloaded resulting in both delay and denial—and denial through delay—of justice. One answer is more and better courts and judges. Some propose that judges should be appointed rather than elected, but it is agreed by most students of the subject that they should be passed on by screening panels composed of citizens of high public repute, including non-lawyers.

Discretion in sentencing results in an enormous range in punishments imposed, unrelated to any reasonable calculation of justice. More sentences should be mandatory, especially when the crime involves violence against persons. At the same time, mandatory sentences should not be so severe that juries would hesitate to convict or judges to pass sentence.

The churches should create a keener public awareness of the vastly disproportionate resources available to the state as prosecutor and the citizen as defendant. If, as is frequently charged, there is today evidence of greater concern for the perpetrator than for the victim of criminal acts, the correction of this imbalance must not be at the expense of society's concern to protect the innocent person accused. As in all conflicts between the rights of individuals and the rights of society, this one is not amenable to scientifically exact or absolutely satisfying resolution. The art of striking appropriate balances is part of the ongoing tasks of politics and public discourse.

It would seem that today some provisions designed to protect the defendant do less to protect his rights than to deny the social need for speedy and certain punishment. The evil of people being detained for long periods without having been convicted of a crime is broadly acknowledged. In many cases, the delay in justice is brought about by the defendant rather than by the court or prosecutor. By inordinate delay the defendant hopes that witnesses and evidence against him will be lost or weakened. In short, the correct proposition that the delay of justice is the denial of justice cuts both ways in the relationship between the state and the defendant.

One proposal now gaining ground in public policy discussion is that we reexamine our somewhat absolutist commitment to the adversarial character of courtroom proceedings and to trial by jury. In some European countries with an impressive tradition of respect for justice and democratic procedure, the approach and structure of criminal proceedings are quite different. There is no morally compelling principle why these alternative approaches and structures should not be carefully considered here. Certainly the problems of our present criminal justice system would seem to suggest the need for fundamental changes.

Especially in the case of less serious crimes not subject to severe punishment, the court's role might be less one of presiding over an adversarial proceeding than one of determining the facts relevant to the crime charged. Some rulings regarding the admissibility of evidence, for example, seem unnecessarily weighted against justice being done. All evidence pertinent to determining the facts should be admissible. In cases of evidence illegally discovered, the law enforcement officers guilty of the illegal act should be speedily and certainly punished. Their action constitutes a separate criminal case and should not be permitted to confound the doing of justice in the case to which the evidence is pertinent.

The courts might also be cleared of much of their present burden if more cases, especially non-criminal cases, were submitted to administrative adjudication rather than to trial. In cases of jury trial, careful consideration should also be given to the present trend in which, through arbitrary challenges and other means, many more thoughtful and educated citizens are excluded, thus raising serious questions about the possibility of "trial by peers."

The operation of the present bail system is grossly unjust, working almost exclusively against the poor. Bail should never be used as punishment, but exclusively in order to assure the appearance of the accused. In cases where public safety suggests custody before trial, that should be effected through explicit law and not through the oblique use of the bail system. To be sure, equality before the law is inevitably compromised at many points by economic inequities. But the difference between the treatment received by the rich and by the poor should be assiduously reduced. Within reasonable bounds, and especially when the crime charged is serious, the public should bear the expense of the defendant's counsel of choice when the defendant cannot do so.

We should be troubled also by the current use of plea-bargaining. Studies suggest that there are frequently cases in which innocent people accused of serious crimes are persuaded to plead guilty to lesser crimes in order to escape a potentially more severe punishment. Such cases are outrageous miscarriages of justice and the remedy must be more urgently sought. We must also protest the state's abuse of plea-bargaining in order to induce defendants to cooperate with the prosecution. Equally unjust is the abuse of judicial power in imposing very severe sentence with the implicit offer of reduction for cooperation with the prosecution. As a matter of general principle the charges and criminal proceedings should be aimed at determining whether the defendant did what he is charged with doing, and at imposing appropriate punishment. Such a principle may sound obvious, but it is obviously not observed in many criminal justice proceedings today. Were it observed, it is likely that some people guilty of commiting crimes would not be charged. That is unfortunate. Were it observed, there would likely be a closer correlation between the crime charged and speedy and certain punishment. That is imperative.

Certainty of punishment is a greater deterrent to crime than severity of punishment. Any effort to reintroduce capital punishment into our society's criminal justice system should be opposed. There is no positive evidence that capital punishment has a deterrent effect. Quite apart from whether it is ruled constitutional or not, it is a cruel and degrading form of punishment that is unworthy of a humane society. In theory the state has the right to impose capital punishment, as the state has the right to wage war. In both instances the action must be justified by compelling necessity. There is no compelling necessity for capital punishment. In addition, the use of capital punishment has been disproportionately against the poor; thus it is in fact, if not in legal theory or court ruling, a violation of the right to equal protection of the law. If, as one hopes will not happen, the courts do not definitely exclude the use of capital punishment, the churches should continue to work for such exclusion or abolition through constitutional means.

The rehabilitation of our criminal justice system requires persistent efforts toward prison reform. It is a sobering fact that there is no such thing as a good prison. The very purposes of criminal justice, which include punishment and the need to isolate those who pose a danger to society, preclude the more sentimental goals sometimes associated with prison reform. Prison reform has a long history, indeed the contemporary prison itself is a product of modern reformist efforts. The "penitentiaries" and "correctional facilities" which are rightly criticized today are, as the names indicate, the products of well-intended reform.

While there can be no good prison, there can be less dehumanizing prisons. Every human being should be dealt with as a sacred mystery of God's creating love and his rights should be respected to the fullest extent possible, except for restrictions necessary to keep him in incarceration and to protect him and the other prisoners. The convicted criminal is appropriately denied voting rights during the period of punishment imposed. While there are no positive requirements for the exercise of citizenship rights, apart from age, the criminal has demonstrated his unwillingness to assume the responsibilities of citizenship and therefore should, for the duration of his punishment, be denied this symbolically important right of citizenship.

Particular care should be taken to preserve the prisoner's ties with his family. Punishing a father, for example, may also impose a severe punishment upon his wife and children. This is undoubtedly unfair and is not the intention of society, but it is also inevitable as long as such offenders are imprisoned. Through support systems and more creative approaches to visitation rights, the blow to the family—and the consequent damage to the prisoner's prospects for rehabilitation— can be softened. Voluntary agencies such as churches can make an important contribution by systematically remembering the forgotten families of prisoners.

While every opportunity for rehabilitation should be offered the prisoner, he should not be forced into therapeutic job training or other rehabilitative programs. The very concept of punishment implies respect for the dignity of the individual and his responsibility for his own actions. The prisoner is not merely a product of the society to be "re-programmed" according to the society's designs.

The rate of recidivism and the escalation in seriousness of crimes subsequently committed by released prisoners suggest that our present prison system may actually be manufacturing crime and criminals. We should therefore welcome the present trend away from institutionalization in large prison facilities. Half-way houses, work-release and education-release programs, and probation should all be used more widely and creatively to help prisoners return to a useful role in society. In such programs, churches and other voluntary agencies, should play an energetic part.

Being deprived of personal freedom should be the sole form of punishment imposed by a sentence to prison. Obviously that deprivation can be gradated in terms of the prisoner's behavior and desire for reform. Social sanctions, both positive and negative, are also necessary in prison "society." But any negative sanction beyond the gradated deprivation of freedom should be strictly forbidden. Such deprivation should never exceed what is necessary in order to protect others or to protect the prisoner from himself.

Reducing the population in the large penal institutions will leave a "hard core" in such institutions. As previously acknowledged, there may be a hard core in any society of people who are not able or do not choose to live in a manner that the society can tolerate. This grim observation, however, must not be permitted to become an operational assumption that there are "hopeless cases." At every point, and even against every probability, every opportunity should be given the prisoner to participate in programs aimed at his return to a constructive role in society.

Prison chaplains have a crucial part to play in humanizing the penal systems. Their work should be more closely integrated into the fullness of the church's ministries. Especially with respect to local prisons, volunteer visitation programs should be strongly encouraged. In addition to assisting the chaplain and other prison officials in meeting the needs of prisoners, such volunteer programs can play a watchdog role regarding the legal and humane operation of the prisons. The churches must constantly combat the widespread and understandable desire to simply block out prisons and prisoners from popular consciousness and concern. Work with offenders, both in and out of prison, should be vigorously encouraged as an especially urgent sphere for Christian vocations.

When the prisoner has served his term, his record should be clean, except for its relevance to subsequent criminal proceedings or especially sensitive positions of public responsibility. All citizenship rights, including the right to hold public office, should be restored fully. The churches and other agencies should work to develop both programs and public attitudes that will expedite the ex-offender's return to a constructive role in society. This is especially urgent in terms of employment.

In all aspects of the criminal justice system, clergy confidentiality must be rigorously respected. What the pastor has learned in the course of exercising his pastoral responsibilities cannot be divulged, either to a court or to other law enforcement agencies, except with the express permission of the person involved or in order to prevent the commission of a serious crime. Even with such express permission, the pastor must judge whether there is compelling reason for such disclosure. In the case of preventing the commission of a serious crime, he should attempt to do so without revealing the identity of the person involved.

The glamorizing of crime, especially of organized crime, in movies and other media should be consistently opposed by the churches as a particularly dangerous manifestation of decadence and of indifference to the neighbor's welfare.

Especially in our large cities, police officers are often viewed as hostile aliens in the communities they are to serve. Law enforcement officers should live at least in the city where they work. Further, steps can be taken toward community control of law enforcement, with only the necessary outside supervision required to combat corruption and assure the protection of legal rights. Within a given community, police officers and citizens should view one another as partners in the common enterprise of protecting the persons and property of the community. Especially in the cities, this goal requires more than better "good will" exercises in community relations. It requires structural change that will bring law enforcement systems into a relationship of greater cooperation and accountability with the communities they are to protect.

This chapter and the last have discussed a large number of issues that dominate our daily newspapers and popular thinking about public policy—crime, drugs, abortion, education, welfare, and the like. Obviously, all the arguments and evidence that influence these exercises in decision-making have not been mentioned. The reader who keeps the theology and principles of Part I in mind, however, will recognize the coherence, if not the absolute consistency, in the approaches and decisions offered in these chapters. While this avoids arbitrariness, it does not mean that the positions suggested here are the only ones that might emerge from the theological and ethical assertions of Part I. Indeed it would be disappointing if others did not explore policy possibilities that are rejected here, or only mentioned in passing, or perhaps ignored altogether.

Now we move to a subject that is more and more important in distinguishing and even dividing Christians who think seriously about public policy, namely, the connection between economics and social change. Here again the considerations mentioned above should be kept in mind. The purpose of the author and of the conversation from which this study comes is not so much to convince the reader of these particular approaches and conclusions as it is to offer a point of reference for the reader's own further thought, study, and decision.

9

Economics for People

There is no area in which expertise has been so consistently humbled as in economics. Experience with both grand theories and short-term prognoses underscores the difficulties in understanding the behavior of "economic man." As in other areas, but especially in economics, we should be respectful of the "postulate of ignorance" (see Chapter 3, "Testings for Decision"). There are points, however, at which choices are contingent upon value judgments, and it is these that are primarily addressed here.

Economic Systems

In pointing to the value decisions involved, the idea of rigid economic determinism in any form must be rejected. It must be rejected not because one can conclusively demonstrate that there are not in fact determinisms outside the purview of political decision but because to operate on deterministic assumptions tends to preclude the role of political and ethical decision. In this rejection is included both the alleged invisible guidance of free market mechanisms and the alleged dialectic of historical forces.

As Christians, therefore, we should be committed neither to socialism nor to capitalism. In fact, we are to recognize that both socialism and capitalism are "ideal types" that have little or no relation to the socio-economic models existent today. All such models reveal a frightening tendency to sacrifice human beings to the advancement of "the system." Operating by the criteria of the concrete, Christians should show the utmost skepticism toward grand designs, whether present or projected, that demonstrate a recklessness in cost-benefit calculation and are too ready to sacrifice human beings and their self-perceived welfare to some impersonal order. In capitalist societies this means skepticism toward talk about "the health of the economy," as though people were meant to serve the economy rather than the economy to serve people. In other societies it means skepticism toward talk about "advancing the revolution," which is too often a euphemism for a redistribution of injustices under the dictatorship of a new class elite.

All existing socio-economic systems are unsatisfactory, some more so than others. In view of our understanding of our moment in relation to the final consummation of history, this is not surprising. It is also no excuse for failing to work urgently toward a more humane economic system. In this struggle, a warning must be issued against the church identifying itself with any socio-economic system, present or projected. In our society this means that the majority of Christians needs to be helped to overcome their phobia of everything that appears "socialistic." It also means that a minority of Christians, largely alienated from the American socio-economic system, should be discouraged from polarizing church membership by their sometimes uncritical attachment to real or imagined socialisms.

Socialism vs. capitalism is not the most accurate or helpful way to pose the issue confronting us. The worldview and values which inform this study throughout can conceivably be sustained under a variety of socio-economic systems, some of which might be called capitalist and others socialist. Today socialism can mean anything from the system of the Soviet Union, to that of Maoist China, to that of Sweden, to the more or less unvarnished nationalisms in some countries of the Third World. It is often more an emotive than a descriptive term. Similarly, few systems today describe themselves as unqualifiedly capitalist. In the western liberal democracies, capitalist theory and practice have been massively modified in the direction of the welfare state. This is true to the point that capitalism in the United States, for example, in many respects bears little resemblance to its "ideal type."

In the modification of socialist theory and practice, the movement among some socialists to devise systems that are truly respectful of the values of liberal democracy is to be welcomed. In the modifications of capitalism, we should welcome those directions that strengthen communal responsibility for human decency and underscore economic, as well as legal and political, rights. In our own society, one is less sanguine about those changes in free market ideology which have entangled the state in rescuing and controlling sectors of the market without any politically accountable design for communal benefit. There is validity in the frequently expressed anxiety about "socialism for the rich and capitalism for the poor." In this area, as in others, developments have outpaced our theory for understanding and controlling them. Christians should contribute to the process by which such developments can be better understood and thus made subject to deliberate decision, before too many decisions are made for us by anonymous persons or forces that escape political accountability.

Humanizing the Economic Order

Economic life need not be a jungle of competition. Its harshness should be ameliorated by public policy at at least three points: 1) where the national interest, clearly defined, is at stake; 2) where it is necessary to guarantee a minimum standard of economic decency for all citizens; 3) where intervention is required to prevent any person or group of persons from being excluded from opportunity to participate in the pursuit of economic reward. All three areas need further and urgent attention. The last two are clearly interdependent. An example of the first area is the lack of adequate public control over energy policy. The second is exemplified in what is accurately perceived as "the welfare mess" and the absence of any coherent policy of income support. The third concern is advanced through more vigorous application of laws proscribing discrimination and through stronger programs of educational and other remediations of past injustices.

If economic life need not be a jungle of competition, neither can it be, at this stage of creation's yearning, a kingdom of freedom in communal cooperation. The "beloved community" is an ideal to which humanity aspires. When it becomes a program to be imposed it has invariably turned out to be the opposite of the beloved community. Christians who believe in the God of history should, of all people, take history seriously. Ideological flights from historical experience have no place in Christian thinking about public policy. Experience demonstrates the possibility of the new emerging from the old. More massively and cruelly in our time, experience demonstrates the need to observe the limits of public policy, especially economic policy, in reordering society.

While Christians affirm the primacy of the political factor over economic and other factors in ordering society, it is far from an absolute primacy. Economic life should not be totally merged into, or subsumed under, political life. As property is essential to liberty, so a large degree of economic autonomy is necessary if the citizenry is to resist the dictatorship of the state. This means that in some form, although admittedly an ever-changing form, the distinction between the private and public sectors of the economy should be maintained. The notion that all property and its power belong to the society represents an idolatrous apotheosis of "Society" and, whether asserted by right or left (and it is asserted by both at times) it is an invitation to totalitarianism.

At the same time we welcome the re-examination of our society's commitment to economic growth and productivity. The churches should help stimulate and contribute to the discussion of "Growth for what?" In addition, there is today in motion a process of redefining productivity in order to include service occupations and people-to-people jobs. We should welcome these developments for several reasons. Some Americans believe there is today an overproduction of needless consumer goods (although, to be sure, were there an equitable distribution of some goods we might discover an underproduction). Second, it is clear that there are many service tasks to be performed that are now neglected. Third, in many instances such people-to-people jobs promise greater work satisfaction than is now to be discovered in the industrial sector of the economy.

If we observe what has been said about implementation through mediating structures, the expansion of people-to-people jobs need not mean an expansion of state control. In addition, it should not be assumed that service occupations are to be financed only, or even primarily, by government funds. Indeed the majority of service occupations today are in the private sector and there is no reason to think the number of services for which people will pay cannot be multiplied. In the past the assumption has been that the economy was based on the production of goods rather than services. If by services are included financial, technological and other organizational services, it is possible that the production of goods can be greatly retracted without economic injury. This does not preclude the possibility that some new consumer products of great benefit might revive or even expand the production of goods. It simply notes the shift toward service occupations and suggests that public policy should not deliberately resist that shift.

Economic policy in the years ahead must pay much more attention to the economy of cities. America's cities are a national asset. A growing number of Americans live in megalopolitan areas and are dependent, whether they recognize it or not, upon urban centers. In addition to the services concentrated in the cities, the cities are essential to the culural, intellectual and political vitality of the society. The churches have a special role in overcoming the anti-urban bias that marks much of American history and public policy. This role is reinforced by the fact that central cities are now the gathering place for many of the nation's poor, especially the black and hispanic poor. It would be naive to pretend that the growing disillusionment with the city is not related to the massive presence there of the poor and marginal. At the same time, much more must be done to correct the perduring anti-urban bias in the church's own life and mission. There is troubling evidence that the much acclaimed "commitment" to the cities which marked much church thinking in the late 1950s and early 1960s is now on the wane. That commitment must be revived and sustained.

We must be sensitive to the complaint of the poor, especially of blacks, that the popularity of "regional planning" has increased precisely at the point when blacks have gained majority or near-majority power in some urban centers. At the same time, considerations of declining tax base and other factors underscore the need for regional interdependence if cities are to survive with any degree of dignity or vitality. While building such structures of interdependence, public policy should not be skewed in such a way as to permit the economic disadvantage of the urban poor to be turned also into greater political disadvantage.

It should be public policy to greatly enhance mass transportation systems in our urban areas. There is a refreshing skepticism abroad about the wisdom of infinitely expanding roads and other facilities designed for the private automobile. Funds previously designated for those purposes might well be transferred in large part to mass transit systems. At the same time, the great majority of Americans is dependent upon the automobile. Indeed one might agree that, in fact, "mass transit" in America is the automobile. Life investments, community structures, and personal life styles have, for most Americans, been premised in large part upon access to the private automobile. It is both politically expedient and fair that these interests be taken into account in future public policy regarding transportation.

Government and Economic Life

A perennial question in American life has to do with the control of the corporations that strongly influence, if they do not control, much of our public and personal existence. Corporations would seem to be controlled in part by stockholders, in larger part by their technocratic management, in increasing part by government regulation, and in immeasurable part by market variables over which corporations have little control. There is no principled reason why control should rest with one party or another. The question is what corporations do to people. Some suggest that all talk about control is illusory since such corporations operate by their own dynamics, as does technocracy itself, in a manner quite indifferent to the decisions of those formally in control. One should exhibit caution against the tendency to demonize the corporation, as one exhibits caution against the current tendency to demonize technology.

It is not true that what is good for General Motors is good for the country. It is true that the collapse of a dozen General Motors would be very bad for the country. Prosperity is better than depression. Jobs are better than breadlines. The valid reasons for governmental intervention in corporate decision-making have been noted. National interest, as well as concern for social welfare, might also justify intervention in order to direct production into new channels. For example, public policy should direct itself more forcefully to the "conversion" of industry from dependence upon, and thus escalation of, military production. This is not to deny that military production is necessary. It is intolerable, however, that defense policy should in such large part be determined by domestic economic considerations. Whatever other values public policy should encourage, it should be aimed at prosperity and employment. Economic schemes—whether they come from the corporate board room or the university seminar—that downplay the importance of mass prosperity and employment reflect an unconscionable indifference to the way the great majority of Americans perceive their own interest.

A cluster of dilemmas that has escaped resolution to date has to do with the role of governmental regulatory agencies in the economy. It is almost universally recognized that the corporations that are to be regulated exercise too much control over the putative regulators. The reasons for this have to do with human venality, but also with the nature and distribution of expertise relevant to the regulating function. To forbid altogether any job movement between industry and regulatory agencies would impose an unfair burden upon the government employee and would likely decrease expertise in government service. Such job movement can, however, be more carefully monitored. Conflict of interest laws can be more consistently enforced. The public can be better informed about the importance and problems of regulatory agencies and thus a climate can be created which discourages currently corrupt or at least ambiguous connections between government and corporations.

The historical development of regulatory agencies as such is in need of careful re-examination. Intended to protect the public against corporate exploitation, it is widely believed today that many regulatory arrangements now work against the public interest, artificially raising prices and limiting competition. This is notably true in such areas as transportation fares, telephone service, and communications networks. Regulations that protect industries from competition more than they protect the public from exploitation are clearly not in the public interest.

The state also has a legitimate responsibility for consumer protection and education. Genuinely dangerous products, as for example, some drugs, should be carefully tested, controlled, and honestly advertised. "Truth in advertising" is a worthy ideal, even though by definition advertising is a promotional enterprise involving hyperbole and suggestions that are hard to match with serious notions of truth. Were every product that could be dangerous removed from the market, and were exaggeration excluded from advertising, there is little doubt the economy would quickly grind to a halt. Prudential judgment on public policy regarding consumer protection should reflect a healthy respect for the common sense and liberty of most Americans. While some government agencies may have a more elevated notion of what ought to be the "national quality of life," consumer education should not be used in a way that restricts the freedom people have to decide upon their own quality of life, also in terms of what they buy and use.

Public policy opinion continues to be divided between those who favor the vigorous application of antitrust laws and those who believe in a convergence of economic activities into quasi-monopolies in a "planning sector" more amenable to public direction. There would seem to be no enprincipled reason for public policy to move in one direction or the other. In either case, economic life should be aimed at sustaining prosperity, employment and pluralism. The value of pluralism would, admittedly, seem to require resistance to excessive centralized control of the economy, either by monopolies or by the state, or by both in combination. On another level, it should be public policy to encourage and help sustain small businesses. In addition to its economic contribution, the entrepeneurial tradition in America has created great benefits for the consumer and has offered freedom and opportunity to individuals outside the corporate mega-structures of our society.

Opinion is also divided about the relative dangers of inflation and depression, with "conservatives" generally more alarmed about the former and "liberals" about the latter. In addition to the business difficulties posed by inflation, it no doubt constitutes a major burden for people on fixed incomes, especially the aged. Depression, on the other hand, would seem to be more universally disastrous and has its most immediate impact in massive unemployment. Full employment is, on paper, the public policy of our country and we should support that goal. Employment should be publicly acknowledged as a right. While one might be sympathetic to the notion that the government should be "the employer of last resort," the notion needs careful qualification. Direct employment by the government in order to create jobs is indeed the *last* resort.

As in so many areas of economic policy, experts are deeply divided over the meaning of "full employment" and the connection between employment and the government's monetary-fiscal decisions. Full employment is a vague goal, subject to changing social factors. For example, some would define full employment as meaning 5 percent of the "labor force" is unemployed, others would say 2 percent, while a few would quite literally insist on zero unemployment in the labor force. Obviously, there is a prior question as to what constitutes the "labor force." It would seem, for instance, that statistically measurable "unemployment" would increase as family incomes rise, as job discrimination against women declines, as job expectations rise among blacks and other minorities, as unemployment compensation is extended and increased, and as inflationary expectations subside. In short, a number of the very changes one might welcome could increase the statistically measured unemployment.

"Full employment" should therefore probably not be understood as getting everyone employed or even guaranteeing everyone a job. If full employment is understood in that way, it begs the questions of the *terms* of employment or even what is meant by "employment." Full employment means providing adequate employment opportunities, fully aware that there is great ambiguity in the term "adequate." It is not, for example, a reasonable public policy that every entrant to the "job market" be guaranteed a starting job, at, say, $12,000 per year with prestige, prospects, and "meaningful" work. Again, as mentioned elsewhere public policy should be aimed at countering misery and at preserving human decency rather than assuring "happiness." A policy of full employment means that no one who wants to work and is able to work should be without a job and that no job should imprison a person in permanent disadvantage against his or her will and ability to contribute to the society.

Even the most ideological laissez-faire capitalist now recognizes that governmental action inevitably affects, for better or for worse, the private sector of the economy. In times of economic downturn and unemployment the government should take action to stimulate the economy, even at the risk of inflation. Since unemployment, especially among the poor and marginal, is frequently caused by factors other than the general state of the economy, the government should—working as much as possible through private business and mediating institutions—support programs of remediation and job training. When there is significant unemployment in the mainstream working force, government initiative should open new jobs and new types of jobs, again utilizing mediating structures. For example, there are many useful services to be performed at the community and family levels in caring for the aged and the sick, and there are almost infinite opportunities for useful employment in the physical rehabilitation especially of urban areas.

In times of large unemployment it would also seem both wise and more fair were massive lay-offs to be avoided as much as possible through wage freezes and adjustments in working hours such as shorter work weeks. In this connection, Christians in labor unions have a special responsibility to bring ethical judgment to bear on union policies that too often work a severe hardship on other workers in order to preserve the full advantages of the employed.

In times of inflation there should be experimentation with various devices to both equalize and minimize the effect. The notion of "indexing" wage and prices in order to reflect the changing money value would seem to be worthy of more serious consideration. For all the complexity of the subject, we are mindful that money is, after all, a human invention dependent upon a human definition of value and ought to be manipulated for human purposes. (One "indexing" activity, although much too partial and cumbersome, is already evident in the adjustment of Social Security payments to the elderly.)

Some factors of the agricultural economy are touched on in our discussion of world hunger and development. Sufficient to say that it ought to be U.S. public policy to maximize long-term domestic food production, to assure a fair market return to the U.S. farmer, to vigorously support increased production in food for poor countries, and to lead the world in generous response to long and short-range emergencies. This is the place to note that schools and other agencies should do a much more effective job than they do at present in educating Americans to the realities of agricultural production. That is, in the U.S. less than 5% of the population is directly engaged in the agricultural production on which all are dependent. This is almost the precise reverse of the ratios of agricultural and nonagricultural employment in many other societies. The result is that too many Americans are indifferent also to the economic needs of American agriculture.

Labor

Because economic life should not be ruled by the law of the jungle and cannot be ruled by the precepts of fraternal cooperation, it is necessary that countervailing forces in the economy be able to deal with one another from positions of institutional strength. Thus labor cannot depend upon the fraternal or paternal good will of management but must have organized leverage with which to advance the welfare of workers. Yet the principle of countervailing force should not be relentlessly conflictual. Labor and management have a common interest in the general economic welfare. In some liberal democratic and socialist societies experiments are being advanced in various forms of "shared management" with labor participation in corporate decision-making. In less formal ways, this same movement toward cooperation is noticeable in some parts of the American economy. As a step toward ameliorating destructive conflict while protecting the several interests involved, further experimentation in shared management should be encouraged.

Although it is not clear that public policy can help remedy the problem, there is today a shameful disregard by "big labor" of the majority of American working people. We witness the development of a unionized "labor aristocracy" that seems to have largely abandoned labor's historic concern for the working poor. One hopes for a revitalization of labor's mission on behalf of "the little people." Christian leadership in labor unions should work toward that end.

Another disturbing development is the growing collusion between political leadership and union leadership created by the unionization of public employees. This is most notable in the cities of our country. Politicians are increasingly dependent upon public service unions for election and public service unions are increasingly in control of city budgets. Thus effective policy-making is removed from the majority of city residents and the political process is demeaned. This dilemma is not amenable to easy remedy. It can be alleviated in part by the devolution of public service jobs to mediating institutions. As noted before, it might also be required that city employees live in the city for which they work. In addition to returning many middle-class white to the cities, the second step would also greatly empower present city residents, notably blacks and other minorities. (It is recognized that such a residency requirement might also intensify the collusion between politicians and organized labor by increasing the urban political base of public employee union. Such a step must therefore be coordinated with other measures advocated for revitalizing our cities, including the expansion of the urban tax base and middle-class population.) Yet another direction deserving more careful consideration is the possibility of cities and other government agencies purchasing or contracting services with the private sector.

While at one time we might have urged simply that the church's witness be on behalf of labor, today the cause of labor and the cause of the poor and disenfranchised are by no means synonymous. The burden of the church's public witness should be on behalf of the poor and disenfranchised. In some instances, such as that of migrant workers, this will be a pro-union witness. In other instances, where powerful unions exclude the poor or resist their political empowerment, the church's witness will be perceived as anti-union. Again, Christians should not permit themselves to be intimidated by such public perceptions of their role but should act confidently and discriminately. The church has no permanent institutional alliances but is guided by the criteria of the concrete in support of policies responsive to human need.

While it would seem that the "cybernetic revolution" of a decade or more ago has been indefinitely postponed, the problem and opportunity of increasing leisure time warrant the church's urgent attention. Increased leisure is produced less by cybernetic revolution than by demographic factors signalling an aging population reaching earlier retirement. Although forced retirement at an age earlier than many workers wish to retire may be required at present to keep the job market open, public policy should aim at expanding employment and thus increasing the worker's freedom of choice about when to retire. As to the use of leisure time, whether voluntary or forced, public policy should aim at increasing opportunities for "second (or third) careers" and the churches and other voluntary associations should devise programs in order to capitalize on such opportunities.

Work itself is not a curse but possesses its own integrity; it should be seen as a critical part of the process of human fulfillment; and, for the Christian, it can be understood as response to divine vocation. Much work is undoubtedly dehumanizing and demeaning of human dignity. It is also reliably estimated that many thousands of workers die each year as a result of hazardous conditions that can be corrected. Job safety is a legitimate and urgent concern of public policy and deserves much more attention than it is presently receiving. Job satisfaction (or job enrichment) is in a more limited sense also within the purview of public policy. With regard to job satisfaction, two cautions are in order. First, jobs that some people may see as demeaning, dehumanizing and deadended are seen by some who do these jobs as satisfying and fulfilling. We dare not despise the work other people do and find worth doing. Public policy concern is aimed simply at assuring, insofar as it is possible, that no one is locked into onerous labor against his or her will. Second, evidence suggests that most workers are much more interested in pay and other benefits than they are in designs for job enrichment. Again, people's own perceptions of what is in their interest should be respected.

Income Redistribution and Tax Policy

Christians have sometimes been accused justly of underplaying the economic factor in such a way as to make other social ideals inaccessible and thus largely illusory for many people, especially for the poor. This criticism should be taken seriously. While condemning materialism, Christians dare not place concern for material justice outside the realm of God's sanctifying and redeeming work. At the same time, Christians should not be so intimidated by the above criticism that they fail to insist that the whole of life does not consist in economic advantage and that justice is more than economic justice.

Today, notably among intellectuals, there is a widespread call for "the redistribution of income" or of wealth in general. Few people advocate an absolute equalization of wealth. Almost no one visualizes an equalization downward. It is rather assumed that such a redistribution would result in an almost universal equalization upwards, with the exception of the super rich. In short, many thoughtful people believe the present income distribution has little plausible relationship to either need or social contribution. This perception is undoubtedly accurate and examples in support of it can be multiplied with ease. In addition, it would seem more just (in the sense both of moral excellence and fairness), were wealth more logically related to need and social contribution. The obvious difficulty is in deciding who will decide which need and which contribution will warrant which portion of economic good. Since the state is the chief, and perhaps the only, candidate for this decision-making role, Christians who have been sobered by the modern history of totalitarianisms will examine with great care the presuppositions undergirding proposals for income redistribution.

As noted throughout with reference to the idea of equality there is a point at which inequities can provoke public scandal in a way that constitutes a threat to social stability. (No value judgment about whether such scandal is created by genuine concern for fairness or merely by envy is made here.) Studies indicate that, apart from a sector of the intellectual elite, Americans are not so scandalized by the present income distribution in our society. Indeed, rightly or wrongly, most Americans seem to view the existence of the wealthy as a welcome provocation toward the promise of their own economic advancement. While we may have differing judgments of this majority perception of reality, we should not impose through public policy a redistribution of wealth that lacks public support and is indeed contrary to the popular understanding of the common welfare. Without exacerbating the human capacities for envy and resentment, Christians should help alert the public to the ways in which it is exploited by the present system and should support remedies for the same.

Unlike income distribution in general, there is a public sense of scandal regarding taxation. The sense of scandal is aimed both at the growth of taxes and the maldistribution in the payment of taxes. We should be sympathetic especially to the middle and lower middle income citizens who seem in increasing numbers to be joining a "taxpayers revolt" against the seemingly endless escalation of taxes. The church's response to this "revolt" should be twofold. On the one hand, people should be helped to see rising taxation within the larger perspective of inflation and rising costs. Misinformation and alarmism about rising taxes should be combatted. In addition, the churches should underscore the increasing and legitimate social welfare tasks undertaken by government and requiring increased expenditure. On the other hand, Christians must be critical of the self-aggrandizing character of governmental services and projects which contribute so much to escalating taxes. A relentless war must be waged against governmental operations that are expensive beyond any plausible social contribution. Christians should avoid both simplistic opposition to "big government" and the equally simplistic notion that increased expenditure by the public sector is a sign of social progress. As emphasized elsewhere, public programs should as much as possible be implemented through decentralized and community-based institutions, thus ameliorating also the fear of "big government."

In addition to rising taxation, there is a sense of public scandal about the maldistribution in the payment of taxes. There are instances, for example, in which the very rich pay less income tax than lower middle-income citizens, and in some instances pay no income tax at all. Sophisticated arguments have been made that in fact this apparent injustice contributes to economic health and thus also to the benefit of all Americans, including the poor. While such arguments have not been (and perhaps cannot be) conclusively disproved, the present situation violates a public sense of fairness and thus tends to undermine the moral and political health of the society. The popular sense of social justice has long since evolved beyond the premise that "America's business is business" or that "What's good for General Motors is good for the country." That evolution must be taken seriously in the making of public policy.

In general, the tax burden ought to be distributed in proportion to the ability to pay. Those who have benefited most from the system have the greater responsibility for maintaining the system. The exercise of that responsibility should not of course negate the benefit. There is legitimacy to the warning that tax policy should not discourage incentive. But we should not be surprised that those who have benefited most—in many cases because of their own response to incentive—tend to be somewhat alarmist about measures that would allegedly destroy initiative in the pursuit of economic advantage.

There are many proposals currently offered for tax reform. Some, from both the left and the right, are quite radical in character. Efforts to replace the escalated income tax with some other basic approach seem somewhat quixotic at present. This does not mean the present linkage (at least in theory) of tax rate to income level is sacrosanct. That linkage seems, however, to be well established and to accommodate a majority's sense of fairness. The proposal that there be a minimum rate of taxation on income, perhaps of 15%, commends itself. This rate would be exacted regardless of tax-exempt investments of other "loop holes." This is one step that might go a long way toward relieving the present sense of scandal about some, notably the very rich, "escaping" income taxation.

Given the present outlines of the tax structure, we should not move toward greater dependence upon sales taxes in the raising of public revenues. Especially when sales tax applies to essentials, it is regressive and unfair, notably to lower income citizens. As discussed elsewhere, we should also resist the increasing tendency to rely upon gambling and similar devices to raise public revenues. Taxation should as much as possible be direct and should be directly accounted for.

To a limited extent tax law is inevitably an instrument for the making of public policy. In the realm of taxation, unlike the economy generally, the logic of distributive justice holds that one person's benefit is at another's expense. In general, taxation should be equitable and across the board. Exemption should be limited to those institutions and activities which are required for the maintenance of a pluralistic society, as, for example, to voluntary associations, educational institutions, churches, and foundations. If it be public policy to encourage, for example, investment in certain business, or to increase the number of rural doctors, or to expand home building, these goals should be supported through positive legislation outside the tax structure. The long standing tendency to make public policy through tax law has contributed to great confusion about what is public policy and even more confusion in trying to understand the tax structure and thus bring it under political control. The present tax structure is a gargantuan thicket of hidden agendas, many of them half-forgotten, many of them obsolete, few of them subject to open scrutiny and debate.

Finally, in discussing these various aspects of economic life we should be keenly aware of our uncertainties and lack of expertise in addressing many of the issues raised. Yet we can be emboldened by the fact that the putative experts seem to know little more, although they no doubt have a better understanding of why they do not understand the economy. Most of all we can be emboldened, however, by the knowledge that important value judgments are involved in economic policies. There may be economic cycles and forces that defy present tools of analysis and decision. We should not, however, resign ourselves to such impersonal dynamics or succumb to the mystification of economic life. The economy is not a Moloch to which human beings should be sacrificed. The "health of the economy" should be measured in terms of the economic welfare of real people. Graphs and figures to the contrary, the economy is not healthy if large numbers of people are economically suffering.

It remains a great historic challenge to bring the economy under human control. In many societies in which the economy has been subject to political decision the result has been both political tyranny and economic disaster. There is limited comfort in the knowledge that the American economic system has, for all its faults and for whatever reasons, been, relative to other systems, remarkably successful in providing prosperity and security for millions of people. Our system, however, is not to be measured only by other systems but by the values we profess as a society. By that measure—and in view of widespread unemployment, economic misery and insecurity—we can in no way rest content with our economic system and the public policies relevant to it. Christians should relentlessly expose and protest the economic failures and injustices in our society; they do this not in order to condemn the society but in order to stir up the imagination and will that can, we hope, lead to a better and more humane economic order.

10

Church and State

The relationship between church and state in American society has already come up at many points in this study. This chapter offers only a few summary remarks and treats a handful of policy issues that do not arise explicitly in other connections.

Institutional Separation and Functional Interaction

Some Christians have in recent years spoken of church-state relations in terms of "institutional separation and functional interaction." That is a helpful formulation, recognizing of course that the line between institutional and functional aspects is frequently unclear. Also, even the qualified use of the term "separation" can play into the hands of those opposed to our understanding of American pluralism.

Since, especially in connection with the First Amendment, popular and legal attitudes tend to emphasize institutional separation, it might be useful to list some of the important dimensions of functional interaction. In the free exercise of its divine mandate, the church relates to the interests of the state in such ways as (1) offering intercessory prayer on behalf of the state and its officials; (2) encouraging responsible citizenship and government service; (3) helping the state to understand, and holding the state accountable to, the sovereign law of God; (4) contributing to the civil virtues which support the state in fulfilling the duties of just government; and (5) championing the human and civil rights of all citizens. (A more detailed description of

the ways in which the church fulfills these tasks is found in Chapter
Two, "Relating Christian Faith to Public Policy: Ways and Means.")

Also under the heading of functional interaction, we note the ways
in which the state relates to the interests of the church: (1) securing
the peace and order conducive to the church's fulfillment of its mission; (2) guaranteeing religious liberty for all; (3) maintaining an
attitude of "benevolent neutrality" toward religious groups in the
context of cultural pluralism; (4) providing on a nonpreferential basis
incidental benefits and financial assistance in recognition of the church's
civil services to the whole society or a part thereof in areas that fall
within the state's mandate to advance the general welfare; (5) acknowledging that human rights are not the creation of the state; and
(6) acknowledging that the church's mandate is not received from
or subject to the state.

As we have seen in connection with particular policies some of these
"functional interactions" lead into highly controversial territory. While
the church must obviously take into account what the state defines as
the law of the land, the church must also cultivate its distinctive perspective on what ought, in particular policy areas, be the relationship
between church and state. In publicly articulating its perspective, the
church speaks on different levels. There is the normative statement in
which the church has a word from the Word of God. There is the
descriptive statement in which the church has the special responsibility
to lift up what it believes to be the nature and consequences of particular policy considerations. And there is the instrumental statement
in which the church participants in formulating the prudential judgment which is the appropriate response to a policy question.

In these various levels of public statement the American churches
have in recent years been excessively timid and docile in relating to
the state. Especially is this the case in connection with the state's
definitions, notably through the Supreme Court, of church-state relations. On policies having to do with education, social welfare, and
the rights of conscience the court has sometimes floundered about in
confused and confusing decisions which have the net result of emphasizing the "nonestablishment clause" of the First Amendment to the
detriment of the "free exercise" clause. The result of such decisions,
largely abstracted from the social realities of American life, tends to

be an unnatural and potentially dangerous separation of social policy from the beliefs and associational ties of the great majority of Americans.

As a result of this unhappy separation, the Supreme Court has been brought into disrepute in the eyes of many Americans. The court is a crucially important part of our constitutional system and should be held in high esteem by all. At the same time, there is a tendency in some circles to view the court as a kind of delphic oracle, making decisions on social policy in areas where the people and their political process presumably lack the necessary wisdom. The Constitution does not establish the Supreme Court as the final word, but rather would explicitly check the court through certain powers of the people's representatives in Congress and through the provisions for constitutional amendment.

A constitutional amendment has never been passed that over-ruled a decision of the Supreme Court sitting at the time of passage. Many believe that this constitutionally established method of overruling the Supreme Court is, while theoretically possible, dangerous and impracticable. Until recently the same belief was widely held about the impeachment or resignation of a president. While there are historical precedents pointing up the dangers of plebiscitary democracy or rule by referendum, this is far from being a real or present danger in American society. There is a danger of judicial decisions increasingly preempting the role of the people in determining public policy and thus further weakening the democratic character of our political process. An experiment in the full exercise of the constitutional process of government by the people, including the power to overrule judicial decisions, might have an invigorating effect upon public confidence in our system of government. Such an exercise should not be viewed as unAmerican or anti-Supreme Court but as a legitimate and important revitalization of one aspect of democratic government. Saying one might welcome such an exercise in principle is not taking a position on the controversial questions on which the power of amendment is currently being advanced, namely, protection of unborn life, educational diversity, and equal rights for women. Those issues are treated separately. Here it is only important to note that the first two questions particularly are closely connected to the concept of "institutional separation and functional interaction" between church and state.

Tax Policy

A major area of concern in church-state relations is that of taxation policy. There is a limited sense in which the church already pays taxes. Sales tax and service-specific taxes in certain localities, as well as real estate tax on unused properties, are examples. Yet a sales tax, for instance, is more precisely a tax on the product purchased as are "taxes" on municipal services more in the nature of payment for purchase. More fundamental issues are raised when it comes to the church's exemption from property and income taxes.

Whether or not the church should pay taxes touches on the complex and frequently tortured history of church-state relations at least since the fourth century. It is not simply a prudential question but involves the church's theological self-understanding within the "two kingdoms" of God's rule. Church tax exemption is, in American law, part of a larger pattern of tax exemption and preference for certain charitable, educational and other activities. As a legal corporation and voluntary association, the church recognizes its placement within this more general pattern, but its position on tax exemption is not limited by considerations which at a given time may be considered appropriate to governmental decision-making.

There are two arguments for tax exemption which are either invalid or of very limited usefulness. The first is that tax exemption is purely a privilege bestowed by the state which can be continued or withdrawn according to the state's judgment of what advances the general welfare. In this sense the church is not merely a voluntary association or charitable enterprise that is to be judged solely by the state's judgment of its social utility. Second, we should reject the notion that tax exemption is to be viewed as a subsidy or "tax expenditure" on the part of the state.

The relatively recent notion of "tax expenditure" should be viewed with great caution. It comes close to implying that the whole of the society's income and wealth is, in principle, subject to the state's direction. Any income or wealth, therefore, that is "exempted" is to be viewed as an expenditure by the state in furtherance of the state's purposes. A corollary says, "That which the state funds (by "tax expenditure") the state ought to control." This direction, pushed far enough and consistently enough, has troubling and even totalitarian implications that could be in serious conflict with the democratic pluralism of American society.

Far from tax exemption of the churches being a subsidy by the state, the taxing of church property and income would constitute a violation of religious liberty and would—in its effect, if not in its intention—betray the "benevolent neutrality" of the state toward the church. In short, the tax exemption of the church is a matter of right rather than of privilege or subsidy. In saying this, we must be aware of the need for careful definition of what is meant by "the church" and by its "property and income." We also must recognize that, just as there can in practice be no abidingly clear line between the two kingdoms, there will be areas of ambiguity regarding taxation policy that will never lend themselves to absolute solution.

The church has a distinctive mandate received from God and in no way derived from or subject to the divine mandate which gives authority to the state. The church, in the sense of all the Christians who are the People of God, renders to Caesar what is due Caesar, including taxes. This is not done grudgingly but willingly as an act of religious obedience. The church as the corporate and institutionalized expression of the community of the redeemed is supportive of, but not subject to, Caesar's role in the exercise of just government. This is a theological statement affirmed with religious conviction and is to be respected by the state. In biblical times and in our own time, a primary symbol of subjection to the state is the payment of taxes. This symbolic act of subjection the church dare not render to the state. This is true for the sake of both the integrity of the church and the integrity of the state.

In addition to the symbolic statement involved, to submit itself to the state's power of taxation would on a more practical level make the church vulnerable to domination by the state. The power to tax is, at least implicitly, the power to control, and even to destroy. In this and other connections, American churches must regain their nerve in confronting the state in no uncertain terms regarding the state's accountability to the sovereign will of God.

The church should not pay taxes on income and property related to its mission. The question of tax preferences, through deductions, for those who make contributions to the church is somewhat different. Tax policy is clearly aimed at encouraging voluntary giving to churches and other non-profit institutions deemed to be socially useful. Were gifts to the churches to be singled out in withdrawing tax preference, that would be an intolerable act of discrimination against religion. Were *all* tax preferences for charitable gifts to be terminated, it would be a severe blow not only to the churches but to all the voluntary and non-profit associations in the society. Minimally it would be an act of enormous imprudence. More likely it would be an unconstitutional policy contrary to the state's "benevolent neutrality" toward religion; it would violate the "preferred freedom" status constitutionally accorded religious liberty; and it would seriously undermine the state's obligation to respect the limits of its mandate, especially regarding its relation to the church and other mediating institutions of governance.

In making its case for tax exemption, the church may sometimes appeal to those considerations which apply to all charitable, educational and other institutions. The church may also appeal to the "secular" utility of the services it renders the society and which ought to be encouraged by the state. And of course the church should be legally adept in appealing to the precedents and rulings in America's judicial history and practice. But finally the church understands its case to rest upon theological premises regarding its own self-understanding and its relationship to "the governing authorities." If the state fails to respect that understanding, the church must contend that the state has violated both the constitutional guarantee of the free exercise of religion and, more ominously, the sovereign will be God. In that unhappy, and hopefully unlikely, eventuality, the church must find appropriate means to change or, if that is not possible, to resist the offending public policy.

The church alone is competent to determine what is required for the fulfillment of its mandate. While "functionally interacting" with the state in as cooperative a manner as possible, the final decision as to what belongs of necessity to the church's work is reserved to the church. Here some distinctions must be made, although they defy exactitude in actual practice. First, there are those activities which are clearly constitutive of the church's very life. These involve the right of assembly, public worship, public promulgation of the gospel, witness on questions of social justice, and the like. The institutions and activities essential to facilitating these goals must be unquestionably tax exempt. A second distinction would involve those activities which are implicit in the church's mission but may be carried out in a wide variety of ways, such as operating educational institutions, hospitals and other agencies of social welfare. Accommodations with the state regarding taxation and other policies in this second area are both possible and desirable. Were the state, however, to place such strictures upon the church's activity in these areas (which are after all, in one form of loving service or another, all inherent in the church's mandate) as to severely inhibit their fulfillment, it would constitute a policy of hostility to religion that is both unconstitutional and, Christians believe, contrary to God's will. In a third category are more marginal "church-related" activities which may be connected with the church largely because of historical accident or because they needed some associational linkage to which the churches were amenable. Here the churches must be more flexible in the kind of principled positions they take. This is not to say that such activities are not important. It is to suggest that in such cases the argument for tax preference or exemption can be made on grounds applicable to all charitable and voluntary activities and not distinctively appropriate to the church.

The public debate over tax exemption and related issues will likely be with us for a long time. Several strategic considerations should be kept in mind. From time to time certain determined secularists stir up the always potent forces of resentments against the allegedly great wealth of the churches. The churches should, as much as possible, rid themselves of forms of ostentation that provoke such resentment. The churches should point out that only a relatively small part of tax exempt wealth is held by the churches. Most important, the churches should make clear what such gross figures regarding wealth actually mean when spread out over the largest associational network in our society, which counts over 120 million members and to which more than eighty percent of the population feels it somehow "belongs." While this course may seem self-serving to some, the churches should make as clear as possible that they are pressing these issues not only for their own advantage but on behalf of institutional arrangements essential to democratic pluralism. Needless to say, this claim will be more believable as the churches' commitment to democratic pluralism in other areas is more believable.

In the public debate on these questions the church should not be belligerent, but it should be firm. With regard to court rulings, the church should have ever in mind that the final interpretation of what is constitutional rests not with the Supreme Court but with the people of this Republic. The churches should not engage in egregious displays of their political power, nor should they seek confrontation with the state or its judicial branch, but neither ought they to be intimidated or to underestimate their potential and responsibility in clarifying the roles appropriate to church and state. Where it does not compromise or confuse the church's distinctive claims, the church should cultivate alliances with other institutions affected by state policy on taxation and related issues.

The singular position of the church and the claim to free exercise of religion can be and have been abused. It is possible that persons claim religious exemption for income or profit-making enterprises in which the claim is fraudulent. In such cases, which are not covered by even the broadest definition of what constitutes legally recognized religion, the state can and should act. But even then it should act reluctantly and with the greatest prudence lest it be found to infringe upon the free exercise of religion. It is much better to tolerate a few marginal instances of fraud than to invite a confrontation between church and state or to have the state establish too restrictive criteria for what is to be legally recognized as religion.

In light of these general considerations, several specific policy recommendations are possible. Excluded from tax exemption status should be church-owned property that is idle or not used for any religious activity. Property used only partially for religious activity or a related business should be taxed proportionately. In today's context, where parsonages usually fulfill no more than general residential purposes, parsonages should not be tax exempt. A corollary of this is that the present practice of giving clergy a tax-free "housing allowance," is, at best, highly dubious. Again, if the housing serves more than general residential purposes, such an allowance could be taxed on a "proportionate use" basis. (Lest a hardship be suffered by some clergy as a result of this proposed change, a closer look should be taken at the present burden of paying Social Security on a self-employed basis. What may be lost in the loss of tax-free housing allowance could be made up for in a more equitable sharing of Social Security payments between the clergy and the employing agency. This compensation could be effected without changing the law or getting involved in the complex issue of whether clergy are indeed "employed" in the Social Security System's sense of that term.) In general there should be no payments to the state "in lieu of" property or other taxes. If a property or activity is genuinely tax exempt, no gesture toward tax payment should be made. If it can make only a very marginal claim to exemption and is capable of paying the full tax bill, it should pay it. If it is not so capable and if the state considers its services socially useful, it may be granted exemption as a matter of prudence and privilege rather than of right.

Church income should be tax exempt, with a few important exceptions. Debt-financed property and wealth should be taxed. Income from profit-making community services and from business operations which for the most part compete with commercial enterprises rather than offering distinctive service to the church also should be taxed. This continues to be an issue, for example, with regard to church publishing enterprises. As mentioned earlier, church-owned property that is idle or not used for any religious purpose should be subject to taxation.

In areas of the church's ministry in social justice, the church must insist without compromise that the state is not competent to judge what constitutes a valid part of the church's mission. Were the state to persist in restricting the church's prophetic ministry through tax regulation, the churches should not in the first instance establish special non-tax exempt funds for such ministry. That may be a necessary accommodation some day, reluctantly and provisionally undertaken. The urgent task now and in the years immediately ahead is for the church to press the public clarification of its God-given mandate in independence from the state. Were the churches forced to make such an accommodation, they should do so only under vigorous protest and with the clear intention of righting such gross injustice through appeal to the people.

Military and Other Chaplaincies

The question of chaplaincies in the military and other public institutions continues to be controverted. Where the state has placed people in an institution or so structured the institution as to limit the free exercise of religion if there were no chaplains, the state is obligated to provide chaplaincy services. Such chaplains are always and primarily fulfilling the ministry of the church and only incidentally part of the state structure to which they are attached, whether it be to the military or to institutions such as prison and hospital systems. It is widely acknowledged that this ordering of priorities has frequently been obscured in practice. The churches should take care to incorporate chaplaincies more fully into the larger ministry. This may mean chaplains are rotated regularly back into the more general ministry. In the military chaplaincy, it may mean that chaplains should not receive their rank and other status from the military but from the church by which they are accredited. In some cases it may mean that, in order to prevent the chaplaincy from becoming merely a creature of a state institution, the chaplaincy should be financially supported by the church rather than by the state. Most of these questions are subject to prudential judgments that need to receive more intensive consideration in the churches. In all this it is important to affirm the state's obligation to assure the free exercise of religion and to favor any steps that would free such chaplaincies to be carried out in clear and primary obedience to the church's understanding of its mission.

These then are some of the issues raised by the "institutional separation and functional interaction" of church and state. (Other issues were treated earlier, see especially Chapter 7.) Indeed, in line with the theological perspective articulated at the beginning of this study, it is not too much to say that the greater part of his whole statement can be viewed under the generic title of church-state relations.

In terms of constitutional debates about the meaning of the religion clauses of the First Amendment, the approach adopted in this study can be described as "accommodationist" rather than "strict separationist." Obviously, all such labels are ambiguous and warrant a robust skepticism. But, in general, many of the concerns that recur throughout this study—such as liberal democracy, pluralism, countervailing forces, mediating structures—require resistance to the literalistic understanding of what Jefferson (not the Constitution) called "the wall of separation between church and state." Religious institutions are among the primary value-generating structures in American life and are, far and away, the largest network of voluntary associations. It is both unwise and unrealistic to devise public policy in indifference to these value-generating and sustaining institutions. "Accommodationism" is another word for realism in acknowledging the role of religion in American life.

With regard to the establishment clause of the First Amendment, public policy should be neutral toward the churches' engagement in certain social programs. That is, if a program of education, health or some other social goal serves a legitimate "secular" purpose, it is a matter of indifference whether that program is implemented by a religious or non-religious agency. With regard to the free exercise clause of the First Amendment, public policy is at present confused by the Supreme Court's contradictory conceptions of what constitutes religion. Some rulings come close to establishing as doctrine what constitutional lawyers have called a "fervency test." That is, if you are sincere enough in your belief your consequent behavior is permitted by the guarantee of "free exercise of religion." Such an approach poses the dual problem of excusing, at least conceptually, almost any violation of law in the name of sincerity, and of completely emptying the word "religion" of any specific content. Some church leaders have urged that the court has no choice but to try to clarify, if not to define, what is constitutionally meant by religion. It is impossible to discuss here the various ways proposed for doing this. It does seem likely, however, that until there is such a clarification or definition we will continue to have confusing and sometimes contradictory rulings from the court as to what is and what is not permitted by the First Amendment.

Finally, it is well to remember that church-state relations in America are not affected only by lawyers' debates or court rulings. The law operates within a larger social and historical context; the law is, quite properly, politics as well as precedents. Therefore our focus should be on reshaping the context, including the moral ethos, within which public policy is determined. The first and most important step toward that reshaping is for the church to assert with new courage and candor —over against the state and all other social institutions—the mission to which we have been called by God and for the world.

Conclusion

Now we have come a long way; yet we have barely begun. I would be disappointed if you referred to this study for "the official answer" on public policy questions. Rather this study seeks to engage you in a continuing conversation that, like a journey, moves through broad expanses of clear vision and the nettlesome underbrush of ambiguities and uncertainty. Frequently, as James Fitzjames Stephen put it, "We stand on a mountain pass in the midst of whirling snow and blinding mist." As difficult as it is to relate Christian faith to public policy, it is also a course of high adventure and urgency, for it is nothing less than one form of response to God's calling that our lives be invested in loving service to the neighbor. For Christians who believe they have a vocation to seek the will of God in the whole of life, the conversation of which this study is part will not be ended until the political task is consummated in the right ordering of his kingdom to come.

This study does not, then, offer definitive answers but some suggestions as to how answers should be sought. One hopes it is a responsible example of fellow Christians in search of answers to some of the more important and perplexing public policy questions confronting all of us today. Lest, it be thought that this is an exhaustive treatment of public policy issues, one might note some of the many items that could not be discussed within the confines of this study. National and regional policies on land-use and zoning raise provocative questions about the right to property, and about the tension between individual, communal and government claims. While supporting compensatory programs for the disadvantaged, the study restrained itself from going into details about various proposals for "affirmative action" in public employment, labor union membership, and higher education. There is also a wide range of questions that might come under the general title of "governmental and political reforms." These would include, for example, public financing of election campaigns, the place of primary elections, the participation of public employees in electoral politics, the value of a constitutional convention, the reorganization of Congress, and such. The list of issues not addressed directly could be readily expanded. This underscores the continuing nature of the conversation of which this study is part. The approach spelled out in Part I and the examples of decision-making given in Part II should enable others to take up the discussion with sustained intensity in parish study groups, classrooms and church offices.

The introduction to Part II highlighted three basic themes that control our exercises in decision-making. They are: a commitment to examine policy in terms of its impact upon the poor, the marginal, and the outcast; a devotion to a more fully democratic process of decision-making; and a high enthusiasm for the pluralistic character of American society. These themes have been evident and controlling throughout, for in large part they sum up the practical meaning of the theological and ethical assertions of Part I. Their further elaboration is crucially important if Christians are to join with others in ordering America and the world in a justice more closely approximating the respect owed to all God's children.

In Context:

How One Tradition Has Tried to Relate Faith to Public Policy

Since the early 19th century observers of the American scene have been struck by the "activism" of the American churches. Whether they call themselves Methodists, Baptists, or Congregational, American churches have characteristically had much to say about almost everything. Only in recent decades have Roman Catholics been securely "Americanized" enough to address themselves regularly to public issues that go beyond more narrowly defined "Catholic" issues. Similarly, the Lutherans, especially the later immigrant Lutherans (as in the Lutheran Church—Missouri Synod and in The American Lutheran Church), have been somewhat reluctant about speaking out on public policy.

The purpose of this appendix is related primarily to the first part of our study, theology and "ways and means." It is an effort to examine the ways in which one church tradition has, through its corporate statements, tried to make the connection between faith and public policy. We have chosen to examine the Lutherans because of our greater familiarity with that tradition, and because, were we to undertake a similar examination of, say, Presbyterian or Methodist statements, the sheer bulk of material would require much more than a brief appendix. The analysis offered, however, should be applicable, mutatis mutandis, to the corporate pronouncements of other denominational and confessional traditions.

By limiting ourselves to "official" statements, we have already cut out a large part—no doubt the larger part—of what Lutherans have actually had to say about public policy. Then, too, we are not even going to deal here with all the official statements. (Readers who want an exhaustive bibliography of all the official statements should see

Byron L. Schmid's *The Lutheran Churches Speak 1960-1974,* available from the Lutheran Council in the U.S.A.)

From this section the reader can get a taste of how Lutheran bodies have formally tried to deal with relating faith to public policy. We will of course pay special attention to the ways in which such formal statements differ from the approach and substance of the present study. In short, then, this appendix is intended as background to help the reader understand how the present study relates to similar efforts in American Lutheranism.

In treating official statements, we limit ourselves to those issued by the American Lutheran Church (hereafter ALC) since its beginning in 1961 and by the Lutheran Church in America (hereafter LCA) since its start in 1963. Statements of the Lutheran Church—Missouri Synod (hereafter LCMS) will generally date from 1960. The above are the three bodies presently members of the Lutheran Council in the U.S.A. We therefore do not take into account statements of the Wisconsin Evangelical Lutheran Synod. (The serious student of American Lutheran social consciousness will certainly want to study the Wisconsin Synod statements, however, since, especially on church-state issues, they are often both distinctive and highly suggestive of another way of understanding the church's role in the American experiment.) And of course we cannot take into account the public policy posture of the Association of Evangelical Lutheran Churches (AELC) now emerging from the LCMS.

We say "more or less official" statements because in fact such statements take many forms. Sometimes church conventions "take a position" on an issue, other times they simply "commend a concern" to their congregations and members. Frequently a board or agency will address a particular public policy question or the Lutheran Council in the U.S.A. will "speak for" its member churches in congressional testimony. Especially in the LCA, officially designated groups frequently undertake "studies" of public policy problems. In some instances these studies are published to "stimulate thought and discussion," and sometimes they eventuate in formal church action. So it is not always easy to tell which statements are more and which less official. As we go along, we will usually note the formal status of the statements mentioned. But in general we have included only those statements which are viewed as normative or at least as mandatory referents by church body staff people who are charged with addressing public policy issues. (With very few exceptions, all statements are listed in Schmid's *The Lutheran Churches Speak.*)

In Chapter Two on "Ways and Means" we said something about the role of formal church statements on public policy. Their place in the larger task of relating Christian faith to public policy was, the reader may recall, pretty far down on our list. Working through the hundreds of statements issued by Lutherans in the last two decades or so has done nothing to change this estimate of their limited importance. Statements by conventions and other groups are necessary and probably inevitable. Often, however, they demonstrate little coherent connection between the theological affirmations with which they almost always begin and the policy conclusions to which they leap. Seldom do they challenge the culturally current definitions of justice, equality, human rights, and the like. With few exceptions, committee efforts to bring out a resolution that will be approved result in platitudinous "reconciliations" rather than forthright statements of disagreement that might provoke further and serious thought. One unfortunate consequence is that these hundreds of resolutions passed give the impression of having "dealt with" many issues, of having "addressed" this problem or that, without having engaged the church bodies or their members in the serious and always disturbing search for God's will for his world. Nonetheless, these are the statements with which we must work and, if it be any comfort, they are probably no more to be faulted than are similar statements by other church bodies.

Finally, in preparing this study I was struck by a number of differences among the three Lutheran bodies. In inviting consultants for the project, it became apparent that the LCA had many more people experienced in dealing with church and society issues than did the other two bodies. The LCMS came off poorest on this score. In addition, the LCA is by far the most energetic and disciplined in doing in-depth studies of various public policy issues. ALC studies and statements have been largely shaped by the enormous vitality of one man, Carl F. Reuss, director of the Office of Research and Analysis. LCMS studies are very few, and its formal statements more frequently reflect the process of ad hoc committee compromise. The LCA study documents, drawing widely upon the talents within that church body, are especially useful in provoking and informing that broader discussion and action that might be only marginally related to formal position-taking. At the same time, in terms of the substance of the positions formally taken, the LCA most often coincides with the conventional reformist wisdom in the culture, the LCMS least often does, and the ALC is more unpredictable.

Theology of the Political Task

Among the most useful of general statements is *A Theology of Politics* by William H. Lazareth, issued by the LCA Board of Social Ministry in 1965. Lazareth has had an inestimable influence on the social statements of the LCA and this booklet represents a succinct presentation of views which pervade other LCA documents. The quotation in our Chapter One, "Luther had to put the church back under God's gospel; we have to put the state back under God's law," is from Lazareth. In agreement with the present study, Lazareth also sees the "two kingdoms" concept as a creative restatement of Paul's understanding of the "two ages." We have, however, pressed the analogy further, giving a much more emphatically eschatological interpretation of the two kingdoms. In treating the relationship between church and state, LCA documents frequently list the various services the church renders to the state and vice versa. One formulation of those mutual services, a formulation which regularly reappears and which we use in a modified form later in our own study, appears in Lazareth (pp. 22f.).

Also issued by the LCA Board of Social Ministry and also written by Lazareth in consultation with others is *Social Ministry: Biblical and Theological Perspectives* (1966). Distinctive emphases in this statement are the focus on the doctrine of the Holy Trinity as the conceptual framework for understanding God's relation to the world and on the Lutheran Symbols' protections against both quietism and activism. This brief and in some respects less satisfactory theological statement is noteworthy for its effort to formulate a Lutheran understanding of social ministry in a way that poses the two kingdoms concept primarily in terms of the distinction between creation and redemption, rather than of the distinction between the two ages. In underscoring the doctrine of the Trinity it suggests yet another conceptual model that could be made primary in spelling out the church's relation to the political task and it thus advances in at least this one respect to the exploration of the several conceptual options proposed in Chapter One.

As the reader may infer from our Chapter One, some consultants to this project thought the two kingdoms model should be dropped in its entirety. That view is hardly rare among Lutheran thinkers who have internalized the meaning of the collapse of Lutheran social ethics during, for example, the Hitler era. Yet others point out that the example of the Scandinavian Lutheran churches during that same era rebuts the argument that the two kingdoms model leads inevitably to the church's impotence before the aggression of the state. This study utilizes the two kingdoms model for two basic reasons. First, because the model is so deeply set in any social ethical approach that is historically identifiable as Lutheran. Second, and as noted in the text, because the *intention* behind the model must inescapably be asserted if Christians are to avoid fanatical politics, on the one hand, or political indifference, on the other. An especially helpful recent discussion of official and unofficial treatments of the two kingdoms model is Hans Schwarz's "Luther's Doctrine of the Two Kingdoms—Help or Hindrance for Social Change" and the spirited response to Schwarz's basically positive argument by Karl Hertz (*The Lutheran Quarterly*, Spring, 1975). The present study's treatment of the two kingdoms model is responsive to some of Hertz's criticisms of its more traditional statement. Hertz is, of course, a consultant to the present study.

Church and State: A Lutheran Perspective is the product of an inter-Lutheran consultation of theologians brought together by the Board of Social Missions of the former ULCA in 1961. It is in many respects an intriguing document, although less critical of secularizing tendencies in American life than is the present study or a number of other studies done since the early 1960s. The treatment of the two kingdoms concept is somewhat ambiguous, moving with dexterity and without explanation between "two aeons" and "two realms." It catches both the positive and negative notes in its posture toward the political task itself: "Christians therefore see political authority, though sinful, as a manifestation of God's hidden rule, an expression of God's will to preserve the world for His redemptive purpose and to curb the egocentricity and wilfulness of His creatures." (p. 31)

The insistence that Christ is Lord of all comes through clearly in "Sent Into the World," a statement adopted by the 1970 ALC convention. "Nothing in the world is neutral or irrelevant to the Gospel. The Gospel does not abandon some dimensions of life and speak to others. It addresses the whole world of relationships: personal, family, community, economic, national, and international. The Gospel addresses the whole creation and invites the whole creation into a new community with God. This is the Gospel with which the church is sent into the world."

Throughout the 1960s the churches were trying, sometimes desperately, to provide a clear theological rationale for the engagement in social issues which seemed so essential were the churches not to be dismissed as "irrelevant." "Our Approach to Social Involvement" was one such ALC effort "commended to the congregations" by the 1968 convention. Invoking the Augsburg Confession, it notes that Lutheran teaching "denies to the church any claims to exercise power and authority over the temporal realm. It sharply distinguishes the powers and functions of both church and state, each under God, and insists that each be free to fulfill its own divine mandate without hindrance from the other."

One of the most difficult problems faced by the churches had to do with *corporate* ecclesial action on social issues. Church leadership generally wanted to assert that the church's involvement must go beyond the individual actions of its members. The 1968 ALC statement reached this formulation: "The corporate church should rely upon its knowledgeable and articulate members for shaping ecclesiastical policies and positions on sensitive issues. Whatever the corporate church decides to do, however, must be consistent with its recognition of the organizational pluralism and proper functions of the several institutions of society, its disavowal of any claims to exercise control over the nonreligious institutions, and its acceptance of its own unique role as the avenue for God's mediating and reconciling Means of Grace." Within those few lines, it might be suggested, are reflected most of the tensions and perhaps contradictions that continue to mark the church's efforts to spell out its distinctive role within the whole of society's governing authorities.

Already in 1962 the LCMS felt it necessary to warn against the church's indiscriminate involvement in questions of social change. Here the two kingdoms intention takes the form of "primary" and "secondary" roles of the church. Thus in "Christian Responsibility in Social

Action," adopted by the 1962 convention, the LCMS says, "The primary purpose of the church—the winning of people for Christ—may become blurred or muted as its concern for the temporal affairs of men is overemphasized." The inference invited is that "winning people for Christ" is somehow removed from "temporal affairs." In its "Social Ministry Affirmations" of 1971, however, the LCMS official resolution puts forth a somewhat different understanding of the church's primary mission. "The goal of Christ's ministry is nothing less than the salvation of mankind; that is, the restoration of all people to that kind of life, both here and hereafter, for which they were created." This suggests an understanding of "salvation" more consonant with that proposed in the present study.

Prior to the above-mentioned 1971 resolution, the LCMS Commission on Theology and Church Relations offered, in 1969, "Guidelines for Crucial Issues in Christian Citizenship." There the eschatological view of the political task is more evident, it being asserted that government is an "interim structure, designed to direct and regulate the political relationships among men during the interval between the Fall and the Lord's return." The process of salvation is involved since "the pursuit of justice and freedom is properly interested in establishing certain manifestations of the destiny God has in mind for His creation." While the statement affirms Christian "subordination" to government, such subordination is always checked by the concept of a "higher law" which is no mere abstraction.

In its 1969 convention the LCMS adopted "Principles of Social Action, With Special Reference to Corporate Positions." It should be remembered that by this time there was a strong reaction in the LCMS against the "Mission Affirmations" adopted by its Detroit convention in 1965. 1969 was the convention in which essentially reactive forces succeeded in displacing Oliver Harms and elected J. A. O. Preus as President of the LCMS. Those critical of the "Mission Affirmations," to which we will return, asserted that the Affirmations taught, among other false notions, some kind of universalistic salvation for the world. The "Principles" try to satisfy this criticism by saying, "God does not wish to destroy that world, even though its ultimate destiny is wrath." It then goes on to say of the so-called secular world, however, "It is His kingdom." The model used throughout is the distinction between "the kingdom of Christ" and the "secular" or "political kingdom." The resolution tries to find its way out of this quandary by saying, "When the Synod concerns itself with the Word of God and the call to proclaim it, it is dealing with what the Confessions call 'the kingdom of Christ.' When the Synod directs its attention to questions of social ministry and social action, it is responding not only to the call to love but to the call to Christians to participate fully in the 'secular' or 'political kingdom.' These two types of response cannot really be separated, for the Christian remains one person, and his ministry must be to the whole man and even to the whole society of men, as the Mission Affirmations state."

In one form or another, then, most Lutheran statements wrestle at least with the intention behind the "two kingdoms" formulation. They all want to assert the full sovereignty of God and to insist that there can be no sharp bifurcation between sacred and secular. At the same time, they usually end up by falling back on distinctions between the church's primary and secondary mission, or between "temporal" and "eternal," or between "spiritual" and "political." Seldom, and usually only by inference, is the political task seen as integral to the saving purposes of God to which the church is witness. The impression one gains is that the serious theological statements do want to assert such an integral relationship, but then the drafters of statements modify the implications of such an assertion in sensitivity to a popular fear that the church will become excessively embroiled in "politics."

In 1966 the ALC adopted "Christians in Politics" which includes this definition of the political task: "Politics is the process by which men exercise God's grant of His authority to foster whatever is good and to curb whatever is evil in society." Given such a definition, the church clearly has a prime role in speaking to that exercise of divine authority. At the same time, however, the resolution acknowledges the provisional character of the political task, pointing out that compromise is essential to it as "an expression of Christian respect for persons and community." The 1966 ALC statement, among others, thus points to what seems to us the happiest formulation of the "two kingdoms" tension—a formulation that maintains both the integral nature of politics to the hope for salvation and, at the same time, the modestly "proleptic" nature of political action at this provisional moment in our realization of the oncoming kingdom of God.

Philip Hefner's "Theological Perspectives on Social Ministry" (LCA

Board of Social Ministry, 1967) might be viewed as something of a minority report on the possibility of rehabilitating two kingdoms thought. "Luther and Lutheran theology after him," according to Hefner, "expected nothing of redemptive significance to happen in the Left Hand Kingdom, the realm of society; and . . . they had a limited view of what Christians should do of a benevolent nature in society." The accuracy of that statement is of course a matter of historical judgment. The point to note, however, is that almost all the Lutheran statements we are dealing with clearly want to assert a more positive assessment of two kingdoms thought, both as to what can be expected from the political process and, more emphatically, as to the Christian obligation to participate in that process. Your author is of the belief that Hefner's is probably the more accurate historical judgment but that the "revisionism" evident in more recent Lutheran statements point the necessary direction for rehabilitating Lutheran social ethics.

In the second half of the 1960s various versions of "secular Christianity" came to dominate much of religious thought in America. This is sympathetically described and welcomed by Hefner who wrote that "for most men, the things of life that pertain to redemption, that is, to the meaning of human existence, to the attainment of proper selfhood, to the fulfillment of human life—these take place outside the church." As a consequence of this understanding of secularization, "the old understandings of the church's relation to the world have been modified, and one can glimpse a new rationale emerging for relating church and world—a rationale that seems more appropriate to the conditions that now prevail." "When men diligently and seriously and courageously seek their own most authentic humanity, they will come to a humanity that is like Jesus' humanity." Although such sentiments were pervasive in "advanced" Christian thought of that time, it should be noted that they find little echo in the quasi-official statements of American Lutheranism. Within a few years, the attractions of "secular Christianity" seemed distinctly faded. It may be that because of the "cultural lag" that has frequently marked American Lutheranism, it would have taken only a few more years for American Lutheran consciousness to reflect the enthusiasm for secularization. A more positive assessment is that Lutheranism contained the theological resources—evident, for example, in the tensions inherent in the two kingdoms concept—to resist the conflation of secular ideas of humanization with the gospel's promise of salvation. In any case, the proposal tentatively set forth in Hefner's "Theological Perspectives" has to date been declined in Lutheran corporate statements.

An earlier attitude toward secularization is reflected in the previously mentioned *Church and State* booklet of 1963. That is, secularization is not apotheosized as equivalent to redemption but it is more or less uncritically affirmed as the facilitator of the pluralism which permits the several churches to go about their business unmolested. *Church and State* suggests a more "mainstream Protestant" view of the American experiment—a view characteristic of the more "Americanized" sectors of the former ULCA, now in the LCA. Thus at several points the Roman Catholic Church is seen as a threat because it asserts "a new self-confidence and aggressiveness" in pushing for public policies in support of religious and cultural particularism. Thus also the public school is seen as the great agency for warding off the devisive encroachments of particular religious traditions upon the public realm.

Both in its fear of Roman Catholicism and in its celebration of the American "melting pot," *Church and State* now seems singularly out of touch with current anxieties about the American experiment. Certainly it suggests a quite different perspective from the emphasis on particularism and "mediating institutions" which marks the present study. *Church and State* is notably uncritical, for example, of the Supreme Court's rulings on the public place of religion in American life. Its authors acknowledge the unspecified "underlying forces" that necessitate a "national and uniform solution" to the problems of pluralism and accept the Supreme Court's decision as "accomplished fact." (Some observers might say that the absence of any perceived threat from Roman Catholicism in contemporary Lutheran statements is not the result of Lutheranism's coming to a more positive assessment of particularism but of American Catholicism's buying into the mainstream secularist consensus.)

"Church-State Relations in the U.S.A.," a statement adopted by the ALC convention of 1966, strikes what some might deem a more balanced approach to the tensions between particularism and "national and uniform solutions." On the one hand it still comes out strongly against public aid to religious schools, even viewing bus transportation and school textbooks as "fraught with such divisive consequences that it is contrary to good public policy." At the same time, however, the state should "condition (its) exercise of its coercive powers . . . in deference to the religious freedom and the religious expression of the people." For public schools to "ignore the influence of religion upon culture and persons" is a "distortion of the constitutional principle of neutrality of the state toward religion." The use of religious symbolism on public property and other such issues are "matters best decided by the responsible authorities in each community. . . ." Statements such as this 1966 document can be seen as transitional toward the 1970's disillusionment with social homogenization and more positive attitude toward particularism.

Combined with the current emphasis upon particularism is a new "populist" politics profoundly suspicious of grand social planning and "centralized government." In 1963 *Church and State* could assert without too much fear of contradiction that, "The state's responsibilities must now be vastly broadened if it is to provide the communal framework of justice within which all the other orders of preservation—home, school, work, recreation, etc.—can also perform their proper functions under God." The present study, for example, would sharply qualify any such assertion about the purview of the state's responsibilities and control.

In defining the limits of the state, there is an interesting contrast between *Church and State* of 1963 and *The United States and Indochina* of 1971 (LCA Board of Social Ministry). In the 1963 statement, the state is seen as operating by its own internal logic of reason and justice. "Hence, not faith and love but reason and justice are normative for the political realm." (p. 39) *Church and State* reflects a basically trusting attitude toward the processes of modern government. After eight years of domestic tumult over the Vietnam war and other crises, the 1971 document is more ready to throw into question the legitimacy of state power. Thus in "A Preface to Dialogue" by Richard Niebanck we have a number of postulates "drawn directly from the classical Lutheran understanding of ethics and politics." One such postulate is that "the legitimacy of a government depends (objectively) upon the extent to which it is fulfilling or seeking to fulfill its proper functions . . . , and (subjectively) upon the degree to which the population perceives it as so doing. A legal . . . government is not necessarily a legitimate one; no government can have legitimacy without a supporting civil consensus." In 1971, unlike 1963, it seemed obvious to many that the U.S. government lacked such a civil consensus. What in 1963 seemed at most a remote possibility was in 1971 a very immediate imperative, namely, that the church should examine critically the legitimacy of the state in America.

Something of this same change might also be inferred by contrasting Lazareth's admirable *A Theology of Politics* of 1965 with "Church and State: A Lutheran Perspective," adopted by the 1966 convention of the LCA. (The latter statement made official a formulation that has since received wider currency in American Lutheranism: "Institutional separation and functional interaction (is) the proper relationship between church and state.") In describing the ways in which the church serves the state, Lazareth's suggestions all imply that the purposes of church and state, at least in America, are congruent, that the church's contribution is, for example, "to create a moral and legal climate . . . in which solutions to vexing problems can take place more easily." In a similar statement of the functional interaction by which the church helps the state, the 1966 LCA statement stresses also "holding the state accountable to the sovereign law of God." We do not wish to make too much of such inferences since the differences between statements are often more accidental than deliberate, but it is worth noting that the accent on "accountability" becomes more and more evident in Lutheran statements from 1966 onward as the sense of crisis about the government's role in the Indochina war and domestic racial injustice became more pronounced. (The formula "institutional separation and functional interaction" of course predates the 1966 LCA resolution, playing a prominent part, for example, in the 1963 document *Church and State*.)

Many of the basic questions addressed by our Chapter One were the subject of a Lutheran Council sponsored consulation in June, 1968, on "Lutheran Views on the Theological Bases for the Relationship Between the Church and the Structures of Society." The consultants, representing a fair cross section of Lutheran leadership groupings, agreed that a "consensus does indeed exist" on that relationship, but they readily admitted it was very much a consensus "among leadership groups in all the major Lutheran bodies." By leadership groups they meant "administrators, professors, church agency staff members, many pastors and some laymen." "But if we look beyond these to the broader ranks of our membership, it is not so clear that a socially prophetic role for the church is genuinely understood or accepted." The consultants were sensitive to the leadership-membership "gap" analyzed in sociological studies such as Jeffrey Hadden's *The Gathering Storm in the Churches* (1969) and Dean Kelley's *Why Conservative Churches Are Growing* (1974).

Although they do not say it in so many words, the consultants sensed that at the root of the problem was the failure to offer a popularly persuasive theological rationale for the church's *corporate* engagement in social change. Such engagement had been readily affirmed in terms of "Christians as individuals, both through their vocations and in their role as citizens." But, the consultants note, "what is now asked for is direct, institutional engagement (on the part of the church)." The leadership urgently wanted to legitimate that corporate engagement of which many laypeople are profoundly suspicious. This does not mean, the consultants say, that "the church need . . . become the primary instrumentality for the political activity of its members." There are many other such instruments for political action in our society. But, they insist, the church—through "research on social problems, testimony before legislative bodies, efforts to influence public opinion, the provision of social welfare services," and the such—is *one* such instrument. The 1968 Lutheran Council consultation relied heavily upon a sociological and organizational understanding of "church." As noted in our text, these dimensions dare not be overlooked. At the same time, one problem would seem to be that this understanding is not held in strong enough tension with the theological definition of church as the community that anticipates now the end time present in the Christ. Again, while it is necessary to say to many Christians that the political task is pen*ultimate,* it may on occasion be necessary to say to some leadership groups that it is *pen*ultimate. (This play on ultimacies is usually attributed to Dietrich Bonhoeffer.)

Although it impinges upon the area of "ways and means" of relating Christian faith to public policy, we mention here yet another facet in the developing understanding of the church, especially as it touches on the possibility of a discretely Lutheran involvement in the political process. The 1968 Lutheran Council consultation, reflecting the religious leadership consensus of the time, evidenced serious misgivings about both the possibility and "legitimacy" of articulating "a *denominational* point of view on public issues." The suggested alternative is to leave such witness to "smaller, ad hoc or special-issue groups with an unofficial status" or to "ecumenical agencies." While our text underscores the importance of such small unofficial groups, it is not envisioned that they would be substitutes for, so much as stimulators of, corporate action by church bodies. In addition, one wonders if the high estimate some leadership groups have of "ecumenical agencies" such as the World Council of Churches or National Council of Churches is not part of their perceived alienation from "the broader ranks of membership" which have a more local and denominational view of "church." (It should be noted that the 1968 consultation posed the issue of "denominational" witness more as question than conclusion.)

The understanding very close to our own is discovered in the 1965 Mission Affirmation of the LCMS, "The Church Is Christ's Mission to the Church": "We affirm as Lutheran Christians that the Evangelical Lutheran Church is chiefly a confessional movement within the total body of Christ rather than a denomination emphasizing institutional barriers of separation." That is, while we would use "church" in the most comprehensive and catholic sense, we recognize that, for reasons of both confessional necessity and historical accident, we must deal with the churches. In the present state of the Christian community's unhappy division, working primarily through "ecumenical agencies" may give the impression of involving more of the church while actually leaving most of the church—that is, the Christian people, in the churches—untouched.

One must hasten to add that in saying "more is less" in this instance we are not downplaying the importance of ecumenical agencies. For many reasons, including the need to underscore the transnational nature of the believing community, such agencies are crucially important. In speaking of "church," however, our approach has relied less upon organizational charts and declarations of comprehensive intent than upon the empirical and institutionalized event of people gathered around preached and sacramental Word in faith and service. (Again it must be noted that already in 1967 the reaction to the 1965 LCMS Mission Affirmations resulted in a convention clarification that the Affirmations "offer no license for other Christians in the body of unionism or separatism but rather emphasize our responsibility to minister also to Christ." It is difficult, if not impossible, to reconcile the traditional LCMS structures against "unionism" with the ecumenical insistence of the Mission Affirmations.)

Relating Christian Faith to Public Policy: Ways and Means

In Chapter Two of our study we describe nine discrete ways in which the church can relate its faith to the shaping of public policy. Obviously there is nothing sacrosanct (at least in this connection) about the number nine. The forms the relationship can take receive various mention in Lutheran statements, although they usually just list "ways and means" without any effort at detailed description. For example, "Our Approach to Social Involvement," adopted by the ALC in 1968, mentions seven ways in which the church "equips its members for mission" in social change. These are called "Avenues for Supportive Involvement." They are followed by five "Avenues for Corporate Involvement" by which the church as a community can have an impact upon social change. Again, these are highly generalized and require the elaboration that is in part, we hope, offered in our Chapter Two.

Of an even more generalized character—and that is probably appropriate to the "manifesto" genre—is "Manifesto: God's Call to the Church in Each Place," adopted by the 1966 LCA convention. In declaring its "joyous conviction that the Word of God is the power to redeem our day," the LCA underscores the imperatives "to be alert to changing needs . . . of the modern world," "to lift its voice (in order to) promote justice, relieve misery, and reconcile the estranged," "to equip its members (for) their ministries in the experiences of daily life," and such. The "Manifesto" is more a call for involvement and even less specific about "ways and means" than the 1968 ALC statement mentioned above.

In the same 1968 convention, however, the ALC adopted "Decision in a Time of National Crisis." That document lists fourteen "channels for action" on the part of the church body, some of which seem repetitious and most of which include the points made in "Our Approach to Social Involvement." Five of the fourteen deal with program funding and the use of investment power. One specific suggestion is that the ALC "strengthen its supportive services" to programs "in the inner city, in dwindling rural communities, and in areas where minority and economically-deprived groups and persons are located." (Especially in the very late 1950s and early 1960s all three bodies passed resolutions emphasizing the urgency of work among the urban poor. By the mid-1970s some obeservers thought that inner-city work had fallen in the churches' priorities in terms of both personnel and funding involved, but no reliable statistics were available. The absence of such data may itself say something about the priority given such work by the church bodies.)

In Chapter Two we emphasize the importance of the church's cultivating civil virtue. "Christians in Politics" (ALC 1966) also takes up that theme, although somewhat in passing. It focuses specifically on the "give and take" nature of the political process, pointing out that in politics "compromise can be an expression of Christian respect for persons and community. (Politics) may require one to yield some of his own advantage for the sake of others and the good of the community." *Social Ministry: Biblical and Theological Perspectives* (LCA Board of Social Ministry 1966) also speaks to the importance of civil virtue or "civil righteousness." Under the rule of God, the law performs two functions: "Its theological task is to judge the self-righteousness of sinful men in the realm of redemption. Its ethical task is to prompt the civil righteousness of rational men in the realm of creation." So also the gospel has the theological task of reckoning the righteousness of Christ to believers while "its ethical task is to empower the Christian righteousness of loving men in the realms of creation." Aside from the moral imperative of engagement itself, both individual and corporate, the statements under consideration have little to say about the nature of civil virtue or righteousness. For the most part it is to be inferred that civil virtue is synonymous with the exercise of reason in the political realm.

While asserting respect for the responsibilities inherent in the vocations of its members, the church bodies also reveal anxiety that individual and group actions should be undertaken cooperatively, especially when such actions might create tensions with the stated "positions" of the church bodies. LCA statements frequently deal with the question of which persons and agencies can in some way implicate "the church" in their actions. And "Christian Social Action Through Public Witness" (ALC 1964) specifically asks members to "consult with the board of your church about the issues. . . . Before there is major involvement in a controversial issue, it would be well to seek the counsel of responsible church officers and of informed civic leaders." Such cautions would seem to have the dual purpose of being "supportive" to members in their actions and of protecting against organizational embarrassment.

The LCMS in particular has been ambivalent about corporate actions or statements, generally limiting itself to expressing concern and urging members to share their informed opinions with appropriate public officeholders. "To Express Concern for War and International Crisis" was adopted in 1967 at the height of domestic controversy over America's war in Indochina. It refers to "extraordinary international crises in Vietnam, the Middle East, and elsewhere" and affirms that Christians should "pray for peace." "Christians," it continues, "are obligated to seek information, to relate moral considerations to political concerns, to counsel with one another." "As a church body we are not a political influence group, identified with a particular program for waging and conducting (nor, presumably, for ending) war. However, we believe that in its desire for peace, justice, and freedom the church should speak in the areas of its competence, according to the measure of its knowledge." While some might consider such statements empty or fatuous, it should be remembered that at that time many opponents of the Indochina war deemed it something of a success to have prevented the LCMS convention from giving an outright endorsement to U.S. policy. In this and other instances it should come as no surprise that most convention statements on social issues are designed chiefly to demonstrate relevance while avoiding controversy. Thus, contrary to the approach advocated in Chapter Two, seldom are issues or disagreements substantively illuminated.

The ambiguities in appealing to member to "take action" are evident, for example, in the 1971 LCMS resolution "Christian Church and World Hunger: To Encourage Legislative Action." The premise is that people are hungry and that is a problem. It is then asserted that "there are uniquely Christian concerns and insights that should be brought to the attention of legislators," although such concerns and insights are not specified. Assuming that an "informed Christian citizen will be active in legislative matters" members are encouraged to "communicate their views to legislators on specific issues concerning hunger . . . inform(ing) lawmakers of their desire for swift and compassionate action on particular bills." To the critic who may find such convention statements meaningless it can be pointed out that, for members who are significantly responsive to the "positions" of their church body, this kind of resolution at least helps "legitimate" the issue of world hunger as an item on the church's agenda. That is a beginning. That convention actions frequently do not move beyond a beginning is the larger problem addressed in part by Chapter Two.

The three bodies frequently affirm the desirability of working together with other churches and with nonreligious groups in the pursuit of social justice. Usually this is a generalized affirmation but it is at times quite specific and discriminating. An example of the latter is the 1969 ALC statement by the Church Council, "The Black Manifesto." In the late 1960s the Black Manifesto, whose chief spokesman was James Foreman, demanded "reparations" to American blacks from the religious communities. The LCA leadership received considerable and uncomplimentary publicity for what was seen as its essentially negative response to the Black Manifesto. The LCMS came up with an affirmation of its own version of "Black Power," which, needless to say, represented a dramatically different view than that of James Foreman and his colleagues. The ALC statement "repudiated" the Manifesto insofar as it was "inflammatory (and) filled with hate" or "seditious" in its advocacy of violent overthrow of "our government." The thrust of the ALC statement, however, is that the Manifesto emerged from "the anguish and frustration in a segment of our society which feels the hopelessness of oppression and man's inhumanity to man." It urges that the Manifesto be read carefully by "each pastor and church council . . . in the light of the need to be informed," and reiterates the ALC commitment "to helping solve the American problems of racism and poverty." Thus the ALC statement may be seen as an example of a critical and discriminating approach to cooperation, an attempt to define the limits of "compromise" in the political process. In the documents we are considering, there are few other instances of such specific address to questions of cooperation in social change.

Similarly, there are few formal statements dealing with cooperation with other church bodies on social questions. This does not mean there is no awareness of such cooperation or the need for it, but simply that the awareness is seldom explicated. Indeed the ways in which particular social problems become "issues" in the American churches and their staff offices might make an intriguing sociological study. There is no

evidence of the Lutheran bodies having addressed a "social issue" that
was not generally recognized as such by the other American churches
and, before that, by the mass media. One example of explicit response
to another ecclesial initiative is the LCA Executive Council's 1971
"Responses to 1970 LWF Resolutions on 'Social Responsibility' and
'Human Rights.'" In this answer to statements from the Lutheran
World Federation's Fifth Assembly, the LCA stresses the importance
of the church's transnational character and highlights the need to be
informed by Christians from other nations and social conditions.

With few exceptions, however, the statements of the three Lutheran
bodies take no note of what other churches have said or done on a
specific issue nor, for that matter, of what the other two Lutheran
bodies have said or done. Reading any one body's statements in isolation, one gains the impression that "the church" is in most cases
addressing the issue at hand for the first time. (LCMS resolutions frequently refer to other statements, but only to those of its own prior
conventions or agencies. The impact of ecumenism is very seldom evident in Lutheran statements on social questions. Lutheran Council
statements are of course more "ecumenical" by definition, at least to
the extent of reflecting the sensibilities of its member bodies.)

In Chapter Two we speak of the "internal politics of the Christian
community" as one way in which Christian faith is related to the larger
political task. The assumption here is that the search for the "right
ordering" of the world is integral to God's redemptive purpose, or as
it is most usually put, to salvation. The Christian community, also by
its own internal ordering of its life, "signals" political possibilities to
the whole of the world. An alternative approach—which, as we have
seen, is dominant in many Lutheran statements—is that life in the
Christian community is quite separate from politics in the secular
realm, the former having a redemptive significance that is denied to
the latter.

The understanding we adopt in Chapter Two is consonant with that
of "Decision in a Time of National Crisis" (ALC 1968). "The church's
involvement in the struggle for justice, equity, and mercy portrays
parables of God's love in action, points to signs of the Kingdom in
our midst, evidences the good works by which men are drawn to see
the Father, and testifies to its faith by deeds of love active for justice.
As the church participates in the struggle for justice and equity it

proclaims with integrity that God is dynamically renewing and trans-forming all areas of life." Specifically on the issue of racial discrimina-tion, all three bodies press nondiscrimination in the church as a sign of the right ordering that God wills for all human society. (See, for example, "Enforcement of Non-Discrimination in ALC Congregations," 1963.)

Because of the necessary tensions asserted by various concepts of the twofold rule of God, Lutherans, unlike some other Christians, do not suggest that the internal politics of the Christian community is *the* model for the right ordering of the world. The Christian com-munity may signal some possibilities for the world, but the hope of salvation is not that the world should become the church or that all society should be "Christianized." Acknowledging the importance of this characteristic Lutheran reserve, however, it is still striking that the Lutheran statements are so unspecific or silent about the ways in which the internal politics of the Christian community signal possibilities for the right ordering of society. We are frequently told Christians should provide examples of moral uprightness, of concern, and of love. But, aside from the issues of racial and sexual discrimination, there is almost no mention of a possible connection between the ways in which the church orders its life and the ordering of society. There are, for ex-ample, no focused statements on democratic decision-making or con-flict resolution and the ways in which the church's handling of these problems might instruct the larger society. If indeed "the Christian church, guided by the Holy Spirit and acting in the obedience of faith, is the primary instrument for the fulfillment of God's eternal pur-pose in the life of mankind," (*The Church and Social Welfare*, LCA Board of Social Ministry 1964), the irrelevance of the church's life to the specific problems of right ordering of society would seem to suggest that God's eternal purpose is fulfilled in indifference to those problems.

This conceptual difficulty plagues most of the Lutheran statements under consideration. On the one hand it is regularly said that Chris-tians must be engaged in the secular political process. On the other, it is just as regularly asserted that, in terms of God's purpose in history, the church's life possesses a primary and even singular integrity quite apart from that process. Thus the judgment that "two kingdoms" thought denies any redemptive significance to societal tasks would seem to be conceptually confirmed even while it is verbally protested.

This dilemma becomes especially evident with regard to "the internal politics of the Christian community" and its significance for the right ordering of the world.

One consequence of this is manifest in the reasoning offered for the church's speaking to an issue of public policy. Thus the church addresses an issue not because it is of great moment for the future of humanity and therefore pertinent to God's eternal purpose, but because it is of moment to the work of the church. For example, in "Federal Aid to Church Schools" (LCMS 1961) we read, "Since federal aid to nonpublic schools would vitally affect the work of the church, we believe that it is appropriate for us to speak on this matter." This kind of reasoning, most frequent in LCMS statements, is similar to that classically employed by the Roman Catholic Church in relation to oppressive public policies. Namely, confrontation with the "powers that be" should be risked only at those points where policies impinge upon the functions and privileges of the organized church. Of course such an approach has the merit of drawing a relatively clear line beyond which the church should not become embroiled in political controversy. Its difficulty is that it would seem to deny any significance, so far as "God's eternal purpose" is concerned, to injustices which do not impinge upon "the work of the church." Certainly it suggests a very restrictive definition of "the internal politics of the Christian community" quite separate from the life of Christians, in interaction with others, in the secular realm. Again, while most of the Lutheran statements considered verbally deny such a restrictive definition of Christian existence and divine purpose, it keeps returning, at least by implication, in specific statements such as the 1961 LCMS document on federal aid to church schools. Except where government policy interferes with the narrowly defined "work of the church," it is generally asserted that "In accordance with Scripture the church is to support government while at the same time serving as an instrument of God's grace and healing." (LCMS "To Express Concern for War and International Crisis" 1967). That challenge or prophetic criticism might be part of God's "grace and healing" is nowhere suggested in this not atypical resolution.

As elsewhere, it is necessary here to note a significant difference between statements by the church bodies and statements by the Lutheran Council. While the church bodies can address the connection between the "internal politics of the Christian community" and the larger political task, the Lutheran Council is one step removed from that issue, being necessarily limited to the explicit authorizations it receives from its member bodies. Thus the Lutheran Council can define the nature of its address to public policy in relatively uncomplicated terms of organizational line of authority: "A social statement is an expression of Christian ethical judgment on a current issue of social policy by a group of Christians acting corporately as the Lutheran Council in the U.S.A." ("Process in the Lutheran Council in the U.S.A. for the Development of Social Statements," Annual Meeting 1972)

In Chapter Two's discussion of "prayer and proclamation" we emphasize that the church's social witness should as clearly as possible emerge from the piety and faith of the Christian community. Both when it is supporting individual members in their citizenship responsibilities and when the church is acting corporately, we propose that the church speak modestly, fully aware of its fallibility and of its being but one participant in the process of ordering society. An alternative understanding is that the church should speak only when it can speak infallibly in the name of the Lord. This approach is suggested in the LCMS "Principles of Social Action" (1969). That resolution refers to a prior commission's statement on "Moot Issues of Our Day" and warns against the church's "issuing superficial moral judgments or urging particular forms of action in complex secular matters for which there is no clear Word of God." As in the case of the narrow definition of what interferes with the "church's work," discussed above, this approach severely restricts the instances in which the church could explicitly address public policy, since there are few public policy choices on which there is a "clear Word of God" as the resolution uses the latter term. As a consequence, the church's corporate engagement in the shaping of public policy is seen as an extraordinary rather than normal part of "the church's work." One hastens to add that other LCMS statements, as well as statements by the other two Lutheran bodies, emphatically affirm the church's continuing and normal responsibility in the shaping of public policy. Again, the contradictions between and within formal statements are almost never explicitly addressed, not to mention resolved.

We have mentioned the anxieties evident in some Lutheran statements about the possibility that individual or small group actions might implicate "the church" in controversial issues. As in all organizations, the formal leadership is nervous about lines of authority and the prospect of being embarrassed or committed by unofficial actions that might be organizationally disruptive. And, of course, the same set of questions arises at the congregational level, especially, when, as was frequent in the 1960s, activist clergy were involved in actions of protest or advocacy on which the church body and perhaps their own congregations had no clear consensus.

"The Role of the Pastor in the Community" (ALC 1970 convention) addresses this question, although in a somewhat ambivalent manner. "Indeed there may be times and circumstances when the pastor must act as the public representation of Christian conscience. When others through their lack of concern permit the perpetuation of injustice, it may be necessary for the pastor, in his sensitivity to Christ's mission, to show his congregation and the community through his deeds the meaning of God's Word for men's lives." While affirming, apparently in exceptional circumstances, this public role of the clergy in social change, the resolution places greater emphasis on the purely private character of the pastor's engagement. "In his private activities as a citizen, the pastor should make plain the personal character of his views and actions. He should be open and candid with his congregation as to the reasons underlying his actions. He should seek to avoid alienating his congregation or jeopardizing his pastoral relations." The resolution goes so far as to suggest that the pastor "may find it wise to forego wearing clergy apparel on certain occasions."

By placing these and other strictures on the pastor's personal and private involvement in public policy questions, the resolution implicitly acknowledges that there is no way in which his involvement can in fact be "personal and private." If, for example, such engagement is truly just "private activity as a citizen," the pastor could presumably tell his congregation or anyone else that it was none of their business as to what positions he takes on public issues. In reality, of course, he is always a pastor and a representative of the Christian community, notwithstanding the somewhat schizoid proposal of this and similar official statements. Unlike "The Role of the Pastor in the Community," our Chapter Two aims at suggesting guidelines for the fulfillment of the pastor's representative role rather than divorcing his public and personal existences. Similarly problematic from our viewpoint is "Institutional Identification in Political Endorsements" (ALC Church Council, 1968) which recommends that pastors, teachers, and other staff people of the ALC "refrain from attaching to their own names the name of the congregation or institution they serve when, or if, they publish statements in support of political candidates." Such resolutions seem excessively preoccupied with avoiding controversy rather than with advancing that lively diversity by which the church's discussion and action on public issues might be shaped. Finally, none of the three bodies has offered formal guidance on the role of bishops and other leaders, a subject which is discussed under official leadership in Chapter Two.

In exploring the way in which Lutheran statements have addressed the "ways and means" of relating Christian faith to public policy, we discover that much of the discussion takes place within the context of studies and pronouncements about "social welfare." This should not be surprising. The churches' institutional engagement in social welfare activities provides a ready "handle" for discussing public policy issues that might otherwise seem extraneous to many church members. By raising diverse public policy questions under the rubric of "social welfare," members more readily agree that such questions are indeed part of "the church's work" and not another instance of "mixing religion and politics."

It is not too much to say that Lutheran thinking about the church's place in social welfare and related public policies is today in a state of acute crisis. An excellent summary of why this is so, and of the unresolved questions facing Lutherans in this area, is "Lutheran Social Services: A Troubled Ministry" (a position paper published in *Lutheran Social Concern*, Fall-Winter 1974). "In reality," this paper asserts, "it is not the church today which decides how it shall operate a serving ministry known as social service, it is the government. The government can and does accomplish this by both its power to fund and its responsibility to license." We agree with the paper's further contention, "All institutions involved in these programmatic aspects of the church's work face enormous problems for which solutions must be found, yet all three church bodies appear to be devoting a minimum amount of attention to these issues."

In studying formal statements on social welfare, it seems not at all clear to the churches whether their agencies are "ways and means" in the formation of public policy. Is the church agency primarily a deliverer of services, an agent of change, or an enabler of congregations? How can laypeople express their faith and citizenship responsibilities through such agencies? Can or should such agencies challenge existing public policy, or are they merely facilitators of such policy? In relation to governmental programs of social welfare are such agencies merely experimental or stop-gap measures, or do they have a continuing, integral and essential place in "the work of the church"?

The most thorough and in many ways still the most useful Lutheran statement on these and related questions is *The Church in Social Welfare*, issued by the LCA Board of Social Ministry in 1964. This 109-page book is important not only for what it says about social welfare but also, as we have already noted, for its theoretical statements on the church's role in shaping public policy generally. While it now seems dated and otherwise inadequate in some important respects, it has not been superseded in Lutheran circles.

Many Lutheran statements on social welfare do not take such programs seriously as "ways and means" for shaping public policy simply because they see such programs as self-liquidating in favor of governmental programs. *The Church in Social Welfare* notes, "Governmental participation in welfare, through social insurance, public assistance, and other legislation and programs, has been substantial for the past three decades, *with no signs of its abatement*" (emphasis ours). It continues, "The problem is not whether government should be an active participant in welfare but rather to what extent and in what ways it should be involved, particularly when its activity serves as a deterrent to voluntary action." More clearly than many other statements, *The Church in Social Welfare* insists that "service is something *essential* to the life and function of the church. Christian service is one form of the witness of the church to the salvation and newness of life available by God's grace in Jesus Christ. . . . Whatever they may finally add up to, specific acts of relevant service are ends in themselves."

"The Church and Social Welfare," adopted by the 1968 LCA convention, begins with the premise: "Neither churches nor voluntary agencies have the capability of dealing with massive, pervasive social problems arising in a highly mobile, rapidly changing society. Therefore governments have rightly assumed increasing responsibility for meeting social need and dealing with its causes." Here and elsewhere in Lutheran statements, the expanding of governmental programs and control is viewed either as inevitable or as morally mandated in the name of social justice. While this 1968 resolution affirms the necessary place of service in the life of the church, it also clears the way for phasing out existing programs and agencies through which that service is offered: "The church should explore new forms of service in its diaconic task since no particular form of service is scripturally or theologically determined." Throughout this study, of course, we have contended that the question is not whether social needs can be met either by the government or by church and voluntary agencies. We have rather advocated that it be public policy that the government work through church, voluntary, and other mediating institutions. Thus the generally defensive posture reflected in this 1968 LCA resolution would seem to result from a fundamentally false posing of the alternatives.

Little help is to be found in "The Role of Government in Social Welfare," a Lutheran Council position paper of 1970. "It is further the duty of the state to provide the proper framework in which other social institutions can freely carry on their appropriate functions. The state must not take on the functions of these institutions but rather assure a context in which all may fulfill their proper roles." The problem, of course, is that "proper" and "appropriate" are never defined, thus begging most of the questions involved in the present confusion. Some idea of what the paper means by proper roles is indicated in its conclusion: "It is a proper role for government to develop standards, grant or withhold licenses, participate in joint planning, and enter into fiscal agreements with voluntary agencies." The only limit placed upon effective, if not total, government control is that "all voluntary agencies (should be) treated equally on a non-preferential basis." Presumably there is no objection to church agencies losing their independent decision-making authority so long as all agencies are weakened equally. The paper sees the relationship it proposes as an instance of "institutional separation and functional interaction" between church and state. This illustrates that the formula is subject to being understood in terms of a rather nominal institutional separation and a one-sided functional interaction. In short, "the Role of Government in Social Welfare" offers little hope that the church's welfare agencies can be viewed as effective ways or means in relating Christian faith to public policy.

A companion document to the above is "A Background Study on the Role of Government in Social Welfare," published by the Lutheran Council's Division of Welfare Services in 1970. This background study is even more uncritical in its endorsement of governmental mega-structures, its indifference to the role of mediating institutions, and its acceptance of what might be called conventional assumptions about social welfare. The thrust of the study is overwhelmingly on the side of expanding government programs. Voluntary agencies may get public funding but such arrangements "should be surrounded by necessary safeguards which assure that the proper development of governmental programs is not thereby thwarted . . ." It is as though government programs are in danger of being displaced by voluntary ones! While the background study affirms the continuing and essential part of social service in the church's life, it, like the 1968 LCA resolution discussed above, talks about exploring unspecified new avenues of service while evidencing little commitment to the institutional avenues the church has already established.

An example of quintessentially conventional wisdom is this statement in the background study: "As resulting knowledge (from government funding of social welfare research) increases with respect to the causative factors in individual and family breakdown, dependency, antisocial behavior, and other related personal and social ills, society will be the better equipped to develop rehabilitative services to individuals as well as those social measures designed to prevent such problems." It is not unfair to suggest that in its view of human nature, in its concept of "society," and in its enthusiasm for expanded government expenditure and control this statement is indistinguishable from the worldview which pervades the myriad agencies of, for example, the Department of Health, Education and Welfare.

One clue to understanding why church social welfare agencies have been so debilitated as potential instruments in challenging and shaping public policy may be that the leadership of such agencies has so thoroughly internalized the culturally dominant assumptions about the nature of social welfare. This is no doubt connected with the enthusiasm for "professionalization" and the acceptance of conventional definitions of "quality." If these agencies are as indistinguishable from other agencies as their leadership says they are, then they have little claim upon continued church support and almost no potential as ways and means for relating Christian faith to public policy.

Again, *The Church in Social Welfare* represents a much more thoughtful and critical approach to the problems discussed here. Our study agrees, for example, with the assertion that "In a democratic society, where the people determine what is to be done, it is never remiss to remind men that justice also includes using the most appropriate means, that is, recognizing the proper responsibilities of family, of voluntary agencies, and of local communities." In a summary statement of "six options" for understanding governmental action in welfare, *The Church in Social Welfare* favors number six: "Government should use its power and funds to help create a situation in which public welfare, the service activities of the church, and voluntary welfare are in creative cooperation in serving the needs of persons." Our own view is even more favorably disposed toward the stated option five: "Government should use its power and funds to promote the services that can be given by church and voluntary groups, especially those on a local level, and should supplement such voluntary services when, and only when, church and voluntary groups are demonstrably incapable of meeting needs." In our text we state it somewhat differently but this is the general approach which we believe can advance both social welfare and the potential of church agencies in influencing public policy on a wide range of issues.

In Chapter Two, then, we describe nine "ways and means" for relating Christian faith to public policy. The formal Lutheran statements we have considered seem either weak or contradictory in terms of all nine. They consistently affirm our Number Four, "individual Christian vocations," but offer few helpful specifics. They are frequently confused and self-contradictory in connection with our Number One, the relation of public policy concern to "prayer and proclamation." That is, most of them are not helpful in understanding why public policy could impinge significantly upon concerns about personal salvation and all things of redemptive meaning. The statements are for the most part silent on the content of our Number Two, "the cultivation of civil virtue and piety." With few exceptions, they seem unsure that "the internal politics of Christian community" might be relevant to public policy. With the notable exceptions of some LCA studies, our Number Five, "research and education," receives little attention. The possibility of church-related agencies playing a strong role in this connection is largely precluded for all the reasons discussed above. Our Numbers Six, Seven and Eight ("advocacy by groups and individuals," "corporate statements," and "official leadership") receive little attention that is not dominated by a tone of organizational defensiveness rather than public effectiveness. Our understanding of Number Nine, "political implementation," finds some expression, chiefly in the Lutheran Council's statements about its responsibilities in offering congressional testimony and such.

In this section we have noted with approval some formal statements that offer positive and suggestive approaches to the ways and means by which Christian faith can be related to public policy. Even these statements, however, are usually contradicted or at least badly fudged by other statements issued by the same groups. The conclusion that suggests itself is that American church bodies need to give much more careful thought not only to *what* positions to take on public issues, but, even more urgently, to *why* such concerns are relevant to Christian existence and to *how* Christian faith can be made publicly effective.

For Further Reading

Why is this book mentioned and not another? It's always a good question. The always unsatisfactory answer was given many years ago by the Preacher of Ecclesiastes, "Of the making of books there is no end." What follows are significant points of reference in the author's own thinking which have a major bearing on what went into this study. This bibliography is therefore somewhat personal and eclectic; it is by no means exhaustive. But, then, no bibliography could be exhaustive; it would be outdated before it saw print. The truth is that one thing leads to another, and the reader can be sure that, if one begins with the books mentioned here, one would be led, through them, to almost all the relevant literature. Some of these books are difficult reading, others are sheer pleasure, some are profoundly wrongheaded, others the quintessence of wisdom, but all are important to contemporary thought about public policy and to the Christian's understanding of that thought.

Church and Society

Abell, Aaron I., ed., *American Catholic Thought on Social Questions,* Bobbs-Merrill, 1968: A reliable and comprehensive survey.

Augustine, Bishop of Hippo, *City of God,* Doubleday Image Books, 1958: It isn't just a classic, it's what "classic" means. Lutherans can and will read into it much that we have discussed in terms of "the intention" of two-kingdom thinking. Our study assumes a more unified notion of history and the salvation promised to history. But, however much one may disagree with Augustine, one never forgets for a moment the option he presents.

Dostoievsky, Feodor, "The Legend of the Grand Inquisitor" in *The Brothers Karamazov:* Crucially important for understanding not only the temptation of the church but of all power in society. Its regular reading and meditation is a regimen conducive to honesty. Were one post-New Testament document to be added to the biblical canon, this might be it, for it tells so terribly much of the story of both church and world since the apostolic era.

Flannery, Austin P., editor, *Documents of Vatican II*, Eerdmans, 1975: Roman Catholics have a large and evolving body of "authoritative" literature relevant to the concerns of our study, of which *Vatican II* and its follow-up documents is the most important recent addition. All Christians will find eminently rewarding a careful study of, especially, "The pastoral constitution on the church in the modern world."

Forell, George, *Christian Social Teachings*, Augsburg, 1971: An admirable anthology and analysis of what the church of various times and places has said about its relationship to society. An indispensable "reader."

Lazareth, William, ed., *The Left Hand of God*, Fortress, 1976: In the Appendix we touch again on Lazareth's influence in contemporary Lutheran social thought. This book is a succinct statement of Lazareth's theological posture, and that of colleagues at the Lutheran Seminary (LCA) in Philadelphia.

Niebuhr, H. Richard, *Christ and Culture*, Harper & Row, 1951: And this is what is meant by a more contemporary "classic." Niebuhr offers several models or "types" for relating Christian existence to the larger culture. Most approaches in Christian social thought can be placed and illuminated in relation to his models, making this a very important book indeed.

Niebuhr, Reinhold, *Moral Man and Immoral Society*, Scribners, 1932: We could have chosen any of a number of his many writings, but this one conveys best the gist of his important contribution. As a leader of "neo-orthodox" or "realist" thinking beginning in the 1920s, Niebuhr represents a protest against what was viewed as sentimental liberalism. He was warmly applauded by many Lutherans. Still today the influence that he and his brother, H. Richard, have on Protestant social thought is likely unmatched by other religious thinkers. Both Niebuhrs are eminently readable.

Ramsey, Paul, *Who Speaks for the Church?*, Abingdon, 1967: We will mention Ramsey again in another connection. This little book addresses many of the issues raised in the "ways and means" section of this study. They are perennial questions about what it means for the church to "address" the world. Although occasioned by problems connected with the World Council of Churches, Ramsey's observations have much wider application.

Rauschenbusch, Walter, *A Theology for the Social Gospels*, Abingdon, 1945: This is, in large part, the liberalism the Niebuhrs saw themselves combatting. In truth, Rauschenbusch was a good deal less sentimental than his later detractors alleged. In any case, it's impossible to understand the history of church and society questions in America without reference to the social gospel movement of seventy and more years ago—and Rauschenbusch is likely the best introduction to what that movement was about.

Richey, Russell and Jones, Donald G., *American Civil Religion*, Harper & Row, 1974: This group of essays covers the ongoing debate about religion and its connection with distinctively American values. For a somewhat different view of civil religion and public values see Richard John Neuhaus, *Time Toward Home*, Seabury, 1975.

Sider, Ronald, *The Chicago Declaration*, Creation House, 1974: In the fall of 1973 a group of leading "evangelicals" issued a statement on Christian responsibility in society. Many observers believe this signals a new impetus toward reflective social engagement among conservative Protestants. See also, Richard J. Mouw's "New Alignments: Hartford and the Future of Evangelicalism," in *Against the World for the World*, op. cit.

Christian Ethics

Bonhoeffer, Dietrich, *The Cost of Discipleship*, SCM Press, 1969 (Second Edition): Bonhoeffer perhaps rivals the Niebuhrs in terms of impact upon contemporary social thought among Christians. His vision gains additional power from the context of the Hitler era in which it was written. In the view of many, Bonhoeffer is a modern saint and martyr, killed by the Nazis in 1945. Others think him something of a romantic with little to say about the American situation today. In connection with what we have called "the internal politics of the Christian community," see Bonhoeffer's little book, *Life Together*, which is surely one of the most compelling visions of Christian community ever written.

Ellul, Jacques, *The Ethics of Freedom*, Eerdmans, 1976: Again, we might have chosen any of a number of Ellul's important works. He is a French layman and very much a disciple of Karl Barth, offering a strong polemic against the church's various accommodations to contemporary culture. His themes are similar to those related to the American scene in *Against the World for the World* (edited by Peter Berger and Richard John Neuhaus, Seabury, 1975). Although *Ethics of Freedom* is a more ambitious and somewhat more difficult work than some of Ellul's other books, he is a joy to read if you are ready to have your assumptions challenged.

Fletcher, Joseph, *Situation Ethics*, Westminster, 1966: Although the influence of "situation ethics" is likely on the decline today, it occasioned much debate in the 1960s, often being condemned as the symbol of rampant relativism. Fletcher's work is premised upon a "love ethic" that is usually placed against the "deontological" approach represented by Paul Ramsey. In recent years both Fletcher and Ramsey have done much important work on medical ethics and related subjects, with Ramsey making an argument much closer to the approach reflected in our study.

Gustafson, James, *Theology and Christian Ethics*, Pilgrim, 1974: Gustafson's many books reflect a very reliable, solid, and irenic approach to controversies in Christian ethics. This very accessible volume deals with the linkage between belief and ethical statement, a subject pertinent to the first part of our study.

Gutierrez, Gustavo, *A Theology of Liberation*, Orbis, 1974: While not a book on ethics in the narrow sense of that term, Gutierrez's is a major effort to recast Christian faith in terms of its political and ethical meaning. To date this is the most carefully systematic statement of the "liberation theology" which dominates sectors of Latin America and has gained a wide following in North America and Europe, especially among those eager for some kind of Christian-Marxist synthesis. For a sympathetic critique of Gutierrez and other liberation theologians, see Richard John Neuhaus, "Liberation as Program and Promise" (*Currents in Theology and Mission*, April and June issues, 1975).

Outka, Gene, and Reeder, John P., *Religion and Morality*, Doubleday Anchor, 1975: A large collection of essays, most of which address the problem discussed by Gustafson above. Its chief contribution is to expose the ways in which religion and morality are confused in some people's minds to mean the same thing, or, in others', to be entirely unrelated. Often difficult, but important reading.

Pannenberg, Wolfhart, *Theology and the Kingdom of God,* Westminster, 1969: Although only two of the essays included are specifically ethical, the theological framework is important to understanding the first section of this study. (Little wonder, since the editing and the extensive introduction is by Richard John Neuhaus.)

Ramsey, Paul, *Deeds and Rules in Christian Ethics,* Scribners, 1967: This represents Ramsey's more systematic approach to the ethical task itself, and that is very systematic indeed. While Ramsey wins no prizes for literary style, he is earthy and relentlessly challenging to those who value substance over flourish.

Yoder, John, *The Politics of Jesus,* Eerdmans, 1972: A Mennonite, Yoder offers a vigorous defense that moves right from the words of Jesus to the decision of this very moment. It is a compelling sectarian vision. (And if you thought "sectarian" is necessarily a bad word, let Yoder instruct you.) For Lutherans, Yoder offers the challenge to come to terms with "the radical reformation" which classical Lutheranism rejected. Also, Yoder's is one of the most persuasive arguments for an absolute pacifist position in situations of conflict.

Basic Approaches to Understanding Society

Becker, Ernest, *The Denial of Death,* Free Press, 1973: In one of the most compelling books of recent years, the author turns psychoanalysis on its head, arguing that anxiety is rooted in the fear of death. Important insights into the "salvific" nature of politics when social change is turned into yet another "immortality project."

Bell, Daniel, *The Coming of Postindustrial Society,* Basic Books, 1973, and *The Cultural Contradictions of Capitalism,* Basic Books, 1976: A steady and promising progression is evident in the author's growing awareness of the role of religion in sustaining "the public household." *Cultural Contradictions* is likely as lucid an analysis of the "crisis" of western democracy as has been written in the last decade.

Bellah, Robert, *The Broken Covenant,* Seabury, 1975: Bellah revived the "civil religion" discussion in the late sixties. Remarks in the present study about "empty transcendence" and the sovereignty of God over the social order will be illuminated by a reading of Bellah.

Berger, Peter, *Pyramids of Sacrifice,* Basic Books, 1975: A novel and refreshingly fair evaluation of the weaknesses and strengths of "socialism" and "capitalism," especially as they relate to ideas of development in poor nations. Cuts through much of the nonsense that usually dominates the socialism vs. capitalism, equality vs. liberty, debates. Some phrases in our study, for example, "cognitive respect," come from Berger.

Berman, Harold, *The Interaction of Law and Religion,* Abingdon, 1974: A readable introduction to the ways in which law is a statement of morality. The approach is similar to that which informs the present study.

Fustel de Coulanges, Numa Denis, *The Ancient City,* Doubleday Anchor: A classic 19th century statement of the religious base of all social order. Fustel's historical treatment of Greek and Roman cities reinforces the sociological and anthropological arguments of Emile Durkheim—as indeed Durkheim was a student of Fustel's. Sometimes hard to get, so look out for it in your used book shop.

Gans, Herbert, *More Equality,* Pantheon, 1973: One of the leading proponents of what is called radical egalitarianism. Although our study is critical of Gans' understanding of equality, he presents his arguments with vigor.

Greeley, Andrew M., *Unsecular Man,* Schocken, 1972: One of the more substantial contributions of this prolific writer. Greeley is often thought to have overstated his case, but his is an information-filled polemic against the notion that society is of necessity becoming ever more secularized.

Harrington, Michael, *Socialism,* Saturday Review Press, 1972: The case for Marxist socialism presented in unusually engaging fashion. Unlike many Marxists, Harrington is strongly committed to democratic freedoms. The tensions—some would say contradictions—in being both Marxist and democrat are a chief preoccupation of Harrington's writings.

Hoffer, Eric, *The True Believer,* Harper & Row, 1951: The axioms of Eric Hoffer, a longshoreman turned philosopher, have become a staple in contemporary conversation about social movements and causes. While often described as a conservative, Hoffer's sword cuts in all directions. Homely and sometimes devastating wisdom.

Marcuse, Herbert, *One Dimensional Man,* Beacon, 1968: The most widely read of the many books by this Marxist guru to many of the revolutionists of recent American history. When someone says your analysis stops short of dealing with "the systematic, repressive, and dehumanizing factors in the capitalistic system," you can likely anticipate the direction of the conversation by having familiarized yourself with Marcuse.

Mill, John Stuart, *Essay on Liberty,* Harvard Classics: In western democracies, possibly the most influential statement of social theory of the last century and a half. In any discussion of "liberalism" and its perennial crises, this is the Bible. It will no doubt be "must reading" for many years to come.

Mills, C. Wright, *The Power Elite,* Oxford, 1959: A precursor of much of the radicalisms of the sixties, the book, as its title suggests, argues that there is an interlocking and oppressive elite in American society that makes a mockery of the official doctrines of democracy. Subsequent research on elites has done much to discredit Mills' thesis, but the mood of his argument continues to be a very important factor in social thought.

Moore, Barrington, Jr., *Reflections on the Causes of Human Misery and Upon Certain Proposals to Eliminate Them,* Beacon, 1970: And if you protested, "But I'll never be able to read all these books. Which are really the most important?," we would reluctantly start paring down the list. But among the last, among the very last, to go would be this little book by Barrington Moore. It is singularly realistic in its understanding of the hopes, limits, and dangers of politics. Our own study has drawn on it for such phrases as "the unity of misery and diversity of happiness"; but, more important, we have been instructed by its tone of sobriety that resists successfully the temptation to cynicism, and arrives at courage.

Neuhaus, Richard John, *Time Toward Home,* Seabury, 1975: Subtitled, "The American Experiment as Revelation," the discussion focuses on "contract" and "covenant" in democratic society. The perspective is explicitly Christian and theological.

Rawls, John, *A Theory of Justice,* Harvard, 1971: If J. S. Mill is the Bible, many liberals have come to view this as the authoritative commentary. The difficult but rewarding argument is for "justice as fairness" with equality as the prime ingredient of fairness. For a criticism of Rawls from the perspective of the present study, see "Justice in a Provisional World," chapter 14 of *Time Toward Home,* op. cit.

Scheler, Max, *Ressentiment,* Schocken, 1972: Written at the beginning of the century, Scheler highlights the seamier, we might say sinful, side of human behaviour in society. He forces the reader to confront aspects of social behavior often evaded by secularized and rationalistic theory. Cries for justice, suggests Scheler, are frequently only the excretions of resentment and even of hatred. Christians who are called to cry for justice need to ponder Scheler's cautions.

Schlesinger, Arthur M., Jr., *The Vital Center,* Houghton, Mifflin, 1949. Until recently, the established liberal view that the genius of the American political experiment is in the avoidance of "extremes" and in the disciplined refusal to press questions to their limit. In the light of the past almost thirty years of confusion, that view seems impossibly superficial and sanguine. But look for its revival if and when there is a "return to normalcy." Weak reed though it be, it is the best that many contemporary social theorists have to lean on.

Schoek, Helmut, *Envy,* Harcourt, Brace, 1969: Like Scheler, Schoeck wants to see society without illusions. Schoeck makes his argument with greater detail and nuance than Scheler and has produced a book that is required reading for understanding the qualified role of equality in any definition of justice that Christians should affirm.

Stephens, James Fitzjames, *Liberty, Equality, Fraternity,* Cambridge, 1967: Written shortly after its appearance, this is intended as a refutation of Mill's *On Liberty.* It remains today a feisty and often convincing challenge to the key assumptions of classical liberalism. (The quotation on the flyleaf of this book is from Stephens.)

Vivas, Eliseo, *Contra Marcuse,* Delta, 1971: A spirited and informed assault on the arguments of Herbert Marcuse, focusing especially on Marcuse's devotion to violence and indifference to democratic freedom.

War, Peace and International Affairs

Bainton, Roland, *Christian Attitudes Toward War,* Abingdon, 1960: A masterful book by a historian who is a pacifist. Especially helpful in understanding the early church's stance toward the state and the differing streams of tradition which later emerged.

Bennett, John C., *Christianity and Communism Today*, Association, 1970: Although written in 1948 at the beginning of the cold war, this remains one of the most readable and useful introductions to the issues in dispute. Temperate and informed, Bennett poses the abiding questions about the possibility of rapproachment between Christianity and communism.

Bock, Paul, ed. *In Search of a Responsible World Society*, Westminster, 1974: An overview of the many documents, studies, and the such issuing from the World Council of Churches. It represents as near as one can get to an "ecumenical consensus" among mainstream Protestants about the issues in international affairs. The influence of John Bennett, see above, is evident at crucial points.

Barnet, Richard, *Roots of War*, Athenum, 1972: Barnet is a leader among "revisionist" writers who contend the U.S. was primarily responsible for the cold war and the many conflicts since World War II. This is one of many influential books supporting the view that war, such as that in Indochina, is endemic and not accidental to the American system.

Clark, Grenville, and Sohn, Louis B., *World Peace Through World Law*, Harvard, 1967 (Third Edition): A standard reference in discussions of international law and the building of a world order beyond the nation state.

Hero, Alfred O., *American Religious Groups View Foreign Policy*, Duke, 1973: An historical catalogue, pretty much what the title says it is. Valuable for the researcher.

Kolko, Joyce and Gabriel, *The Limits of Power*, Harper & Row, 1972: Gabriel Kolko is often thought the most hard line of the revisionists (see on Barnet, above). To understand this viewpoint, however implausible it may seem, is to understand why many intellectuals, in America and elsewhere, believe that overthrow of American power is the first item on the agenda of global justice.

Mueller, John, and Barnet, Richard, *Global Reach*. As mentioned in this study, multinational corporations are a major and relatively new force in international affairs. In conformity with the revisionist argument, Mueller and Barnet see multinationals as extensions of

American imperialism and almost totally negative in their impact upon the poor.

Potter, Ralph, *War and Moral Discourse,* John Knox, 1969: A marvelously sensible and balanced discussion of the various ways in which Christians and other ethically concerned thinkers have wrestled with the horror of war. Included is a very comprehensive and annotated bibliography on most of the relevant literature, making this little book doubly useful.

Sakharov, Andrei D., *My Country and the World,* Knopf, 1975: A dissident Soviet physicist writes about his hopes and fears for freedom in the world. He urges westerners, and Americans in particular, to a more urgent and sober appreciation of their responsibility for the future of liberty in human history.

Solzhenitsyn, Aleksandr, *The Gulag Archipelago; Lenin in Zurich; From Beneath the Rubble; The First Circle; Cancer Ward;* and, one prays, many more. For every age God, in his grace, raises up prophets. Solzhenitsyn is a prophet. Profoundly Christian, committed to "the criterion of the concrete," unintimidated by fashion and fame, Solzhenitsyn, like most prophets, is often hard to take. Perhaps more than any person writing today he has seen, and understood, the horror of our time. We may be inclined to protest his seeming excesses, but it is an inclination to be kept in close check. Solzhenitsyn may be the measure of who in our time has ears to hear.

Simon, Arthur, *Bread for the World,* Paulist/Eerdmans, 1975: The author, head of the organization by the same title, offers the most knowledgable, compassionate and succinct statement of what we can and should do about global poverty. This inexpensive book has been circulated by the many, many thousands in homes, parishes and classrooms throughout the country. The treatment of poverty and development questions in the present study largely parallels that found in Simon's book. (That may not be unrelated to the fact that the author of the study is a founder and director of the Bread for the World organization.)

Race, Medicine, Crime, Revolution, Ecology, and Related Crises

Banfield, Edward C., *The Unheavenly City,* Little, Brown, 1968: Essential reading for those concerned with urban problems and poverty in America. As the title suggests, Banfield comes across as something of a pessimist, and some of his attitudes are hard to square with Christian commitment to the poor. But in terms of the difficult questions of policy, Banfield is an important counter to the notion that all that is needed is good intentions. Se also Banfield and James Q. Wilson, *City Politics* (Vintage 1963), which is a provocative defense of "political machines" in America.

Callahan, Daniel, *Abortion: Law, Choice, and Morality,* Macmillan 1970: The most thorough survey to date of laws, practices, and arguments, ethical and otherwise, regarding abortion. International in scope. Written, of course, before the Supreme Court decision of 1973, but continues to be of great value.

Commoner, Barry, *The Closing Circle,* Knoph, 1971: One of the leading voices of environmental concern, Commoner takes a strong commonsensical and humane approach against those who see excess population as the chief cause of environmental pollution.

Derr, Thomas, *Ecology and Human Need,* Westminster, 1975: Altogether the most readable and balanced treatment of the subject available. Warmly recommended for use in classrooms and study groups.

Genovese, Eugene D., *Roll, Jordan, Roll,* Pantheon, 1974: Although, as a history of slavery, this book may seem marginal to our study, it is in fact an utterly engaging study in the role of religion in bringing injustice under judgment. It is more convincing because the author has strong Marxist sympathies which presumably would preclude such an understanding of religion's role in society.

Fuchs, Victor, *Who Shall Live?,* Basic Books, 1974: Like Illich, see below, Fuchs debunks many of the myths of modern medicine. His is a temperate treatment of the subject, however, and includes more positive proposals for redesigning the medical establishment in a way more closely related to human health.

Hardin, Garrett, *Exploring New Ethics for Survival,* Viking, 1974: Among the chief proponents of "triage" and "life boat ethics" approaches to ecology and population. The antithesis of the direction advocated by this study and by Derr, above.

Hong, Edna, *Bright Valley of Love,* Augsburg, 1976: A beautiful story of Christian care for retarded children in Germany during the Hitler era. The lessons drawn by the author are painfully relevant to current discussions about abortion, euthanasia, and other issues dealing with the definition and protection of human life. Eminently read-able, the book deserves wide circulation among church members and others.

Human Life Review. A journal edited by Christians and begun after the 1973 Supreme Court decision on abortion. Offers legal, historical, and ethical articles of both a scholarly and more popular nature on the whole range of life-related issues. Edited from a "pro-life" viewpoint but the presentation of alternative positions is both careful and well informed.

Illich, Ivan, *Medical Nemesis,* Pantheon, 1976: A hard hitting and informed exposé of the myths of modern medicine. Argues persuasively that public policy should take a careful look at present "health care delivery systems" before bankrolling them with billions of public dollars. Illich also demonstrates great sympathy for Christian and other religious approaches to sickness and health which may present alternatives to the conventional wisdom of the present.

Jencks, Christopher, *Education Vouchers,* Center for the Study of Public Policy (Cambridge, Mass.), 1970: Jencks headed up the study group that produced this report for the federal government. It deals with most of the questions that have been raised about "education vouchers" as a way of achieving educational diversity and is particu-larly sensitive to issues of racial and economic discrimination.

Kahn, Herman, *The Next 200 Years,* Morrow, 1976: Spirited pro-growth, pro-technology "scenarios" for a world 200 years from now with five times its present population and everyone living at the pres-ent level of North Americans. Some find the scenarios implausibly optimistic, but they are carefully thought through and deserve very serious attention.

Lader, Lawrence, *Abortion,* Beacon, 1966: A prominent proponent of "abortion reform" in the sixties, Lader sets forth in succinct fashion the standard arguments against legal restrictions. Although events have outpaced his proposals, the arguments used today have not changed significantly.

Lewis, David, *King: A Critical Biography,* Praeger, 1970: To date the most adequate, or least inadequate, study of Martin Luther King, Jr. and the civil rights movement he led. Flawed by the author's ten-dency to read his own Marxist sympathies into King's thinking, the book is nonetheless a very helpful introduction for those to whom

King and the civil rights era are only legend. And, of course, the issues raised continue to be strikingly pertinent to America's continuing racial dilemma.

Lindsay, A. D., *The Modern Democratic State,* Vols. I and II, Oxford, 1962: Perhaps the best historical and theoretical study of the origins of modern democratic thought and practice. Lindsay is especially strong in his understanding of the connections between religion and politics.

Michaelson, Robert, *Piety in the Public Schools,* Macmillan, 1970: A very solid historical study of public policy regarding religion and education, especially as it relates to court decisions.

Morgan, Richard E., *The Supreme Court and Religion,* Free Press, 1972: A splendid overview of the subject, concluding with an argument for greater governmental "neutrality" toward religion in public life. At present, Morgan believes, the emphasis on the non-establishment clause of the First Amendment is seriously restricting and confusing the meaning of "free exercise."

Neuhaus, Richard John: In addition to numerous articles on many of the topics dealt with in this study, *In Defense of People* (Macmillan 1971) is a critical examination of the environmental movement as it relates to social justice. Also *Movement and Revolution* (with Peter Berger, Doubleday, 1970) deals at length with the meaning of revolution as viewed from the perspective of the classical Christian measures of "justified war." "No More Bootleg Religion" (in *Controversies in Education,* edited by Dwight Allen, Saunders, 1974) is a treatment of current law relating to the teaching of religion in the public schools.

Palmer, R. R., *The Age of the Democratic Revolution,* Princeton, 1959: A brilliant analysis of the historical developments leading up to the modern democratic state. Especially strong in underscoring the differences between the French and American revolutions and in noting the role of values in shaping democratic thought.

Ramsey, Paul, "The Indignity of 'Death with Dignity,'" *Hastings Center Studies,* May, 1974: A convincing critique of the arguments for euthanasia sometimes advanced as "death with dignity." The publications of the Hastings Center (Hastings-on-Hudson, N.Y.) are must reading if one is to stay on top of the wide range of debates regarding medical ethics today. The Center includes people of all viewpoints and ethical approaches and is headed by Daniel Callahan, mentioned above.

Ravitch, Diane, *The Great School Wars,* Basic Books, 1974: Surveys the various conflicts, including conflicts over religion, which have shaped public education since the middle of the 19th century. Although focusing on New York City schools, the book is broadly applicable to urban education elsewhere in America.

Ruether, Rosemary, ed. *Religion and Sexism,* Simon and Schuster, 1974: In this large volume essayists from many religious traditions and none explore the ways in which religion has been responsible for allegedly "sexist" attitudes and behavior. While the focus is not primarily on public policy, the public policy implications are evident throughout.

Schoeps, Hans Joachim, *The Jewish Christian Argument,* Holt Reinhart, 1963: When we speak of "the mystery" of living Judaism and of its relation to the State of Israel and to the church, it is necessary to know something of the history of those questions. Schoeps is an eminently sound and thoughtful introduction to that history. There is of course an enormous amount of material on American-Israeli relations written from a diplomatic and strategic viewpoint, but the present study assumes that the discussion of American-Israeli relations presupposes an understanding of Jewish-Christian relations.

Smythe, Mabel M., ed. *The Black American Reference Book,* Prentiss-Hall, 1976: Articles and data covering almost every aspect of the black American experience past and present.

Wilson, James Q., *Thinking About Crime,* Basic Books, 1975: Imagination, learning, and a common sense touch combine to make this perhaps the best single volume on "the crime crisis" available today. Wilson helps us rethink basic assumptions about punishment, rehabilitation, and the world of the criminal. His answers, where he has them, are lucid and humane. Where he does not have them, he is honest and provides wisdom for muddling through.